The

Bantry

Murder

By

Pat Doran

Cover designed by
Pat Doran

ISBN-13-979-8-3543-7327-7

This Book is dedicated to

Lauraine and Sam.
Thanks for
Your Continuing Support and Patience.

And to

all the unnamed journalists whose great reporting on
this story over 120 years ago
gave me an immeasurable amount of information.

Table of Contents

Bantry and West Cork

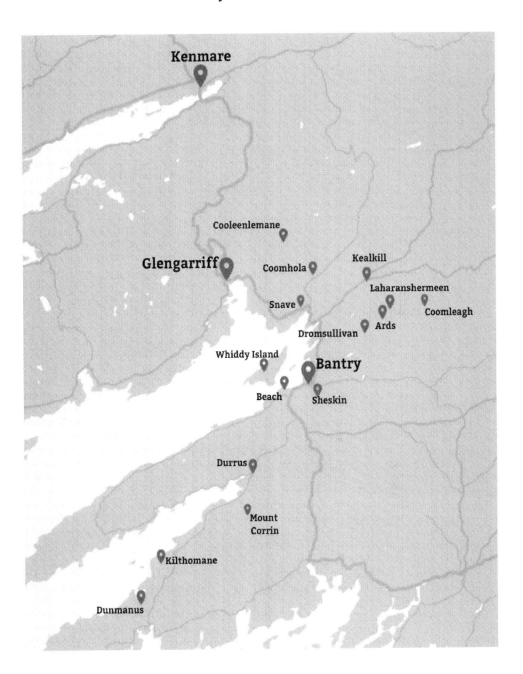

Bantry Town Centre

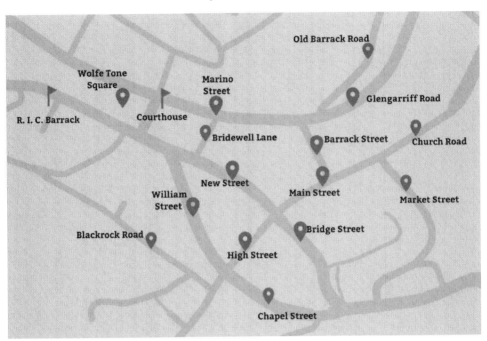

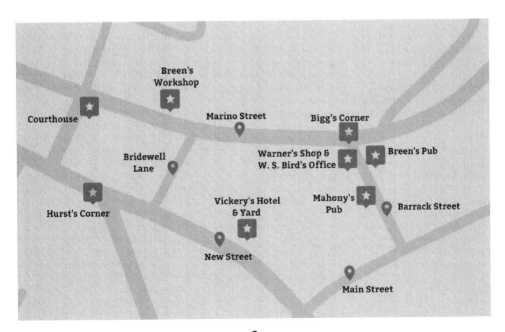

Background

"When a man takes a farm from which another has been evicted, you must shun him on the roadside when you meet him, you must shun him in the streets of the town, you must shun him at the shop-counter, you must shun him in the fair and at the marketplace, and even in the house of worship... you must shun him your detestation of the crime he has committed... if the population of a county in Ireland carry out this doctrine, that there will be no man ... [who would dare] to transgress your unwritten code of laws." Charles Stewart Parnell.

In February 1898 the United Irish League was established in Westport County Mayo. One of the organisations founders was the former M.P. and veteran of the Land Wars of 1879-82 and the Plan of Campaign from 1886-91, William O'Brien. The League had three main objectives, the first was to revive a popular grassroots movement in the countryside in order to heal the rift and divisions which had split the Irish Parliamentary Party since the death of Charles Stewart Parnell in 1891, secondly, to mount pressure on landlords to transfer land to their tenants on a permanent basis, and thirdly, to redistribute land from grazing to tillage to meet the needs of impoverished farmers. By 1900 the United Irish League had branches in towns both large and small around the country.

As well as those three main objectives another important issue was dealing with so called "land grabbers". These were people who took over the farms of evicted tenants. During the Land War ordinary citizens were encouraged to boycott these people rather than resorting to violence. This was in order to make it impossible for them to exist on the land they had taken over. At the other end of this scale were the Moonlighters, these were bands of masked men who roamed the countryside at night attacking the farms of evicted tenants which had been rented out again by landlords. These attacks often resulted in the burning of buildings and on some occasions murder.

In Cork at the time reports from the newspapers and the R.I.C. suggested that most league branches were being driven by anti-land grabber feelings which were either expressed by those tenants who had been evicted or by the branch officials on their behalf. Many of the areas in Cork where the United Irish League was active provided fertile ground for their ideals. These areas had been prominent in previous land disputes and police reports stated that there was a close association between the league and a number of prominent members of the Irish Republican Brotherhood. Newspapers also reported that in the poorer parts of the county, the west and northwest, these feelings had been exacerbated due to the treatment of some tenants on the large estates in the area. Branches of the League were established in towns like Skibbereen, Macroom and Kanturk and then in more rural locations.

A meeting of the United Irish League was held in the Square in Bantry on Sunday the 18th of February after last Mass. The purpose of the meeting was to establish a branch of the League in the town. The meeting had been due to be held a week earlier but had to be postponed due to heavy snow. A large vociferous crowd attended and the meeting was addressed by William O'Brien and James Gilhooly the local Nationalist M.P.. Six days later, on the 24th of February, a local land agent and landlord was murdered while working in his office on a busy street in the town. His name was William Symms Bird.

The Judicial System

Before going any further I would like to briefly outline the procedures that followed a murder in 1900, many which are similar to today. First a Coroner's Inquest was held, this usually took place a day or two after the murder. If the verdict returned by the inquest jury confirmed a murder had indeed taken place and a suspect had been arrested, this suspect was taken before a magistrate who determined if there was enough evidence to forward the suspect for trial. If the suspect was forwarded for trial he/she could be held on remand while the authorities gathered more evidence. Since there was no Director of Public Prosecutions at the time, the police acted as public prosecutors for a lot of less serious cases than murder. The evidence was then placed before a Grand Jury and if this jury found a "true bill" against the accused, he or she were sent for trial. Criminal cases were prosecuted by Crown counsel while the accused was represented by counsel which was usually paid for by the state unless the accused had funds to defend himself. In order to qualify as a jury member, the individual concerned had to hold property of a certain rateable value. Most juries were known as "common juries" but on some rare occasions "special juries" were used at criminal trials. These juries consisted of men with greater wealth and higher social standings than common jurors. No women were allowed on juries.

Criminal cases were normally tried in the county where the alleged offence had occurred. Several times a year judges from the superior courts in Dublin travelled on a circuit to preside at county assizes to hear important criminal cases. The trials themselves are broadly speaking similar to ones held today, although a lot shorter. An opening statement was made by the prosecuting counsel (Crown counsel) then witnesses for the prosecution were called. Each witness was examined by Crown counsel, cross-examined by defence counsel and could be re-examined by Crown counsel if it was felt necessary. Jurors could question witnesses if they wished. Once the Crown had finished presenting its case, the defence made it's opening statement and proceeded in a similar manner. When all the evidence had been presented and all witnesses examined, counsel for each side would make closing statements. The jury would then listen to the judge's charge, which included a summary of the evidence presented as well as his own view of the case.

Like today, in all cases the prisoner was presumed innocent and the burden of proof was with the prosecution. The jurors had to be satisfied beyond any reasonable doubt that the accused was guilty in order to convict. Witness testimony was governed by several principles, those of competence, reliability and compellability and was limited by evidentiary rules like the best evidence rule and the rule against hearsay. If a guilty verdict was returned by the jury in a murder trial, a mandatory capital sentence was imposed, which might be commuted to life on appeal.

A Murder in Bantry

On Saturday the 24th of February 1900 it was market day in Bantry and a large number of people were in the town. That morning William Symms Bird, aged forty-nine, a local land agent and landlord was collecting rents in his office which was located above a shop belonging to Mr. J.S. Warner on Barrack Street. Mr. Bird, who was also a local magistrate and Justice of the Peace, left his office at approximately half past one to go to the Bantry Conservative Club which was located on Wolfe Tone Square. He then returned directly to his office and resumed his business shortly after two o'clock. A private hallway led from the street to his office. This hallway was thirty feet in length and could also be accessed from the shop through a storeroom.

Between ten past and a quarter past two, clerks in the store below heard a noise like that of the stamping of feet from the office above, the noise grew louder and one of them, Robert Warner, a seventeen-year-old nephew of the owner J.S. Warner, thought it sounded like a scuffle. He then heard two shots and conferred with the other clerks. Subsequent to this conversation he went to the shop next door, which was also owned by his uncle and where his uncle was. After a short delay he informed his uncle of what he and the others had heard and his uncle sent two of his office staff, James Swords and Edward Brooks to investigate what was happening. Brooks opened the door to the hallway and saw nobody. After a short pause he went up the stairs to investigate. The door to Mr Bird's office was open and when he looked in he was greeted with the sight of Bird lying dead on his hands and knees in front of the counter. A strong smell of gunpowder hung in the office. Naturally enough Brooks was stricken by fear at this moment and it was only when he was joined by Swords did he enter the office. They looked cautiously around but no one else was about. They then turned their attention to the motionless body of Mr Bird. They saw two bullet wounds, one close to the heart and another to the back of the head. The scuffle heard by Warner must have taken place near the door for all the furniture, books, papers etc were all untouched. No firearm was found. The police and doctors were summoned immediately and the medical opinion was that the shots had been fired from very close range. A rumour swept the town that the victim had committed suicide but this was soon discounted due to the facts that no gun was found and the wounds could not have been self-inflicted. Others believed the assassin was the victim's brother Dr. Robert George Bird. Those were the facts to the murder of William Symms Bird according to reports which appeared in the newspapers over the following days.

Within hours the police believed they knew who the killer was, a man named Michael Hegarty, a farmer from Dunmanus who had paid rent to Mr. Bird minutes before he was shot. Mr Bird had only half completed the entry into his ledger when he was murdered and the ink was still wet. Hegarty was questioned regarding his movements. He said he had gone to Mr Bird's office at around two o'clock to pay £10 rent and stayed for five or six minutes before leaving with a receipt. He stated that he was seen by two people who could swear to this fact. Hegarty said that Mr Bird was alone when he left. He then joined his wife who was waiting outside and visited several places in the town. While having their dinner that evening in Miss O'Shea's establishment on Wolfe Tone Square he heard that "Master Willie" had shot himself some five minutes after he had left his office. Hegarty was kept in custody for several hours before he was released, having evidently satisfied the police as to his movements. Early on Sunday morning, the 25th of February another man, named Timothy Cadogan aged thirty-five, was arrested in a house in Laharanshermeen which was approximately six miles from Bantry. The previous night Dr. Robert Bird, the victim's brother was heard to say that "If Timothy Cadogan was in town on the day of the murder, 'twas he who did the deed.". It was due to this statement that the police went looking for Cadogan and charged him with the murder of William Symms Bird.

The news of the murder soon reached London and was mentioned in the House of Commons as well as in the newspapers. The London Evening Standard indicated that the murder had something to do with the revival of the Irish Land Question under the auspices of the United Irish League in an article published a couple of days after the murder.

"We would not suggest that the United Irish League instigated the murder of Mr. William Bird in Bantry last Saturday. But it is impossible not to trace the same sort of connection between the recent revival of murderous agrarianism in Bantry and the inauguration there of a branch of this society as we proved to exist between the Land League and outbreak of crime in the earlier period. In a letter which today we print, a correspondent quotes some expressions from a speech made at Bantry by Mr. William O'Brien only a few days ago. When a frenzied orator urges his listeners to "get rid of landlordism," and preaches the example of the Boers "who took down their guns," the results on an impressionable audience are only too likely to be dangerous. We are aware that Mr Gerald Balfour's (Chief Secretary of Ireland) illness may be a cause of some difficulty to the governance of Ireland just now, however, this kind of speech making on Mr O'Brien's part requires to be watched and its effects noted. When the landowners of Mayo approached the Chief Secretary eighteen months ago and asked him to proclaim the United Irish League under the Crimes Act he declined to do so. Sterner measures have since become more necessary. The sentiments professed in parliament by Irish politicians do not so much matter. What they say on the hillsides is of serious importance."

On the day this article was published, the 26th of February, the Coroner's Inquest into the death of Mr Bird was held. Coroner Richard Neville presided. District Inspector Armstrong represented the constabulary and County Inspector Hamilton was also present. A seventeen-man jury was sworn in and they then went to the deceased's residence at Beach House Bantry for the formal identification of the body. This was performed by Mr Bird's brother; Dr Robert Bird, who then gave his evidence.

"I am the brother of the deceased. I last saw him alive at five minutes past eight last Saturday morning. He was then at the hall door in the house. I now recognise the body as being that of my brother."

Coroner Neville. "Have you anything to add?"

"Nothing except what may be required afterwards in a court of justice."

Mr McCarthy, a jury member. "Did your brother carry a revolver?"

"He was not in the habit of carrying a revolver in recent years, at least not for the last nine."

The inquest then adjourned to the courthouse in Bantry where the first person deposed was Michael Hegarty from Dunmanus.

"I remember last Saturday going to the office of Mr William Bird on Barrack Street. I got there sometime after half past one and found the office door locked. From there I went down to Mrs Sullivan's house on New Street where my wife was. After about fifteen minutes I returned to Mr Bird's office. When I got to the street door I asked a girl of about twelve years of age whether Mr Bird was upstairs in his office, she replied that she didn't know. I then proceeded inside and up the stairs and found him in his office. Mrs Hourihane, a harness maker's wife was inside the office speaking to Mr Bird. She left a few minutes after I arrived and I then paid him £10 rent. While I was paying the rent some man came in on my right-hand side, who I did not look at. He and Mr Bird had a conversation about twigs or spurs for thatching purposes and Mr Bird took some money out of his pocket, I saw a shilling and some coppers, but I will not swear that he gave this money to the man. The man then left before me. I don't think it could have been more than three or four minutes after him when I left. If you wish me to repeat what took place between Mr Bird and myself I have no objection in doing so."

Coroner Neville. "How long were you in the office?"

"I was there altogether from about six to ten minutes."

"Would you be able to recognise the man who came into the office after you?"

"I never looked at the man."

"Did you get a receipt for the £10?"

"Yes."

"Where did you go after leaving the office?"

"I went to Mr Cullinane's shop on Main Street where my wife was waiting for me. I was not five minutes in Mr Cullinane's when I saw three policemen running up the street and then I heard someone say that Master Willie had shot himself."

District Inspector Armstrong. "Besides paying the rent, had you any other business with Mr Bird?"

"No."

"What kept you so long then?"

"We had a long conversation."

"About what?"

"When I arrived in the office he was writing some letters but he put them aside and asked me how Mrs Hegarty and the children were and I said that they were very well. I asked him how he and the doctor were and he said the doctor had gone out near my place shooting that day and he wondered had I met him on my way to town and I told him I had not. He then asked me if I had a bull from the Congested District Board and if I had any calves for sale. When I was leaving he seemed like he wanted to prolong the conversation but I left and he said good morning Mr Hegarty."

Mr Swaine, another member of the jury. "Did you meet anyone as you were coming down the stairs?"

"Not a single soul."

District Inspector Armstrong. "Were you and Mr Bird friends?"

"Yes."

"When did you enquire whether it was true that he had been shot?"

"About three quarters of an hour afterwards I went to enquire whether he had shot himself."

"Was it you or your wife who made the enquiries?"

"My wife made some enquiries and she was told that Mr Bird had been shot. I did not make any enquiries until after my dinner."

"Where did you enquire?"

13

"When I returned to Vickery's Yard and Pat Crowley was fixing my horse to the trap."

"You did not go back to Mr Bird's office to find out whether it was true?"

"No."

"Why not?"

"I can't give an answer to that. If he had been a relative of mine I would have went back, but I only collected some rents for him."

"Were those the rents you paid him that day?"

"No; the rent I paid was my own. There is no man in the County Cork who will miss him more than myself. Not only on one occasion, but every occasion he was a very good and useful friend to me. When my wife told me that Master Willie had shot himself I said it was not possible he did, for I had never seen him in better health and he was in his usual good humour. He didn't say a cross word to me or the two people who were in the office during the time I was there."

Mr McCarthy. "Did you go directly to Mr Cullinane's after leaving Mr Bird's office?"

"Yes."

Coroner Neville. "How much time elapsed between you leaving the office and seeing the policemen run up the street?"

"About a quarter of an hour."

James Swords was next deposed.

"I was working in Mr Warner's shop last Saturday and at around twenty-five past two Mr Warner called me and told me to go immediately to Mr Bird's office, which is above Mr Warner's other shop next door. When I got there I found Mr Bird lying on the floor outside the counter in his office, he was on his hands and knees and his head was on the ground. There was blood flowing from a wound in his head. I checked for a pulse to see if he was alive and I found none. I then examined the room and around the deceased for firearms, as I thought it was a suicide, but there were none.

14

After an interval of five- or six-minutes Mr Breen's two sons arrived on the scene and one of them suggested we try and give him some air, which we did. We opened his shirt and found a wound on his left breast. The police then arrived on the scene and took charge."

Coroner Neville. "Was there any other public door open to the office besides the street door?"

"There wasn't."

The next witness was a man named John Leary.

"I was working for Mr Warner last Saturday and shortly after two o'clock I went to Mr Bird's office to get some money due to me. Mr Bird was there and he paid me."

Coroner Neville. "Was Mr Bird alone?"

"No; there was a man there; who I now know was Mr Hegarty."

"Were they talking?"

"Yes."

"Can you describe the tone of their conversation?"

"Well; I heard no angry words between them."

District Inspector Armstrong. "Did Mr Bird seem his usual self?"

"He looked angry."

"Did you anger him?"

"No; I said or did nothing to make him angry."

"What made you think he was angry?"

"I knew by his face he was angry."

"Did you see anyone else as you were leaving the office?"

"I saw nobody on my way down from the office."

"How long had you left before you knew something was wrong?"

15

"About five or six minutes, when I saw the policemen running up the street."

"Were you aware then of what had occurred."

"Someone said that Dr Bird had shot himself and I told them that the doctor was not there when I was inside."

Dr Thomas Popham was next to be deposed.

"I was called to see the deceased and arrived at his office at about twenty minutes to three last Saturday. My son had proceeded me. When I got there I found Mr Bird lying at full length between the counter and the door of his office. He was quite dead. His clothes in front were open and I could see a wound on his left breast. He had blood on his body and his nose and there was also some blood on the floor. Then I found a wound on the back of his head. In conjunction with Dr Bennett I carried out a post mortem yesterday."

Mr Swanton, a member of the jury. "Could the wounds have been self-inflicted Doctor?"

"No. On making a superficial examination of the body we found a circular wound on the outside of the right arm caused by a bullet's entrance. On the inside of the same arm we found an exit wound. Corresponding with this there was an abrasion of the skin on the seventh rib. We found a second wound about three inches above the left nipple and a half an inch on the outside of the nipple line. This wound was scorched. We found a third circular entrance wound on the skull. The back of the right hand was scorched extensively and the fingers blackened. There was also a recent bruise over the right ear. We then removed the scalp and found a circular hole five eights of an inch in diameter through the bone corresponding with the scalp wound. We then removed the skull cap and found a flattened bullet lodged in the base of the brain close to the spinal column, and a circular piece of bone corresponding to the size of the hole in the bone, and a fracture at the base of the skull. We then examined the wound on the chest. It was a circular entrance bullet wound over the second left rib. We traced this downwards and found it entered the chest, notching the lower border of the third rib. On opening the chest we found a circular wound through the left lung corresponding to the notched rib. This continued through the base of the heart, diaphragm, liver, and lower abdominal cavity. We found the bullet lodged in the abdominal wall above the right hip that would have caused these injuries. We found all the other organs healthy. Either the wound through the heart or the brain would have caused instant death."

District Inspector Armstrong. "How long do you think Mr Bird would have been dead before you saw him?"

"I would say about twenty-five minutes."

Dr Bennett who had assisted Dr Popham with the post mortem then corroborated the evidence given by his colleague. That was the last evidence given before the coroner briefly summed up the case for the jury.

"On the evidence that has been heard you can only come to the one conclusion that the deceased was foully murdered and the only verdict you can bring in under the circumstances is that the deceased was murdered by some person unknown. I am sure I speak for you as well when I say I strongly condemn this outrage and hope that the perpetrator will be speedily brought to justice."

The jury agreed with the coroner and returned a verdict to the effect that William Symms Bird was murdered on the 24th of February in Bantry by some person unknown.

The following morning an eighteen-year-old man named Walter Dennis, who worked in the shop below Mr Bird's office, was taken into custody under unusual circumstances. It was believed that he may have been an eye witness to Timothy Cadogan leaving the scene of the murder. After making his statement to police and identifying Cadogan on Tuesday the 27th of February, Dennis was brought to Cork under protective custody and placed out of the reach of the press.

A Magisterial Inquiry

On the Friday following the murder, the 2nd of March, a magisterial inquiry was opened to investigate the murder of William Symms Bird in the Bantry Courthouse. The police and authorities were unusually reticent about their intentions and had the press and public barred from attending the proceedings. The only information the press received was from anonymous sources, however, they were still able to cover the hearing in a substantial enough manner for the following morning's papers.

The inquiry was held before Mr B.R. Purdon R.M. and it's purpose was to justify the Crown's application for a further remand of Timothy Cadogan. Mr H.T. Wright C.S. of Cork represented the Crown while a local solicitor, Mr P. O'Leary defended the prisoner, who was present for the hearing. The first witness called was Dr Lionel Popham from Bantry. He deposed that he had known the deceased, Mr Bird, and then recalled his activities on the day of the murder.

"At about twenty-five past two I received a message off a messenger belonging to Mr Warner. In consequence of this I proceeded to Mr Bird's office on Barrack Street, the office is above Mr Warner's shop. Upon entering the office I found Mr Bird lying on his back between the counter and the door. I examined him and ascertained that life was extinct. I found three bullet wounds on the body, one through the upper part of his right arm, a second in his left breast just above the nipple line and the third in the lower left part of his skull. When I arrived at the scene, acting Sergeant Driscoll was in charge of the body and the room. My examination only took a few minutes and I left after my father Dr. Thomas Popham arrived."

The said gentleman was next deposed and he corroborated the evidence of his son regarding the wounds on the body. Acting Sergeant Driscoll was next to take the stand and he also said that Mr Bird was known to him.

"In consequence of a communication made to me I proceeded to the deceased's office. When I arrived I looked at my watch and it was twenty-five past two. I found Timothy Breen and James Swords there on my arrival. The body was lying between the counter and the office door. I remained there until Dr Lionel Popham arrived and I helped him with his examination. After he had concluded his examination it was half past two."

Mr. O'Leary. "How do you regulate your time?"

"By the Post Office."

"And is it in time with the Post Office?"

"I found I was three and half minutes faster than the Post office."

Mr. Wright. "After the doctor completed his examination what did you do?"

"District Inspector Armstrong and myself searched the clothes of the deceased. In his vest pocket I found a gold watch and chain, a card case in the ticket pocket of his coat, two Bank of Ireland £5 notes in his coat pocket and a pair of spectacles and a case in another pocket. I still have possession of these articles. After Dr Thomas Popham came and also examined the body I was left in charge of it for some time."

"Did you carry out any other duties that day?"

"Yes; that evening at eight o'clock I went in search of the prisoner and I found him at about a quarter past five the following morning in the house of Richard Sullivan of Laharanshermeen, he was in bed. When I roused him I asked him was he Timothy Cadogan and he said he was."

"Did you know of him before?"

"I did not."

"Please proceed."

"I gave him the usual caution about his answers being taken down and I then asked him about his movements the previous day. He said he had gone into Bantry at around half past ten in the company of a John Sullivan, a mason from Ards. He said they reached Bantry at about one o'clock and went into Tommy Hurst's pub with another man named John Sullivan from Coomleagh and had two glasses of lager beer each while the other Sullivan had two half whiskeys. He said they remained at Hurst's for about an hour before separating. He then said he walked about the town and bought some biscuits before heading for home at around six o'clock. I then read over his

20

statement and he signed it. I told him to get out of the bed and to get dressed and once he came downstairs I arrested him in the kitchen for murdering Mr Bird, he replied that he had no further statement to make."

Mr. O'Leary. "Did he ask you anything prior to you arresting him?"

"When he entered the kitchen he asked me what charge I had against him."

The brother of the deceased Dr Robert Bird was next deposed.

"I am the brother of the late Mr W.S. Bird. We resided together at Beach, Bantry. Since my return from the navy I have been in the habit of assisting him as land agent. Amongst other positions my brother held that of agent and receiver over the estate of R.H.E. White. Esq."

Mr Wright. "Do you see the prisoner?"

"I do."

"Do you recognise him?"

"Yes; he was a tenant on a portion of the White Estate at Cooleenlemane."

"Had your brother any dealings with the prisoner?"

"Yes; in consequence of his rent falling into arrears, my brother instituted proceedings against him by ejectment for non-payment of rent. I produced an ejectment decree against the prisoner dated the 23rd of October 1894 and I was present on the 19th of August the following year when possession was taken and handed to my brother."

"What happened the prisoner?"

"He was evicted."

"Have you seen Cadogan since then?"

"Yes; I was present on three occasions when he made applications to my brother to be reinstated on the land. I remember two occasions vividly, the last only being six months ago."

"On each occasion your brother refused his application?"

"Yes."

"What was the prisoner's demeanour on the last occasion when he asked to be reinstated, this was only six months ago?"

"Yes; I remember he appeared sullen and rude. Other meetings may have taken place between them but I was not present."

Mr. O'Leary. "Where were you at the time of the murder?"

"I was shooting on my brother's property at Kilthomane."

"You were there all day?"

"Yes; I left my brother at about ten minutes past eight that morning and I did not return home until between six and seven o'clock that evening."

Further evidence was then heard from two men who gave evidence at the Coroner's Inquest, Michael Hegarty, who was believed to be the last man to see Mr. Bird alive before he was murdered, and James Swords one of the first men to find him afterwards.

Mr. Wright. "I would like to ask for the prisoner to be remanded for a further eight days."

Mr O'Leary. "I object to remand being granted. I submit that no evidence has been given to connect the prisoner with the murder and a remand is not justified on the evidence which has been given."

Mr Wright. "Mr O'Leary has not heard all the evidence that has been given. Today is only a continuation."

Mr O'Leary. "When the prisoner was being remanded a few days ago in the police barrack he asked for the assistance of a solicitor and his request was denied."

Mr Purdon. "If the application had been made to me I would have allowed it."

Mr O'Leary. "The application was made to the police."

Mr. Wright's application for the remand of Timothy Cadogan was granted and he was removed to Cork by train in handcuffs.

The magisterial investigation resumed on Saturday the 10th of March. On this occasion Mr. Purdon was joined on the bench by two fellow magistrates, Mr S. Hutchins and Mr James Gilhooly J.P. who also happened to be the local M.P. and was one of the so-called controversial speakers, along with William O'Brien, at the United Irish League meeting in Bantry on the Sunday before Mr Bird was murdered. Mr. Wright once again appeared for the Crown. Mr O'Leary resumed his role as counsel for the prisoner and on this occasion was assisted by Mr J. Flynn. Once again the proceedings were closed to members of the press and the public, however, the press succeeded in obtaining a full report of events at the close of the day from an individual who had been present in the court. At the beginning of proceedings Mr O'Leary asked that the evidence be taken in open court.

Mr Gilhooly. "As I intend to adjudicate on the case, I also believe that the evidence should be heard in an open court."

Mr Wright. "I object to Mr Gilhooly, or any other magistrate who was not present at the previous hearing, adjudicating on this case."

Mr O'Leary. "Any magistrate is entitled to take part in the inquiry and express his views on the evidence."

Mr Gilhooly. "I agree."

Mr Purdon. "I agree with Mr Wright and I think that Mr Gilhooly should leave the room."

Mr Gilhooly. "That I will not do."

Mr Wright reiterated his objection to the presence of Mr Gilhooly, however, despite that, Gilhooly remained in the court. It is obvious that the Crown believed that Mr Gilhooly would have been prejudicial to their case, for they were aware he had previous history with the Bird brothers. In 1891 he asked a question in the House of Commons concerning the brothers overlapping roles as land agents and magistrates in some specific cases and in 1892 William Bird was one of the proposers of a Unionist candidate, Mr Somers Payne, who ran unsuccessfully against Gilhooly in that year's general election. Mr Gilhooly defeated Mr Payne by 3,155 votes to 329. Interestingly another of Payne's proposers was Mr J.S. Warner who was the owner of the shop on Barrack Street over which Bird had his office. The first witness called was a sheriff's bailiff named John Sullivan. (not either of the men bearing the same name who were in Bantry on the day of the murder with Cadogan) Sullivan deposed that he had evicted the accused from his holding on the 19th of August 1895 and handed over possession of it to Mr William Symms Bird.

R.I.C. Sergeant George Cooper of Glengarriff next stated he was present at the eviction of Cadogan along with two constables. He went on.

"The late Mr. W.S. Bird and his brother Dr. Bird were present and possession was handed to Mr. Bird by the bailiff. I saw the prisoner there and heard him addressing Mr. Bird when he came on the scene about the way the bailiff was handling his belongings."

Mr. O'Leary. "I object on the grounds that any statement made by my client then was not evidence as there is nothing to connect it with the present case."

Sgt. Cooper continued. "The prisoner asked Mr. Bird not to go ahead with the eviction that he would pay him the rent as soon as possible but Mr. Bird replied that it had to go ahead. The prisoner then muttered something and became rude and dogged in his demeanour, he went towards a heap of bottles and crockery wares which had been removed by the bailiff from the house. He grabbed some of them and threw them violently, smashing them against a wall. Mr. Bird said to him. "Cadogan, you are a bad boy". The prisoner made no remark and continued to smash the bottles. I remained with Mr. Bird in consequence of these actions."

Richard Sullivan, Laharanshermeen, Bantry, was next deposed.

"Timothy Cadogan had been in my employment for two months up until the end of January. I informed him then that I would no longer require his services. He asked me to accommodate him until he could find a new master. On the morning of the 24th of February he said he was going to the market in Bantry to try a find new work and he left after breakfast. I gave him a pound that I owed him in wages and told him to bring back a paper. He returned that night after ten o'clock and knocked on my door which I had bolted before going to bed. I let him in and he sat down and took off his

24

boots. I asked had he brought back the paper and he replied he hadn't. I asked him had he any news and he said he had not but there was a great war in South Africa. I said I heard that Mr Bird had been shot and he said he heard that too. I believe I gave him a drink before I went to bed."

Patrick Cronin from Snave was next to take the stand.

"I was in Bantry on the 24th of February. I was standing on the corner of Barrack Street outside Mr. Biggs's shop at about half past two when I heard that Mr. Bird had been shot. I am sure I saw the prisoner that day outside Mahony's shop on Barrack Street around an hour before Mr. Bird was shot. Mahony's shop is about four doors away from Mr. Bird's office on the same side. This was the only time I saw him that day."

Cornelius Sullivan, a brother of the prisoner's employer, Richard Sullivan, was next to give evidence.

"On the morning of the 24th of February I spoke to Timothy Cadogan on the road near my house which is about six miles from Bantry, it was about eleven or half past eleven. I saw him again that night just before I was going to go to bed and I told my wife to bring him a drink. I asked him had he any news and he said he had not. He did not mention anything about Mr. Bird being shot."

The next person deposed was a small farmer from Caherdaniel named Michael Regan.

"I came into Bantry at about twelve o'clock on the 24th of February. I went up to the chapel and I spoke to Father O'Connell and Father Hea for a minute or so. I came down Pound Lane and I met Dan McCarthy of Newtown at Mr. Vickery's Corner. The two of us then proceeded to Mr. Hurst's public house. After we arrived the prisoner and John Sullivan came in and had a drink. I stayed there for a half an hour and then went down to the Bridewell Lane where they sell cabbages. While there I saw the prisoner going into Vickery's Lane. During this time a man spoke to me and I remained talking to him for a few minutes. I then set off for Cronin's the saddler on Marino Street and as I did I saw the prisoner come back out of Vickery's Lane. The prisoner went ahead of me and stopped outside Breen's workshop on Marino Street and spoke to a countryman with a cart. I got as far as the saddler's but I didn't go in. Instead I came back through Bridewell Lane and out into the Square where the baskets are sold. I had only stopped there when a few boys came down the street and said that Mr. Bird had shot himself. I saw the prisoner around the town afterwards."

Mr. O'Leary. "How long were you in the Square before the boys came along saying that Mr. Bird had shot himself?"

"I had only gone a few yards into the Square."

"Do you know where Mr. Cadogan was at this time?"

"He would have been near Breen's workshop."

Mr. Wright. "What this witness told Constable Daly was that he was standing at the corner of Bridewell Lane for a quarter of an hour before he went on to Marino Street and when he returned from Marino Street he only stood at the corner of the lane. Who is your brother married to?"

"The prisoner's sister."

Henry Breen the owner of a public house on Barrack Street and a coach building workshop on Marino Street was next deposed.

"I saw Timothy Cadogan on the 24th of February after two o'clock opposite my workshop while I was talking to another man. At about half past two a man named O'Shea passed by and told me that Mr. Bird was after shooting himself. I rushed up Barrack Street as quick as I could then and I did not notice or see the prisoner on my way."

Henry Breen's twenty-one-year-old son Timothy also gave evidence of seeing Cadogan outside their coach building workshop on Marino Street.

Publican Thomas Hurst was next called to the stand.

"I knew the prisoner by appearance but not by name. He came into my shop on the 24th of February with two others, one of them a man named Sullivan. They had two drinks each, the prisoner paid for one and Sullivan the other. It was about half past one at the time. They remained in the shop for about a quarter of an hour and I did not see the prisoner again. Sullivan came back

26

a short time after in the company of two others, none of whom were the prisoner."

Mr. O'Leary. "Are you sure it was Sullivan who returned and not the prisoner?"

"I am sure."

Constable William Daly was then called and asked about the statement he had taken from the witness Michael Regan on the 7th of March. He stated that he read the statement back to Regan and then Regan had put his mark on it.

This closed proceedings and Cadogan was further remanded, despite the protests of Mr O'Leary, until the investigation resumed on the following Tuesday, the 13th of March. On its resumption Mr Wright once again objected to the presence of Mr Gilhooly, who made no reply, and was supported in his objection by Mr Purdon. Like the previous hearings the press and the public were excluded. Mr O'Leary applied for an assistant to aid him in taking notes of the evidence. Mr Wright objected to this unless an undertaking was given that the notes would not be passed to the press. Mr Leary said that he would not give such an undertaking and Mr Purdon said that he could not permit a shorthand writer into the court.

The first person called to give evidence was Edward Brooks.

Mr Wright. "Where do you live?"

"I live in Glengarriff."

"And where do you work?"

"I am employed as a clerk by Mr J.S. Warner in Bantry."

"Do you remember February 24th last?"

"I do."

"With regards to the murder of Mr Bird tell us what you remember of that day?"

"I work in Mr Warner's shop which is next door to the one in which Mr Bird had his office. In consequence of a communication made to me by Mr Warner, I went to Mr Bird's office at about half past two. I ran until I entered the hall door then I walked up the stairs. Robert Warner, another clerk, was on my heels as I went up. I got as far as the office door, which was wide open and looked inside. I saw Mr Bird on the floor apparently dead. He was on his knees and his head was covered under his chest. I saw blood on the floor under where his head was. I did not touch him. I stayed for about a minute before going back down the stairs where I met Mr Swords and another clerk in Mr Warner's employment coming up."

"Did you return to Mr Bird's office?"

"Yes."

"Shortly after?"

"No; not until nine o'clock that night when the police were in charge of the office."

Robert Warner was next to be deposed.

"I was working in my uncle's shop which is underneath the late Mr Bird's office. I remember sometime between two and three o'clock on the day in question hearing a noise from upstairs. It was like the shuffling of feet and then I heard shots. Miss Dukelow, a shop assistant, was then in the shop. I spoke to her and in consequence of what she said to me I went down to the shop my uncle was in. There was a good many customers around him and it took me a little while to get his attention. When I told him what I had heard he went into the office in the shop where Mr Brooks and Mr Swords were. He gave them certain directions and they went up to the house that Mr Bird's office was in. I accompanied them. Mr Brooks was the first to go in, he went up the stairs to Mr Bird's office, I followed him. When I went up I saw the body of Mr Bird lying on the ground. Mr Swords came up behind me and Mr Brooks went back downstairs. I saw Mr Swords lifting Mr Bird's head up and I noticed blood underneath where it was. I came back downstairs and was instructed to go and get Dr Popham."

Mr Wright. "Did you go back up to the office?"

"No; I did not go back to Mr Bird's office again."

The next witness called was Henry Breen Jnr. The twenty-year-old son of Henry Breen and brother of Timothy Breen.

"I live in Barrack Street over my father's public house and opposite the building where Mr Bird had his office. On the 24th of February I remember setting my clock at twenty-five past two. I found out afterwards that it was five minutes fast. After setting the clock I walked to the pub's door, and while standing there I heard some report coming from the direction of Mr Warner's shop; this is the upper shop next to Mr Biggs's. When I heard the report I looked in the direction of the shop and then I looked down the street. I remained at the door for a couple of minutes and then I went upstairs for my dinner. After going upstairs I went to the front window and saw Mr Edward Brook's coming quickly out of Mr Warner's upper shop.

Mr Wright. "How many reports did you hear?"

"I am sure I heard two reports."

"Not three?"

"I couldn't say if I heard a third."

Mr O'Leary. "What did you do after seeing Edward Brooks come out on to the street?"

"I came downstairs and crossed the street and went up the stairs to Mr Bird's office."

"Were you on your own?"

"My brother Timothy was immediately after me."

"Who did you see up there?"

"Mr James Swords was standing in the door of the office when we went up and I saw Mr Bird lying on the floor in the office, apparently dead, he was on his face and hands and there was blood underneath him."

"What did you do then?"

"I was sent for the police and I got acting Sergeant Driscoll who came to the office immediately."

The next person deposed was John Sullivan, who had met the prisoner on the way to Bantry on the morning of the murder and walked with him to the town.

"When we reached the town we went straight to Mr Hurst's pub for a drink after our walk. Each of us had two drinks, I paid for one and he the other. John Owen Sullivan from Coomleagh joined us for the drinks. After that myself and the prisoner went outside and stood on the corner for a little while. Then a man named Tom Sullivan came along and on his invitation the two of us went back inside for another drink. After that the two of us went back outside and stood on the corner talking for another while, this was about half past one. I met a man named John McCarthy and after talking to him I went away leaving the prisoner standing on Hurst's Corner and I didn't see him in Bantry again that day."

Mr O'Leary. "When did you hear about Mr Bird's murder?"

"I saw a crowd of people running up Barrack Street towards Mr Bird's office."

"How long was this after you had left the prisoner on Hurst's Corner?"

"About a half an hour."

"What time did you leave Bantry for home?"

"I left at around seven o'clock for home."

"Were you on your own?"

"No; I was in the company of two men named Timothy Sullivan and Patrick Mahony until we reached Dromsullivan West at about half past eight. I then caught up with Tim Cadogan around ten minutes later."

"Was Cadogan on his own?"

"He was."

"What did the two of you talk about?"

"On the way into Bantry that morning Cadogan told me he was going into town that day to look for employment and he asked me if I knew of anyone looking for a man. I said I didn't but when I caught up with him I told him that an old master of his, Con Sullivan of Maularaha, was looking for him; he had work for him. Cadogan said he would go see him after Mass on the following morning."

Mr Wright. "Did you speak regarding the death of Mr Bird?"

"I said to him was it not awful about Mr Bird and the way he had done away with himself or whatever happened or words to that effect."

"What did the prisoner say to that?"

"He said that the rumour around town was that Mr Bird had done it himself or his brother the doctor had done it. We said no more about it after that."

"When you reached your house did he say anything to you?"

"Yes; he asked me if I had a newspaper, that he had forgotten to get one himself. I told him I had got one and if he had the time he could come in and we could read it."

"Did he come in?"

"Yes and I read the paper to him."

"What time did he leave your house?"

"He left at about half past ten and said he wanted to be home before they were gone to bed; that he didn't want to be rapping on the door."

"Was the short conversation the two of you had about the death of Mr Bird on your way home the only time the subject was mentioned?"

"Yes sir, we didn't talk about it again."

A man named Jeremiah McCarthy was next questioned.

Mr O'Leary. "Do you know the prisoner?"

"Yes; I know him for the last eight or nine years."

"Did you see him in Bantry on Saturday the 24th of February last?"

"I believe so."

"Where did you see him?"

"I remember passing through Bridewell Lane coming on dinner time and I turned left onto Marino Street where I saw a man named Cronin and a woman talking to a man who I think was the prisoner."

"Mr Wright. "Were you present at the United Irish League meeting in Bantry on Sunday the 18th of February?"

"I was."

"Did you see the prisoner that day?"

"I did."

"Did you observe what he was doing during the meeting?"

"I saw him shouting and taking off his cap."

"Did you ever know the prisoner to have possession of a gun?"

"Yes."

"When and where?"

"About seven or eight years ago when I was taking care of a farm for the late Denis McCarthy of Bantry, the prisoner lived close by and I saw him on the mountain with a gun."

"Was he often on the mountain with a gun?"

"I saw him more than once with one."

"Did you ever see him fire the gun?"

"Yes."

"What was he firing at?"

"Birds; woodcocks or grouse."

"Was he a good shot?"

"I couldn't tell you that."

"Did you know where he kept his gun?"

"No."

"How long were you minding the farm for Mr McCarthy?"

"For four or five years."

A labourer from Bantry named Jeremiah Keohane was deposed next.

Mr Wright. "Were you in Bantry on the 24th of February last?"

"Yes."

"Did you meet a man named Michael Regan that day?"

"Yes."

"Where abouts did you meet him?"

"I met him where they sell the fish in baskets in the Square near Bridewell Lane."

"Did you talk to him?"

"Yes; for about five minutes and then we walked slowly up New Street and Main Street as far as Timmy McCarthy's Corner on Barrack Street."

"What happened once you reached McCarthy's Corner?"

"We saw a crowd and heard what had happened regarding Mr Bird."

"Was Michael Regan still with you at this time?"

"Yes."

Mr O'Leary. "I object to this evidence as it is not evidence against the prisoner, it has simply been given to contradict the evidence of Michael Regan."

Mr Purdon. "Overruled."

"It appears there is no point in objecting to any evidence tendered as you will overrule all my objections."

The R.I.C. Head Constable of Borrisokane in County Tipperary, a man named McBride was next deposed.

"I was stationed in Glengarriff from August 1887 until June 1893."

Mr Wright. "Do you know the prisoner?"

"I do."

"How do you know him?"

"I often searched his house for firearms."

"Did you find any?"

"No."

"Do you recollect the murder of a man named Denis Harrington on the 12th of February 1891?"

"I do."

"Did you have a conversation with the prisoner regarding Harrington's murder?"

"Yes; on the 23rd of March that year the prisoner made a voluntary statement which I took down in writing. "

The Head Constable then took this statement from his pocket.

"It is as follows…"

Mr O'Leary. "I object to any such statement being received as evidence; it has no connection with this case."

Mr Purdon. "Overruled. Proceed Head Constable McBride."

"If Harrington had taken a fool's or a friend's or a neighbour's advice, the damned thing would never had happened to him, but he was too covetous. I last saw his sister in New York about six years ago. I got two months imprisonment and hard labour for firing at a man named Hallissey of

Dunkerron West, Kenmare. The only evidence against me were two caps found in my waistcoat pocket an old one and a new one."

Mr O'Leary. "The sooner you take that statement back to the North Riding of Tipperary the better!"

(Denis Harrington was a twenty-one-year-old gamekeeper and was shot dead while carrying out his duties. Four men were arrested shortly after the murder. Timothy Cadogan was not one of them nor was he ever charged in connection with this murder.)

Patrick Lenihan, a farmer from Farranfadda next deposed that he had been in Bantry on the day of the murder and had spoken to Mr Bird outside the courthouse as he was coming from his club and heading in the direction of his office. He thought the time was about half past one but could not swear to an exact time. Mr Wright then applied to have the prisoner remanded for a further eight days while Mr O'Leary sarcastically said there was no point in him objecting. Cadogan was then removed and returned to prison in Cork. He would be remanded on another three further occasions before the investigation resumed on Wednesday the 25th of April, two months after his arrest. Once again the hearing was held in camera and the principals in the case were the same. The first person deposed was a woman named Mary Hourihane who lived on Marino Street in Bantry.

"On the 24th of February I went to the office of the late W.S. Bird on Barrack Street at about a quarter to two to pay rent. I went up two or three steps of the stairs and then noticed the office door was closed. I turned around and as I went out the street door I met Mr Scanlon, who was a rent collector for Mr Bird. We spoke for a little while at the door, about ten minutes. I then went down Barrack Street as far as the corner leaving Mr Scanlon at the door. A short while later I returned again and Mr Scanlon told me that Mr Bird was now upstairs in the office. I went upstairs to the office and I found Mr Bird alone writing a letter. I paid him the rent and was only there a minute or two when Mr Hegarty entered the office. As I left I heard the two of them talking. I walked down the stairs and out the hall onto Barrack Street without seeing anyone else and went straight home. This was shortly after two o'clock."

Michael Scanlon, Mr Bird's rent collector was next to be deposed.

"I was standing at the street door of Mr Bird's office at about two o'clock and I was speaking to Mrs Hourihane for a few minutes. After she departed down Barrack Street I remained at the door and I noticed Mr Bird coming around Biggs's Corner. He spoke to me and then we both went upstairs and transacted our business. I was in the office for about five minutes before I left. I met nobody on my way out to the street. A short time later I heard that Mr Bird had been shot."

The next witness called was John Leary, Old Barrack Road, Bantry.

"At about two o'clock on the afternoon of the 24th of February I went to Mr Bird's office on Barrack Street. I entered by the street door and went upstairs to the office. As I was going up I could hear two people talking and when I went into the office I found Mr Bird and Michael Hegarty, they were the only people there. Mr Bird was sitting on a chair behind the counter and Hegarty was standing at the front of it. They stopped talking when they heard me approach, I thought Mr Bird seemed a bit agitated. He gave me some money that was due to me and I then went down the stairs and out the street door."

R.I.C. District Inspector Armstrong was then called to give his evidence.

"I arrived at Mr Bird's office at five minutes to three. Acting Sergeant Driscoll was there in charge of the body which was lying between the counter and the door. I examined the body without moving it and saw the wounds. I noticed the back of the right hand was scorched and yellow. I thought clutching the barrel of the revolver being fired would account for this scorching. I searched the clothing of the deceased with the assistance of acting Sergeant Driscoll and found some money in a trouser pocket and a bullet in the lining of his coat. I was present the next day when the doctors were examining the body and a bullet which was removed from just above the right hip was handed to me by Dr Popham. On the 9th of March last I met Timothy Breen outside his workshop on Marino Street and we walked from there through Bridewell Lane, New Street, Main Street to his father's public house on Barrack Street, which I entered and walked to the foot of his stairs. I then turned round and walked a distance of about fifteen yards into the middle of the street. As I did so I saw Head Constable Brennan and Sergeant Burke coming out of Mr Bird's office through the street door. By arrangement with me they had started at another place to get there. It had taken me three minutes from Breen's workshop to where I was standing when I saw them come out of Mr Bird's office. The Head Constable had taken the direct route from Breen's workshop along Marino Street which was a distance of 137 yards to Mr Bird's, while the route I took was 304 yards."

Head Constable Brennan was next called and he collaborated the evidence of District Inspector Armstrong regarding the experiment carried out on the 9th of March. After the Head Constable stepped down Mr Wright said that was the end of the evidence and asked for the prisoner to be returned for trial at the next Assizes on the capital charge of wilful murder.

Mr O'Leary. "I object on the grounds of insufficient evidence. Timothy Breen saw the prisoner within 137 yards of Mr Bird's office, but as that was a market day you could find 150 people who were nearer. In fact, I myself was in my office the same day and cannot see why I should not be charged as well as the prisoner."

Mr Purdon. "Mr O'Leary has not heard the important evidence which was given at the beginning of this case. I return the prisoner for trial to the Summer Assizes."

The important evidence which Mr Purdon was referring to was then placed in evidence in the form of two depositions which were read into the record. The first was from Walter Dennis which he deposed on the 27th of February.

"I was in Mr Warner's shop on the day in question. Mr Bird's office was above it. I heard some noises as if footsteps running around the office. I then heard two shots and went to the door that leads into the hall. I saw a man coming down the stairs, that man was Timothy Cadogan. He had a revolver in his hand next to me. He put it back into his pocket. I went back into the shop and looked out the window. Cadogan rushed along the Glengarriff Road. I knew him from coming into town for the last two years but I did not know him by name."

The second deposition was by a Miss Fanny Dukelow, an employee of Warner's shop, she stated that when Walter Dennis came back into the shop he was very pale and frightened.

Prior to the trial a defence brief was written and filed by Mr Ralph Brereton Barry Q. C., the defence counsel who would defend Timothy Cadogan at his trial.

"As counsel will see from the depositions, in this case the late William Symms Bird was murdered in his office at Barrack Street, Bantry on Saturday the 24th of February sometime between a quarter past two and half past two. Saturday is Market Day in Bantry and the streets were also pretty crowded with people and cars, especially Barrack Street, Main Street, New Street and The Square, where they sell fish, baskets, and cabbages, and around Hurst's Corner (Mr Hurst's public house is almost opposite the fish market.) On the other hand Marino Street and along the courthouse wall opposite Breen's workshop where the prisoner was seen standing is very quiet as the people do not gather there at all. It is unlikely to be the way a person about to commit murder would select to come to Mr Bird's office, whereas, if a person came by New Street, Main Street, and Barrack Street, he would have a better chance of escaping unnoticed and could pass along easily until he came to the office.

From Mr Bird's office door down Barrack Street until it joins with Main Street, it is generally lined on Saturdays with horses and carts and a person could be scarcely seen by anyone on the opposite side of the street. A person could easily have waited in Barrack Street within sight of Mr Bird's office door and slipped in after Mr Bird had gone in, with much less chance of being seen then standing opposite Breen's workshop where it will be alleged that the prisoner was seen waiting. In the former place he was in a position to see if the coast was clear and that nobody was standing at Mr Bird's hall door, while in the latter he would have no such opportunity; in as much from Marino Street he had no view of the office door and could not see whether anybody was around the place until he came around the corner from Marino Street onto Barrack Street and right up to the office door. Then, as to Glengarriff Road, where it is alleged the prisoner was seen running up after the murder as proved by the witness Dennis; it runs across the top of

Barrack Street where people gather on Saturdays as a rule. If a person ran across there, he could not but be seen by a lot of people and running would certainly attract a lot of attention particularly after shots were fired. Along the Glengarriff Road there are mostly tenement houses for about 300 yards on one side and 400 yards on the other, and all the old women and young children are for the most part of their days and especially on Saturdays, at their doors or sitting at the front chatting and taking stock of all the people passing by. And although the police have visited each one of these houses they have failed to find one who saw the prisoner running out that way on that Saturday. Several of these people must have known the prisoner for this is the road he has taken in and out of Bantry all his life.

As to the prisoner being seen on Hurst's Corner, that is nothing unusual as it is a recognised corner for corner boys and country fellows on a Saturday. Then as to the evidence given by the witness Michael Regan, who swore he saw the prisoner alone a little below the Bridewell Lane where the empty carts are stored, that is also a place where corner boys and others congregate and sit on the empty carts, and as to the prisoner being seen subsequently standing in Vickery's lane where Patsy Kelly has the horses, that particular place is a kind of public urinal for all the loafers and idlers of the town as it is a lane running behind a lot of backyards which have a number of stables and which was at one time the entrance to Vickery's own stables connected to the hotel. Unfortunately in this case the prisoner cannot account for himself after the time he was seen standing outside Breen's workshop talking to a man and woman by the witness Timothy Breen. He has said in a number of interviews with Mr. Flynn that he walked around the town aimlessly and did not meet or speak to anyone he knew. In this respect it should be mentioned that the prisoner was always a morose distant sort of fellow and associated with very few people.

My principal case will be to try and break the Crown's evidence and show to the jury that it would have been impossible for the prisoner to have had the time to commit the murder between the time he was seen by Timothy Breen standing opposite his father's workshop and the time the murder was committed. As it has been sworn by Timothy Breen, that he left the prisoner standing opposite or a little below the workshop and walked up Bridewell Lane up New Street onto Main Street and then Barrack Street, and that when he got to the foot of the stairs in his own house, which is directly opposite Mr Bird's office, he heard the shots and swore that it must have been between ten minutes past two and a quarter past two, that he left his workshop and left the prisoner there, at the time the prisoner seemed engrossed in conversation with a man and woman and apparently had no intentions in immediately parting with them. Henry Breen Snr. also swore that it must have been ten minutes past or a quarter past two when his son left the workshop. Then to a walking experiment carried out by Timothy Breen and District Inspector Armstrong as sworn by the latter's deposition. Tim Breen and the District Inspector also walked up Marino Street and the latter opened the two locks and Tim Breen walked into the office and behind the counter. District Inspector Armstrong then told him to go down to the door and see if he could see the police coming. Breen did so and the police were only coming around the corner of Barrack Street from Main Street further down. It is thought the police were sent around by New street and Main Street to know if it would tally with Breen and Armstrong getting there previously, if so, it did not.

As to Walter Dennis, who is the principal witness against Timothy Cadogan, we believe threats were made against him by the police to give the evidence he has given. He was taken by acting Sergeant Driscoll from Warner's shop on Tuesday the 27th of February to the police barracks where his deposition was taken in front of the accused. There was no test of identification as the prisoner was not put among any number of people to be identified by Dennis. Mr O'Flynn is also informed that Mr O'Leary, the prisoner's solicitor, was also refused admission when Dennis was giving his evidence. The next evening Dennis was driven to Durras Road station, the next station to Bantry, and taken to Clontarf in Dublin and is there ever since under the charge of acting Sergeant Driscoll. Dennis is about nineteen years of age and Mr O'Flynn is informed by his parents that he is very easily frightened, fond of drink, quarrelsome to his parents at home as he wouldn't get money when he wanted and he wouldn't go to school. It is not known how Dennis could be so well acquainted with the prisoner as the prisoner was such a reserved type of man that very few people knew him and he did not frequent the town much. The evidence of Harry Breen in a great measure contradicts the evidence of Dennis, as Breen has stated he set his clock at twenty-five past two that day and that it was five minutes fast. He then came

40

and stood at his own door and heard the shots. He looked in the direction of Mr Bird's office and down the street and then remained at his door for a couple of minutes after. If that is so and Dennis's evidence is true, he should have seen the prisoner come out of Mr Bird's office.

The witness Patrick Cronin swore he saw the accused outside of Mahony's shop on Barrack Street at around one o'clock. That cannot be, even on the evidence of the Crown and on the witness John Sullivan, who accompanied the prisoner to town that day, they went straight to Hurst's pub when they arrived in town and it has been sworn that the prisoner remained around Hurst's up to all events half one or later.

The action of the witness Michael Hegarty is rather mysterious. He is not considered a man of very upright character. He was at one time an emergency blacksmith and was for a long time under police protection in the days of the Land League. He was at that time considered a man of notorious character who would stop at nothing. He, of course, carries firearms. In later years though, he has changed and now poses as a full-blown Nationalist. Apparently that day he was the last man seen with Mr Bird before he was shot and according to the evidence of the man Leary, he thought he heard angry words as he went up the stairs and that Mr Bird appeared to him to be angry looking. There is discrepancy between the evidence that Hegarty gave at the inquest and at the inquiry. At the inquest he said he first heard about the murder at about Cullinane's or Vickery's, while in his deposition he said it was much further down, "opposite the late Philip Wolfe's house.". Then again if he was such a great friend of Mr. Bird as he wished people to believe, why did he not go up to Barrack Street and find out for himself the truth of Mr Bird's death. Sometime later that evening he was taken to the police barracks and kept there until Dr Bird came home. He was let go then as Dr. Bird said that the only man who could do it was Timothy Cadogan. Another strange thing too, Dr Bird was out shooting in Dunmanus, where Hegarty was living. Mr O'Flynn also believes there was an unfinished entry in Mr Bird's books regarding the payment from Hegarty. This Hegarty was an emergency man and a bailiff nearly all over County Cork. He acted as a bailiff on the Ponsonby Estate in East Cork and use to take a type of travelling forge with him to shoe boycotted horses. He was well used to using a revolver at all events. In fact if Cadogan committed the murder, Hegarty should have met him on the stairs after leaving Mr Bird. Hegarty is certainly bad minded to do anything.

With regards to the witness Robert Warner, he, it is thought could be got to swear that Hegarty entered the shop where he was and that he then went up to Mr. Birds office and then he heard the shuffling and the shots. It is said that the witness Dennis said to the witness Swords several times between the day of the murder and the following Tuesday, when he volunteered the evidence, that he did not know or had no idea who committed the murder. It is also stated that he said the same to other parties."

End of Brief

The Grand Jury

The Commission of Assize for the County of Cork was opened on the morning of the 16th of July in the County Courthouse by Mr Justice William Kenny. The Justice was a former Liberal Unionist M.P. for the constituency of St Stephen's Green in Dublin. He had won his seat in 1892 by defeating George Plunkett, the father of Joseph Mary Plunkett, one of the leaders of the 1916 Rising. He was appointed Solicitor General in 1895 and served until 1898 when he resigned as both Solicitor General and as an M.P. in order to be appointed as a High Court Judge. In his memoir "The Old Munster Circuit" published in 1939, Maurice Healy, a solicitor and author, described Kenny as "stern and inflexible, somewhat lacking in empathy for those poorer than himself, but also a sound and learned lawyer with a strong sense of justice."

Addressing the Grand Jury with regard to the murder of William Symms Bird, Mr Justice Kenny said.

"This homicide is one that in its calculated deliberation and its deadliest of purpose has left an indelible stain on your county. The murdered man was a gentleman named Bird, a well-known land agent. On the 24th of February last between the hours of two and three o'clock, in the broad daylight, he was shot dead in his office in the town of Bantry. He was seen alive and well shortly after two o'clock on that day; his dead body was found between half past two and three o'clock. The reports of at least two shots were heard by people in the vicinity of his office, and evidence will, I believe, be laid before you that the accused man, Timothy Cadogan, was seen coming down stairs from the direction of the office with a revolver in his hand. It would appear that Cadogan had been evicted some years ago from a holding on an estate over which the deceased was agent, and that on several occasions; the last being about six months before the murder, he had applied to the deceased gentleman to be reinstated and had been refused. If, gentlemen, you see no reason to doubt the evidence of these circumstances that will be laid before you, it will be your duty to find a true bill against the accused. Whether he be a guilty man or not the fact remains that a murder of a most cowardly and terrible character has been committed.

While I trust that it does not indicate a recommencement of that form of crime that has disgraced this country in years gone by and led to untold misery. I cannot avoid referring to a circumstance appearing on the deposition; that a public meeting was held in the town on the Sunday before this awful occurrence took place, at which observations were alleged to have been made in regard to the estate on which the eviction of the accused man took place. That, gentlemen, was a meeting to establish a branch of a body that calls itself the United Irish League, and it was addressed by two gentlemen, both well-known, one of them being a member of Parliament. I cannot imagine from the past experience of this country anything more dangerous to the community than meetings of this character, especially in a county like this, where, I am informed by the officials, that there are large number of evicted farms and that people are under police protection.

My own experience at the last Spring Assizes has supplied me with one of the strangest illustrations of what I said, in a case of malicious burning of hay which came before me as Assize judge in Enniskillen March last. The farm was an evicted one, and its occupation by a tenant was followed by a threatening letter, and to that succeeded a meeting of the United Irish League held alongside the farm, which was addressed by a member of Parliament, and at which this tenant was denounced. Then came the burning of the unfortunate tenant's hay, and finally the night before I heard the claim for compensation, the principal witness for the claimant was brutally murdered on his way home from the court. (Mr Justice Kenny was referring to a sixty-year-old man named Hugh Thompson who was beaten to death on the night of March 8th, 1900, near Belcoo in County Fermanagh) These facts, gentlemen, were all proved before me, and no one has been made amendable for that awful crime, and no motive for it was apparent save that the victim was a friend of the tenant of the farm. Gentlemen, the right of public meeting in one that is a free country like ours has unquestionably to be guarded, but like every other right it is capable of abuse. There may be utterances, which, under one state of things, may produce no injurious results, while in other surroundings, with perhaps an inflammable audience, intemperate expressions may lead to consequences

44

most mischievous to the community at large. I think I am bound to call attention to this aspect of crime at the present Assizes, and it would give me very great satisfaction indeed if I thought my words would have any effect in connection with the association I have referred, and which, according to the police reports, have an organisation represented by over seventy branches in this county, all of which have come into being within the last year."

The Grand Jury then retired to consider the bill and returned shortly after with a true bill against Timothy Cadogan. Consequently he was sent forward for trial which was to begin on Wednesday the 19th of July. Mr Justice Kenny announced that he expected the full panel of jurors to be in attendance and warned that any absentees would incur a heavy penalty.

The Trial of Timothy Cadogan

The trial of Timothy Cadogan for the wilful murder of William Symms Bird opened at half past ten on Wednesday the 19th of July with Mr Justice Kenny presiding. Chief counsel for the Crown was the Solicitor General, Mr George Wright Q.C.. Mr Redmond Barry Q.C.* and Mr J.F. Moriarty B.L. assisted the Solicitor General. The defence team was led by Mr Ralph Brereton Barry Q.C.* who was assisted by Mr P.D. Lynch B.L..

*(In order to try and avoid confusion, since we have a Barry representing both sides, from here on Mr Redmond Barry for the Crown will be referred to as Mr Redmond, while Mr Ralph Brereton Barry for the defence will be referred to as Mr Barry.)

A common jury was sworn in consisting of Daniel Hunter, a sixty-year-old business manager from Blackrock, who acted as jury foreman. Edward Hoare, also from Blackrock, who was a thirty-seven-year-old veterinary surgeon. Redmond Reali aged forty, a farmer and landowner from Glanworth. Richard Jonas Smith, a forty-six-year-old farmer from Ballincollig. George Walton aged forty-four, a farmer from Carrigaline. Frederick Stopford, a forty-one-year-old produce broker from Monkstown. William Ross from Glanmire, a fifty-nine-year-old stationmaster. William Hawkes aged thirty-four, a farmer from Knockavilly and the only Roman Catholic on the jury. James Wilson, a fifty-year-old master painter from Grand Parade. George Duke from Shanakiel, a forty-five-year-old cattle dealer. James McDowall, a fifty-eight-year-old brewery agent from St Patrick's Hill and Robert Cleburne from Monkstown, a fifty-seven-year-old merchant tailor.

Mr Justice Kenny opened proceedings by asking the defendant how did he plea to the charge that he did wilfully murder William Symms Bird on the 24th of February 1900. Timothy Cadogan replied in a strong voice.

"Not guilty sir."

The Solicitor General then rose to his feet to deliver his opening address.

"On the 24th of February of the present year in the town of Bantry in the west of this county, occurred a murder so cold, so cruel, so premeditated in its character, that I do not believe the history of this county or any other county in Ireland furnished any parallel to it. It occurred in the middle of the day, a little after two o'clock in a well frequented street in the town on market day. It was obviously a murder carefully planned, carefully thought out and executed by a man who had some motive for carrying it out. A motive strong enough to impel him to risk his life for the object he had in his view. What that object was, I will tell you shortly. It was carried out by a man who evidently knew the place and the victim well. The victim was Mr William Symms Bird, a land agent in this county; the place was his office where the murder was committed between fifteen and twenty minutes passed two. Before twenty-four hours of the crime had elapsed, Timothy Cadogan, the prisoner at the bar, was in the custody of the police and charged with having committed the murder. It will be my duty to submit to you evidence that will bring home clearly and beyond all doubt that the prisoner at the bar is guilty of having committed this murder.

People in the street and about the place were attracted by the sounds of two or three shots and when they ran into the office they found Mr Bird lying on his hands and knees on the floor with his head under his chest. One bullet had passed through his forearm and was found in the lining of his coat, another bullet entered the left breast and was found afterwards in the body. Probably the second wound either caused death or was sufficient to cause it. However, the man who went there was determined to leave nothing to chance, he fired a third shot into the head of his victim. This bullet was found in the base of Mr Bird's skull. It will be necessary to trace the movements of the prisoner, to tell you who he is, what was his connection to Mr Bird, and what is feelings towards Mr Bird were. We will show he came into the town of Bantry that day at the hour of one o'clock with the single object of taking Mr. Bird's life and having accomplished that, he left that night.

Mr Bird was a Justice of the Peace for this county, a Grand Juror on many occasions, a landlord in a small way and a land agent. He was a quiet and inoffensive gentleman that has ever drew the breath of life. Mr Bird was receiver for a property at Glengarriff known as the White Estate, and under the Land Court he had to follow their directions on every matter concerning the estate. I mention this to show that once a man had been appointed receiver, his own independent volition was taken away. A tenant on this estate was Timothy Cadogan, the prisoner. He got into arrears with his rent and in 1894 Mr Bird, by direction of the court brought a civil bill against him and a decree was pronounced in October 1894. It appeared by the decree that four years rent was due, in fact it was high time that those proceedings were brought. Possession was taken on the 19th of August 1895. From that time until the time of Mr Bird's death, Timothy Cadogan nourished feelings of deep resentment towards him. Possession was taken by a bailiff named Sullivan. Mr Bird and his brother Dr Bird, who was at one time a surgeon in the navy and since his retirement had helped his brother, went out to see possession taken. The bailiff and Sergeant Cooper will tell you what the demeanour and the conduct of the prisoner was on that day. The prisoner was extremely violent; he was blaming Mr Bird for being the author of his eviction, he smashed the furniture and so violent was his demeanour that Sergeant Cooper had to remain beside Mr. Bird for his protection. Before leaving Mr Bird felt the need to say. "Cadogan, you are a bad boy". Cadogan is a man extremely fond of firearms, I do not mention this as a point of evidence in this case. It is merely a circumstance to say that he was very fond of shooting about the mountains, and with a revolver was a very good shot. He was clever in evading the visits of the police. Over and over again for years past, week after week, the police used to go to Cadogan's house to search but could never find anything.

In this case we have found it incredibly hard to gleam information because as you will understand very well, no one wishes to come forward to help in the prosecution of a person in a case like this. I mention this because it was with the greatest difficulty that we secured evidence from a man named Levis, whose evidence was given a short time ago and after the prisoner had been returned for trial. In his evidence Levis states that he met the prisoner on the mountain a short time after his eviction and he was cussing and swearing and saying he was going to take Mr Bird's life and other things of that kind. Now, I do not ask you to take these remarks literally, because an angry man often uses such expressions without meaning them. The prisoner from being a small farmer became a farm labourer. On several occasions he visited Mr Bird's office in Bantry; an office he knew perfectly well, for the purpose of getting reinstated. The last time he came to the office was about six months before the murder and on that occasion Dr Bird happened to be in the office. Cadogan in somewhat of an aggressive manner demanded to be reinstated as a tenant. Later we found he got employment with one Richard Sullivan, living about six miles from Bantry. This employment lasted until the end of January past. He asked Sullivan to allow him to remain in his home until he found new employment, which Sullivan agreed to. However Cadogan was now a man without work or a home and his feelings towards Mr Bird intensified.

Now we come to the 17th of February last. On that day Cadogan came into Bantry and took a night's lodgings with a woman named Ellen O'Donoghue. Why did he come to stay in Bantry that night? Because on the 18th of February a meeting was held in the vicinity of Bantry; a meeting under the auspices of an organisation which was called the United Irish League, and there the usual speeches of an inflammatory character were made, speeches made by men who probably think little of their words, speeches by men who thought little of the consequences of their words or cared less. Speeches by men who probably never owned a sod of land in their lives. Men who want to alter the relationships between landlords and tenants. At a particular part of this meeting, when the speeches were at their most violent, Timothy Cadogan was seen with his hat off waving it in his hand. At that meeting allusions were made against the White Estate and the management of it. Timothy Cadogan heard those allusions and Timothy Cadogan cheered these speeches, and remember Timothy Cadogan vowed to have Mr Bird's life and had threatened him on three occasions. When he went home these speeches were ringing in his ears. As to cause and effect, the speeches were like that of a lighted match on dry timber and it roused the smouldering vengeance that lay in Cadogan's mind for the last four or five years.

Now let us come to the day of the murder. I will ask you to follow the movements of Timothy Cadogan on that day and the movements of the murdered man on that date. On that day the prisoner, with a man name Sullivan, walked a distance of about seven miles to the town of Bantry and when they arrived in the town they went into a public house owned by a man named Hurst. According to Hurst, Cadogan stayed about a quarter of an hour or twenty minutes. We suggest that Cadogan did not come to town that day to make purchases for himself, nor to buy a newspaper for his master Richard Sullivan, but with the object and purpose of taking Mr Bird's life. See how he watched Mr Bird's movements that day. By standing outside Hurst's pub you can see from Bird's office to the Bantry Conservative Club. We suggest that Cadogan was on the watch all day for Mr. Bird. He had had his drink in Hurst's and had then come out and watched, for he was seen standing outside for a considerable time, and what was he doing? He was dogging and watching for Mr Bird, his victim. Cadogan was seen going into the public house, was seen to have a drink, was not seen going about looking for employment, was seen standing outside Hurst's public house, apparently with a perfect view of Mr Bird going down to his club and back.

There is a family named Breen in Bantry, the father Henry, holding a public house in Barrack Street, almost exactly opposite Warner's shop. Lower down in Marino Street, he has a coach workshop, and that workshop is almost directly opposite where Bridewell Lane opens into Marino Street. Two o'clock is the dinner hour in Bantry and this was a very critical time as the murder was committed in a few moments after that time by a man who was no burglar, and who having done the work made off as quickly as he could. Just after two o'clock that day when the employees had been sent off, Henry Breen Snr. and his son Timothy, were standing outside their workshop, and on the footpath on the other side they saw and took particular notice of the prisoner. You will find that the prisoner followed Mr Bird through Bridewell Lane and when seen by the Breen's was only a minute or two behind him. The distance from where Timothy Cadogan was seen standing to Mr Bird's office was 137 or 138 yards, which a man walking quickly would cover in only a minute or two. You now have to follow the movements of another person in this critical drama. Young Timothy Breen for some reason of his own, started from the coach workshop and went to his father's grocery establishment by the longer route, by Bridewell Lane through New Street, Main Street and down the whole length of Barrack Street, a distance of about 380 yards. To a man walking rapidly it would take about three and a half minutes, but for a lad walking like young Breen it might have taken five minutes. The importance of this matter is this, just as young Breen reached his home above his father's shop he heard two or three shots emanating from the upstairs office in the building opposite, Mr. Bird's office. In Warner's shop underneath Mr. Bird's office there were three people, a girl named Fanny Dukelow, Walter Dennis, and a nephew of Mr. Warner's. Fanny Dukelow had only come back from dinner about ten minutes, and from a public clock on her way in she saw it was ten minutes past two. Both Dennis and herself heard something which they described as like dragging or the shuffling of feet overhead. A piece of mortar fell from the ceiling. They then heard what they thought were two shots but it was in fact three that they heard. Young Dennis, who was behind one of the counters, went to the back door which led into the hall leading to Mr. Bird's office and saw a man coming down the stairs in the broad daylight with a revolver in his hand. The man who came down was undoubtably the man who had fired the shots. That man according to Walter Dennis was the prisoner, Timothy Cadogan. You have often heard that a great deal depends on a person's power of identification - he might see him on a dark night or he may see him a long distance away- but Walter Dennis had known the prisoner by appearance for a considerable time and knew him by name for about twelve months. He saw him frequently in the shop and saw him that day in broad daylight at two o'clock. Young Dennis, like the prisoner, is a native of this county, coming from Whiddy Island. He is not motivated by any sordid reason to give any false evidence against Timothy Cadogan and I challenge any of my learned friends to suggest that he is. He saw the man coming downstairs with a revolver in his right hand before putting it into his pocket and exit by the front door. Walter Dennis had at this time figured out in his own mind that this was the revolver which had fired the shots that he had heard. He came back to the shop according to the girl Fanny Dukelow, pale and frightened. Then standing at the window so he could see out, he saw the same man running down the Glengarriff Road, from where he apparently disappeared. Of course, the news quickly spread and people rushed to the office. The police were sent for and were there at twenty-five minutes past two.

Now we shall seek the motive for the murder. Mr. Bird was a land agent and was collecting rents in his office that day, so I ask, was robbery the motive that day? We shall examine the last people to see Mr. Bird alive in his office. Mrs. Hourihane was there and a man named Hegarty, who paid Mr. Bird a sum of £10, for which Mr. Bird gave him a receipt. Hegarty then left the office and met his wife and went to a shop owned by a man named Cullinane. When people arrived they found the deceased's watch and money still in his possession, the office was not ransacked in the way a thief would go about his business looking for valuables. This rules out the motive of robbery. What was the motive then if it was not revenge? Was the prisoner stimulated by the reckless speeches that he had heard the Sunday before? To give effect to the vow he had given in the mountains some years before. He came to town that day to take Mr. Bird's life. It was the work of a man who knew his way into and out of the victim's office and knew the use of firearms and the vital importance of concealing them. At about half past eight on the night of the murder the prisoner was overtaken by the same man he had gone to town with that morning, John Sullivan. Cadogan never said a word about the murder, which was the talk of the town, until Sullivan said to him. "Wasn't it an awful thing about poor Bird." And what was Cadogan's answer? "It must have been he killed himself or else the doctor did it." Whether it was he wanted to suggest that the man had been killed by his brother, with whom he lived with in the closest friendship, I do not know. Although Cadogan said he remained in town until six o'clock that evening, he forgot all about the paper his master told him to buy. On the way home he appeared to have met another man, Cornelius Sullivan. Having heard from John Sullivan of the murder of Mr. Bird and having brought the extraordinary theory that the victim had either shot himself or had been done away with by his brother the doctor, he went into Cornelius Sullivan's house for a drink of water or something of that kind, Sullivan who had not been to Bantry that day, asked was there any news from the town. Cadogan's reply that there was none but that there was a great war in South Africa! Is this answer consistent with Cadogan being an innocent man? Was there a man in Bantry that day who talked less about the murder than Cadogan? Would not the first thing he would have told Sullivan was that Mr. Bird had been shot dead if he had a had no hand act or part in the crime. He had no word to say about this awful tragedy, instead he mentioned the war in South Africa. Putting all these things together, were they the sayings of an innocent man or were they the sayings and language of the man whom Walter Dennis saw coming down the stairs with a revolver in his hand. After this Cadogan went to the home of his employer, arriving there after everything had been locked up for the night. When he came in he was asked had he got the paper and he replied that he had not. Not a single word did he say about the tragedy that had occurred in town. Was there any other explanation for this behaviour other than a guilty man wanting to conceal his guilt.

It cannot be suggested that the police were lacking in the matter. The morning after the murder acting Sergeant Driscoll set off from Bantry to look for Cadogan and at half past five or six o'clock found him in the house of Richard Sullivan. The acting sergeant asked him to account for his movements the previous day. Cadogan said he went into Bantry at such and such hours and had some drinks and so on; but on his movements up Marino Street and Bridewell Lane he said nothing. He said he was in the town up until six o'clock. You know it would be easy to get evidence to help the prisoner but as far as we know there were no sightings of him from when he was seen running down the Glengarriff Road at half past two. Cadogan is a practiced shot. He has been a poacher for years; he has being shooting grouse and any other game he could find on the mountains for years. In that time he has avoided being caught by the police in possession of firearms and above all he was particular conscious of the consequences of being caught with firearms and ammunition.

Cadogan had been in America and when he came home he got a farm but was unable to keep it and ended up being evicted. He had not only cherished feelings of resentment but he had given utterances to those feelings. On the 18th of February his blood had been fired by the speeches he had heard. On the 24th of February he came in to Bantry nominally to do two things neither of which he did. The man who took William Bird's life was a man who had a very strong motive of revenge. Cadogan had such a motive, the man who took it was a man who dogged and watched Mr Bird's movement. Cadogan is the man; the man who did it was a man who knew Mr Bird's office, Cadogan knew it. The man who did it was a man who well understood weapons and how to use them. Cadogan is such a man, and above all what was the meaning of the prisoner concealing to the three Sullivans any knowledge of the tragic event.

Putting all these things together, is it not true that in that fateful hour as Timothy Breen was going around the three sides of the building, Cadogan was advancing up the fourth and was the man that Walter Dennis, who has no motive but to swear what he saw, saw coming down the stairs. It is not a case where Dennis did not divulge this knowledge for a long time. It is not a case that a long time elapsed before Dennis told what he saw. Cadogan was arrested on the Sunday and was before the magistrates on the following Tuesday, and on that day Walter Dennis was examined under oath and identified Timothy Cadogan as the man he saw three short days before coming down the stairs with a revolver in his hand.

Such is the outline of the Crown's case. If what I have stated is borne out you will have no doubt that a cruel, cold, and deliberately planned and premeditated murder was committed by a person who had the worst feelings against Mr Bird. If the jury is satisfied that it was carried out in this cold and determined fashion and if they are satisfied that the man who stood over the victim and fired those shots into his victim was Timothy Cadogan, all pity should be displaced and it will be their duty to respect their oaths and find the prisoner guilty."

This concluded the Solicitor General's opening statement. Mr Harding Ryan, a civil engineer from Dublin was then called to prove the accuracy of a map produced of the streets of Bantry. The first witness called was the Sheriff's Bailiff John Sullivan, who repeated the evidence he gave at the magisterial inquiry regarding the eviction of Timothy Cadogan in 1895. He was followed by Sergeant Cooper who also repeated his evidence, he was cross examined by Mr. Lynch.

"On that day did the prisoner promise to pay the rent he owed?"

"I could not say."

"Yet at the magisterial inquiry you swore that he indeed did promise to pay what he owed if Mr Bird would stop the eviction."

"I thought he did, but that is only my opinion."

Dr Robert Bird, the deceased's brother was next to take the stand and he also repeated the evidence he had given previously at the magisterial inquiry. He then went into further detail in regard to the last encounter he witnessed between his brother William and Timothy Cadogan in the former's office.

"Mr Cadogan was very eager in his desire to be reinstated on his farm but my brother refused him. He told him that the land was now in the possession of Miss White and she could not be deprived of it."

Mr Redmond. "Do you recollect what Cadogan then said?"

"On thinking it over I recollect what he said was. You have done your worst; you can't do anymore, or the devil thank you and something in the way of you may be sorry for it."

"You swear now that you distinctly remember that?"

"I do; it has come back to me."

"What was the prisoner's demeanour on that occasion?"

"Sullen."

"When did you hear of your brother's murder?"

"I was out shooting all that day, fourteen miles from Bantry on my brother's property and did not hear about his murder until I was about three miles from home on my return that evening."

Mr Barry. "What else did you hear that evening?"

"When I came back to Bantry I heard a man named Hegarty had been detained by the police in connection with the murder. I ascertained that Mr Hegarty had been in my brother's office between two and half past two that afternoon."

"Did you know of Mr Hegarty?"

"Yes; his farm is near Kilthomane where I was shooting that day."

"Did you hear anything else about Mr Hegarty?"

"I heard that he had been in Bantry that day and had been in my brother's office shortly before he was murdered and had been arrested that night in connection with the murder."

"Did you know he had been boycotted in the past and also held firearms?"

56

"Yes."

"Did you know at one time he belonged to the Property Defence Association and afterwards he joined the Land League?"

"Yes."

"Was it you who suggested to the police that Cadogan should be arrested?"

"It wasn't"

"Who suggested it first?"

"It was the policeman; Mulcahy is his name I think."

"What did you say to Constable Mulcahy when he mentioned Timothy Cadogan's name to you?"

"I said if Cadogan was in town that day it was Cadogan who did it. Hegarty had no cause to."

"Tell me Dr. Bird, have you a boy in your employment by the name of Michael Leary?"

"We had."

"Where is he now?"

"I don't know; but I have a letter telling me that he went away last Monday."

"Very well; the importance of this will be seen later on."

Dr Bird. "He has left since I came here to Cork."

The next witness was an old man named William Levis and he was examined by Mr Moriarty.

"Do you know the prisoner well?"

"I knew him previously but I can hardly recognise him now."

"Do you remember meeting him shortly after he was evicted from his holding in 1895?"

"I do."

"Where was this?"

"In the mountains."

"And what did he say to you?"

"He said he would get revenge on Mr. Bird from turning him out of his farm and I said to him that it was not like old times when you could gather a mob and gain satisfaction from him. The law was too strict now and he replied Oh, we have another way of doing it."

"Did he say anything else or make any type of gesture?"

"Yes; he made the gesture of firing a gun."

Mr. Lynch. "When did all this occur?"

"About two or three years ago."

"And what do you believe Cadogan meant?"

"I knew he meant using a gun."

"Did you often see Cadogan in the mountains?"

"No."

"How far do you live from Bantry?"

"About eight miles."

"Did you give this evidence before the magisterial inquiry?"

"No."

"Even though you had heard that Cadogan had been arrested for the murder?"

"Yes."

"When did you give this information to the police?"

"About a month ago."

"And to which policeman did you give the information to?"

"To Sergeant Cooper."

"You made the statement about a month ago to him?"

"I did."

"Yes you did and that is the reason we were not served with notice till two days ago."

The next witness was Ellen Donoghue, the owner of the lodging house in which Timothy Cadogan stayed for a night the week before the murder, this was on the night before the meeting of the United Irish League was held. Mrs Donoghue stated that Cadogan was not in her house while the meeting was on and she also said in answer to a question from Mr. Barry that the reason he gave for staying was because of the snow, that a man had already being found dead in the mountains that week. The next person to take the stand was Jeremiah McCarthy.

Mr. Redmond. "Where do you live?"

"At the present I live in the town of Bantry."

"Where did you live before that?"

"I had charge of a farm belonging to Denis McCarthy, a merchant in Bantry, which was around nine or ten miles from the town."

"Do you know the prisoner?"

"Yes; he lived three or four miles from that farm."

"Did you ever see him with a gun?"

"Yes; on two or three occasions, on the mountain."

"Did you ever see him fire a gun?"

"Yes; on one occasion."

"What was he firing at?"

"I don't know; he was too far away."

"Did you ever see him shoot birds?"

"No."

"Well that flatly contradicts what you said before the magistrates."

Mr. Redmond then read out the witnesses previous deposition where he stated that he had seen Cadogan shooting at grouse and other birds on more than one occasion.

"Did you swear before the magistrates that you saw him shoot birds?"

"I was asked what was he shooting at and I said I suppose at birds."

"Did you say they were woodcock or grouse?"

"I may have; they were a long way away."

"Were you present at the meeting of the United Irish League on the 18th of February past?"

"I was."

"Who did you see there?"

"I saw Mr. William O'Brien and Mr. Gilhooly there."

"Did you see the prisoner in attendance?"

"I think I saw him there with his cap in his hand."

"What was he doing?"

"He was standing in the crowd."

"You have no doubt that he was there?"

"I think he was."

"Well if you saw him in the crowd there is no doubt that he was there?"

"Someone like him was there."

"Do you not know the man?"

"Well I did."

"Was he not the man you saw in the crowd?"

"I think he was."

"Was he doing anything in the crowd that attracted your attention?"

"No more than anyone else."

"What was he doing?"

"Standing in the crowd with his cap in his hand."

"Was he doing anything with his cap?"

"No."

"Did you hear him shouting?"

"It would have been hard for me, there was so many people."

"Did you hear him shouting?"

"There were many shouting."

"Did you hear Cadogan shouting?"

"I think I did?"

"Did you hear him shouting?"

"I think so."

"Did you swear before the magistrates that you saw Timothy Cadogan shouting and taking off his cap while the speeches were being made?"

"I don't think I said that; it was mad though."

"Did you see or hear the man shouting?"

"I saw him with his cap in his hand."

"What did you mean when you swore before the magistrates that you heard him shouting?"

"I don't think I did, but it was mad."

"Was it true?"

"It was."

"Were you in Bantry on the day Mr. Bird was killed?"

"I was."

"Did you see the prisoner that day and if you did where did you see him?"

"I went on to Marino Street from Bridewell Lane and as I did I saw a man with his back to me and I thought at the time it was Timothy Cadogan, but I don't know whether it was or not."

Mr. Lynch. "How long ago was it since you saw the prisoner in the mountains with a gun?"

"Eight or nine years ago."

"Did you see a man named Cronin talking to the man you thought was Cadogan on Marino Street that day?"

"I can't remember."

At this stage the court adjourned for lunch. When it resumed Bantry publican Mr. T.R. Hurst was called to take the stand. He confirmed he knew the defendant and that on the day of the murder he came into his premises in the company of two other men.

"One of whom was John Sullivan, the mason. They had two drinks each, one of which Cadogan paid for with a pound note."

Mr. Redmond. "At what time was this?"

"About half past one."

"How long was he in your pub?"

"For about a quarter of an hour or twenty minutes."

"Did you see him again that day?"

"No."

Mr. Barry. "Did you see the prisoner earlier that day on your premises with Sullivan?"

"Not that I remember."

"Do you remember any other detail about their visit?"

"Well, when they were ordering their first drink, Sullivan also ordered a bottle of whiskey to take away that evening."

"Was the third man Timothy Sullivan."

"I don't know, but I would recognise him if I saw him again."

The next witness called was a woman named Kate Harrington who lived near Mount Corrin about seven miles from Bantry. She stated that on the day of the murder she thought she arrived in Bantry at about twelve o'clock.

Mr. Redmond. "What did you do when you arrived?"

"I went to the fish market first and from there I could see Hurst's Corner."

"Did you see anyone you knew standing on the corner?"

"Yes I saw Timothy Cadogan."

"Was he with anyone?"

"There was a group standing there but I don't know if he was a part of it."

"Have you known him long?"

"For about fourteen years."

Mr. Lynch. "When you completed your business at the fish market did you notice if Cadogan was still on Hurst's Corner?"

"He was."

"Is it unusual for a crowd to lounge around on Hurst's Corner on a market day?"

"No."

"Did you see him again that day?"

"No."

"Where were you when you heard the news about Mr. Bird?"

"I was in Biggs's shop when I heard he had shot himself."

Henry Breen Snr was next called. He stated that his public house was opposite Mr. Bird's office.

Mr Redmond. "Where were you at two o'clock on the day of the murder?"

"A little after two o'clock I was standing outside my coach workshop on Marino Street?"

"Did you see Timothy Cadogan?"

"Yes."

"Was he alone?"

"No; he was walking and then he stopped to talk to a man and a woman whom I did not know."

A Juror. "In what direction was he walking?"

"From the Bridewell Lane in the direction of the courthouse and Square."

Mr Redmond. "What did you do then?"

"I went back into the workshop and sent my son for his dinner; all of the other employees had already gone. A man named Murphy came into the workshop soon after my son left. While we were talking another man, named Shea came and told us something that as a result of I went to Mr Bird's office."

Mr Justice Kenny. "How long was this after you told your son to go for his dinner?"

"I can't be sure but I think it was over a quarter of an hour."

Mr. Redmond. "And how long was it after you had seen the prisoner?"

"I cannot say."

Mr. Barry. "How many employees have you in your workshop?"

"Nine; including three of my sons."

"What time did the men go for their dinner?"

"At two o'clock."

"And how much longer after that did you see the prisoner?"

"About ten minutes."

"Was anyone with you when you saw him?"

"My son Tim was."

"Did your son leave immediately after you seeing Cadogan?"

"No; he went back into the workshop before leaving about five minutes later."

"Did you see your son leave?"

"No; I did not."

Mr Justice Kenny. "How long after your employees had gone for dinner before you saw Cadogan?"

"I could not say."

Henry Breen's son Timothy was next to give evidence. He corroborated his father's testimony about seeing Cadogan in Marino Street near their workshop. He stated that the prisoner was nearer to the courthouse then to the workshop when he saw him and he thought that this was at about ten past two.

"After that I went to dinner by Bridewell Lane, New Street and Main Street to my father's home on Barrack Street. On my way upstairs I heard the reports of shots nearby and when I got to my room I looked out the window and saw Mr Warner and his clerk, young Mr Warner, on the opposite side of the street in an apparent excited mood. I went back downstairs and crossed the street to where they were standing. I followed a Mr Swords inside and went up the stairs to Mr Bird's office. Mr Bird was lying partly on his knees with his face downwards, leaning in the direction of the door. I lifted him up and opened his shirt and put my hand on his chest. The chest heaved a little bit and I thought that I heard a sigh from Mr Bird, but he changed at once and turned black in the face."

Mr Lynch. "What was the accused doing as you went for your dinner?"

"He was talking to a man and a woman on Marino Street."

"Did you recognise the man and woman he was talking to?"

"I think it was Dan Cronin and his wife from Sheskin."

"Did you tell anyone this?"

"Yes; I told District Inspector Armstrong."

Mr Justice Kenny. "Were you in a hurry to get your dinner?"

"Yes sir."

"Then why if you were in a hurry did you not take the shortest route to your house?"

"I had no reason in the world."

R.I.C. Constable Daly was next on the stand. He stated he had been on beat duty between ten o'clock and two o'clock on the day in question.

"At about half past one I was at the top of Barrack Street and I saw Mr Bird come out of his office. He then turned down Marino Street in the direction of his club."

Mr Barry. "How did you know what time it was?"

"I looked at my watch a short time before I got to the top of Barrack Street."

"Have you any idea how long it would have took Mr Bird to get from his office to his club?"

"If he walked at an ordinary pace, less than five minutes."

Frank Costelloe, a steward in the Bantry Conservative Club on Wolfe Tone Square was next called and he confirmed that Mr Bird was a member and that he was in the club on the 24th of February.

"I saw Mr Bird on three different occasions, the last was at ten minutes to two when I saw him in the reading room and we had a brief conversation. I left the club shortly afterwards on business and upon my return Mr Bird had left."

A labourer named Patrick Flynn then testified that he met Mr Bird heading in the direction of his office at about two o'clock walking at a smart pace. He was cross examined by Mr Barry.

"Was it after two o'clock or before two o'clock when you passed Mr Bird?"

"I think it was after two."

"But in your deposition before the magistrates you swore it was ten minutes before two when you passed Mr Bird."

"I am a bit confused."

"Think hard, was it after two o'clock like you say today or was it ten minutes to the hour as you swore in your deposition?"

"It was ten minutes to two."

One of the last people to see the deceased alive, Mr Bird's rent collector, Michael Scanlon, was next to give evidence.

"At about five minutes to two on the day in question I was standing at the street door to Mr. Bird's office awaiting his return."

Mr Redmond. "Were you alone?"

"No; a tenant of Mr Bird's named Mrs Hourihane was there waiting to pay her rent and we spoke for a few minutes. After our conversation she left and went down Barrack Street."

"What did you do?"

"I continued to wait for Mr Bird who arrived a few minutes later."

"What time did he arrive?"

"In or around two o'clock."

"Did he speak to you?"

"Yes; he said "Scanlon, what is the matter with you?" He then went upstairs and I followed him and completed my business with him and after a brief conversation I then left."

"Did you meet anybody on your way out?"

"Yes; I met Mrs Hourihane again out on the street, she was on her way to see Mr Bird."

"Where did you go then?"

"I then went home."

"Where do you live?"

"On Blackrock Road."

"When did you hear of Mr Bird's death?"

"I was sitting at home reading the newspaper at about half past two."

Mrs Mary Hourihane was next to take the stand.

"I went to Mr Bird's office at about a quarter to two on the 24th of February last to pay my rent. When I arrived there I found the office locked. While waiting outside I got into conversation with Mr Scanlan, Mr Bird's rent collector."

Mr Redmond. "Did you stay long?"

"For about ten minutes."

"What did you do then?"

"I walked down Barrack Street and around the corner on to Main Street before retracing my steps and returning to the office from where I met Mr Scanlon leaving. I then went upstairs and transacted my business with Mr Bird. After a brief conversation I left after a Mr Hegarty came into the office."

Mr Barry. "Could you hear the two men talking as you left?"

"Yes."

"Where did you go then?"

"I went home."

"Where do you live?"

"On Marino Street."

"Near Breen's coach workshop?"

"About three doors down."

"And what time was that."

"Not long after two."

Michael Hegarty, the owner of three farms, one of which he paid rent to Mr Bird for, was next to take the stand. He stated as well as farming he worked for Mr Bird, acting as a receiver, and collecting rents from small holdings in Dunmanus.

"On the 24th of February I was in Bantry. At about half past one I called to Mr Bird's office which I found locked. I then went down to Bridge Street to Mr Sullivans shop and from there to Cullinane's on Main Street. After some time there I returned to Mr Bird's office where I found him seated at his desk facing the counter speaking to a Mrs Hourihane. After she left I paid my rent of £10 with two £5 notes, I was speaking to him for some time and he gave me a receipt for my payment. Before I left a man named John Leary came into the office and Mr Bird gave him some money. Leary stayed for a few minutes and left before I did. When I left I went back to Cullinane's where my wife was waiting for me. We then went to Vickery's yard for my horse and from there we went to Miss O'Shea's on the Square for dinner. It was on our way to dinner that I heard about the murder."

Mr Lynch. "Did Mr Bird enter your payment into a book?"

"He had a book open in front of him but I could not say whether he entered my payment in it."

"Did Mr. Bird write in the book while you were there?"

"Yes."

"Had he given you your receipt before John Leary came into the office?"

"Yes."

"Who left the office first, you or Leary?"

"I was last to leave."

"Did you not swear at the inquest that you heard "Master Willie" had been shot as you went down Bridge Street?"

"I did not."

"How did you hear he had been shot?"

"My wife told me that she had overheard two girls saying that they heard he had shot himself."

"How did you feel when you heard this?"

"I was terribly shocked but I did not believe he had shot himself."

"At what time did your wife tell you that she had overheard the two girls?"

"At twenty-five past two."

"And at what time did you have dinner?"

"When we went to Miss O'Shea's for dinner it was three o'clock."

"It took you thirty-five minutes to walk there?"

"Yes."

"And you never made enquiries about Mr Bird?"

"No."

"Did you order dinner the same as if nothing had happened?"

"It was Miss O'Shea who told me that he had been murdered."

"And you stopped at O'Shea's for twenty minutes and never went to ask about it?"

"No; he was not a relative of mine and I did not think it was any of my business."

"You had a revolver some time ago?"

"Yes."

"Where is it?"

"At home."

"Have you a license for it?"

"Yes; for the last eighteen years."

"When did the police come look for you?"

"About an hour and a half after the occurrence."

"Did you make a statement to them?"

"Yes."

"Did they question you for long?"

"I was three hours in the barracks."

"In custody?"

"Not in custody."

"Do you suggest you could of went home at any time you wanted?"

"I didn't suggest the like."

"Why did you say you were not in their custody?"

"I thought I was not."

"Do you think you could have left?"

"I don't believe so."

Mr Moriarty. "Were you arrested?"

"I was not."

"Were you charged?"

"I was not."

Mr Justice Kenny. "It would have been a gross dereliction of their duty if the police had allowed the witness to go home."

John Leary then took the stand and confirmed to the Solicitor General that he had visited Mr Bird's office shortly after two o'clock and had left Michael Hegarty with him when he left.

Mr Barry. "Could you hear the two men talking as you went up the stairs to the office?"

"Yes; but they stopped when they heard me."

"How did Mr Bird appear?"

"He appeared angry."

"Who did he appear angry with?"

"I couldn't tell sir."

"There was only Mr Hegarty and himself in the office?"

"Yes."

"How long did you stay in the office?"

"Less than a minute."

"Did you hear them speak as you were going back downstairs?"

"No."

The next person to be examined was the Crown's most important witness. Walter Dennis, the man who swore he saw Timothy Cadogan coming down the stairs from Mr Bird's office holding a revolver after the shooting. He was examined by the Solicitor General.

"How old are you?"

"I am nineteen years old."

"Where are you from?"

"I am from Whiddy Island."

"Are you employed?"

"Yes; I have been employed by Mr. Warner in Bantry for the last four years."

"On the 24th of February at around two o'clock were you working?"

"Yes; I was working in the shop under Mr Bird's office."

"This is the shop next to Biggs's?"

"Yes."

"Was there anyone else with you?"

"Yes; there was a girl who works there as well named Fanny Dukelow."

"Tell me what occurred?"

"Shortly after two o'clock I heard footsteps upstairs in Mr Bird's office."

"What did you hear next?"

"I heard a shot."

"And after that?"

"I heard another shot."

"When you heard the sound of the shots where did you move to?"

"The back sir."

"Is that away from the street towards the hallway?"

"Yes; back from the door."

"How does the door open?"

"There is a cord on it and a weight attached."

"Did you go out into the hallway?"

"Yes."

"From the hallway could you see the two flights of stairs leading to Mr Bird's office?"

"You can mostly see them all."

"While you remained standing there did you see anyone appear on the stairs?"

"Yes sir."

"From what direction was this person coming?"

"He was half-way down the stairs."

"Had you a good view of him?"

"Yes."

"Who was he?"

"Timothy Cadogan sir."

"Is that the man in the dock?"

"Yes."

"Did you see anything in his hand?"

"Yes."

"What was it?"

"A revolver."

"In which hand was it?"

"The right hand I believe."

"Did you remain in the hallway while Cadogan came down the lower flight?"

"No I did not sir."

"What did you do?"

"I just looked at him and then went back into the shop."

"But before you went back into the shop did you see Cadogan do anything with the revolver?"

"When I was looking at him he was putting it into his pocket."

"When you went back into the shop did you look out a window?"

"Yes."

"Did you see anyone coming out?"

"I saw the like of him; the same fellow crossing the street."

"Was it the same fellow?"

"I am not sure sir; it was like him."

"Where did he go?"

"Towards Glengarriff."

"How did he go?"

"Running."

"Did you notice anything about what Cadogan was wearing?"

"A coat sir; and a cap."

"Was the man running across the street dressed the same way?"

"Yes."

"Did you form any opinion at the time whether it was the same man or not?"

"I did not at the time."

"What did you think?"

"I thought afterwards it was because he ran from the door straight across."

"Now, you say the man you saw standing between the two flights of stairs was Timothy Cadogan, the prisoner?"

"Yes."

"How long did you know Cadogan?"

"I knew him by sight for the last two years."

"How long did you know him, not alone by sight but also by name?"

"About twelve months."

"During the last twelve months have you seen Cadogan in Bantry?"

"I saw him a few times there."

"The murder of Mr Bird occurred on the 24th of February. You were examined on the 27th, three days after, before the resident magistrate Mr. Purdon. Did you identify Timothy Cadogan on that occasion?"

"Yes."

"Had you seen him between Saturday when you saw him coming down the stairs from Mr Bird's office and Tuesday when you identified him before the magistrates?"

"No sir; I had not."

"Did the prisoner ask you a question?"

"Yes."

Mr. Barry. "How long did you say you have worked for Warner's?"

"For four years; I am a messenger now."

"Did you ever see Timothy Cadogan in Warner's shop?"

"No never; he was never a customer of Mr. Warner's."

"Your only acquaintance with him was you knew his appearance?"

"Yes."

"Was Cadogan often in Bantry?"

"I don't know that."

"You did not see him often?"

"Yes."

"You did not know him to speak to?"

"No."

"You never spoke to the man in your life?"

"No."

"You never saw him in Warner's shop?"

"I saw him outside the shop but I never saw him inside the shop."

"How many times?"

"I saw him about once outside the shop."

"Who told you his name?"

"I don't know that. I don't know who told me his name. I know a great many people and I can't say who told me their names."

"You had no particular reason for fixing the appearance of this man more than any other man in Bantry."

"No; but I knew him well enough."

"You said a moment ago that you looked out the window and had a fair enough view?"

"Yes."

"Did you go outside the door and into the hallway?"

"I went through the door into the hallway."

"A flight of stairs or six or seven steps goes up from the hall, is there a window at the head of these steps?"

"There is one at the landing."

"Is that the first landing?"

"Yes."

"Do you swear to that?"

"Yes."

"At the top of the first flight of steps?"

"No; but at the landing, where Mr. Bird's office is."

"There is nothing but the back wall of the house at the first flight of steps?"

"That is all."

"From where you looked out you could not see the man come down the first flight at all?"

"It was at the top of the first flight that I saw him."

"Coming from the top flight to the landing?"

"Between the two."

"You could not see him come down into the hall at all?"

"No."

"You did not wait to see him descend the first flight of stairs into the hall?"

"No."

"The only view you had of him was for this moment of time was on the landing between the first and second flights of stairs?"

"Yes."

"Do you think whoever was there saw you?"

"I don't know that."

"Could he not see you from where he was; were you not between him and the door?"

"I was not between him and the street door, I was at one side of the stairs."

"Then the stairs were between you and him to some extent?"

"They were."

"Was it through the bannisters of the stairs you saw him?"

"Yes; over them."

"You were looking up and saw him over the bannisters?"

"Yes."

"Could you see all of his body over the bannisters?"

"Through the bannisters and all."

"How much of him did you see over the bannisters?"

"I saw his face over the bannisters."

"Was that all you saw?"

"That was all I looked at too."

"Did not the bannisters of the stairs cover the man partially at all events except for his head?"

"Yes."

"He had a cap on?"

"Yes."

"When you saw the man running away did you remain in the shop?"

"Yes."

"Mr Warner was there?"

"Yes."

"Mr Swords was there?"

"Yes."

"And young Mr Warner was there?"

"Yes."

"Did anyone follow the man down the Glengarriff Road?"

"I don't know that."

"When did you see Cadogan again?"

"On the Tuesday after."

"Was it in the police barracks that you identified him?"

"Yes."

"Did the police put him in a line up with other men?"

"They didn't."

"Who was there when you identified him?"

"The District Inspector."

"Was acting Sergeant Driscoll there?"

"Yes."

"Did acting Sergeant Driscoll come for you that morning to go there?"

"No he did not; he came for me in the middle of the day after I had told him."

"I suppose you had heard by that time that Cadogan had been arrested?"

"Yes."

"And you knew at the time you had told it first that Cadogan had been charged with the crime?"

"Yes; I did."

"Did acting Sergeant Driscoll tell you when he came for you on Tuesday that Cadogan had been charged?"

"No; he did not."

"But you knew he had?"

"Yes."

"And you knew Cadogan was in jail?"

"Yes."

"And you knew when you were brought by the police you would be asked to identify Cadogan as the man you saw come down the stairs?"

"I didn't know it then."

"What did you think you were being brought to the police barrack for?"

"I didn't know what for."

"Why did you go to the police barrack?"

"I was told I should go there."

"By whom?"

"By acting Sergeant Driscoll."

"When the acting sergeant told you that you should go there you went there?"

"I went to the barrack and told them all about it."

"And that was the first time?"

"Yes."

"Did you hear on Saturday that Michael Hegarty was been kept in the barrack?"

"No."

"When did you hear first that Timothy Cadogan had been arrested on the charge?"

"Sometime on the Sunday."

"And did you know when acting Sergeant Driscoll came for you on the Tuesday he wanted you to identify the prisoner as the man you saw coming down the stairs?"

"No; I did not."

"What did he want you in the police barrack for?"

"I don't know."

"Do you swear to the jury at this moment that you do not know what acting Sergeant Driscoll brought you to the barrack on that Tuesday for?"

"He took me there to make some statement."

"What was the statement about?"

"About seeing the man come down the stairs."

"And you knew you were to say that the man you saw coming down the stairs was Cadogan?"

"Yes."

"And it was acting Sergeant Driscoll who took you to the barrack?"

"Yes."

"Tell me; after this did you and the acting sergeant go away together?"

"Yes."

"Where did you go to?"

"We went to Dublin, but he did not go with me at first."

"When did he join you?"

"About a week later."

"Have you and acting Sergeant Driscoll being living together ever since?"

"Yes; we have."

"And do you still swear to this jury that you didn't know what acting Sergeant Driscoll took you to the barrack to do on that Tuesday?"

"No."

"Who examined you before the magistrates?"

"I don't rightly know who put the questions to me."

"Do you mean to say that you do not know whether it was acting Sergeant Driscoll or District Inspector Armstrong who put the questions to you?"

"It was the District Inspector."

"Why didn't you say that first? Didn't you know well that it was the District Inspector who put the questions to you?"

"I didn't know well."

"Did you forget it?"

"I didn't forget it."

"Do you know it well or do you not?"

"I know it well enough."

"Then; when I put the question to you why didn't you answer?"

"He only put some of the questions to me."

"Who put the rest of the questions?"

"I don't know who the other man was."

"Was he a policeman?"

"No; it was not."

"Was it a magistrate?"

"It must have been I suppose."

"Are you sure it was now?"

"I am not."

"On that occasion did you hear the prisoner, Cadogan, ask for his solicitor to be present before you made your statement?"

"I did not."

"You did not hear anything like that said?"

"No."

The Solicitor General. "We will prove distinctly that nothing of the sort was said."

Mr. Barry. "It was on Tuesday you told acting Sergeant Driscoll?"

Walter Dennis. "Yes."

"Do you know a man named Michael Leary?"

"No."

"Did you ever know him?"

"No."

"Did you ever hear of him?"

"No; I don't think I ever have."

"And you never had any conversations with O'Leary about this case?"

"No."

"I suppose you know Mr Swords?"

"Yes."

"On your oath did you tell Mr Swords that you did not know who the man you saw on the stairs was?"

"I didn't tell him I saw any man on the stairs."

"Did you tell him you saw a man on the stairs but you didn't know who he was?"

"I didn't."

"When you went out into the hall and saw this man and then came back in was Mr Swords there?"

"No; he was not."

"When did he come in?"

"I don't know when he came in."

"Didn't he come in very soon?"

"He did."

"And you did not tell him what you saw?"

"No."

"And Miss Dukelow was there and Mr Warner's son and nephew were there and Mr Swords was there and yet you never said a word about what you had seen?"

"No; I did not."

"And it was only when acting Sergeant Driscoll came to you the next Tuesday that you told anyone about what you saw?"

Walter Dennis did not answer this question.

The Solicitor General. "Approximately how high was the bannisters?"

"About breast high."

"What could you see over it?"

"I could see the face and a portion of the body."

"Could you see the revolver?"

"Yes."

"Did you ever have a quarrel or disagreement with Timothy Cadogan?"

"No."

"Did he ask you a question on the day you identified him?"

"Yes."

"What was it?"

"He asked me was I sure."

"And were you?"

"Yes."

Walter Dennis then stepped down and his work colleague Miss Fanny Dukelow was called to the stand. She stated that she was employed in Mr Warner's shop which was located below the office of Mr Bird. She then went into detail about the day of the murder.

"On the day in question I had dinner as usual at Mrs Wiseman's and on my return to the shop I saw by the town clock it was ten minutes past two. I went up Marino Street on to Barrack Street and into the shop. About a quarter of an hour after my return I heard noises coming from upstairs in Mr Bird's office like that of stamping or the moving of furniture. At the same time I noticed a small piece of mortar fall from the ceiling. Then I heard a noise like someone striking a door with a rod which was followed with a sound like somebody falling downstairs."

The Solicitor General. "Was Walter Dennis in the shop with you at this time?"

"Yes."

"After hearing these noises did Walter Dennis do anything?"

"After hearing the noises he went to the door leading from the shop to the hall and opened it. He then went into the hall."

"Did the door close after him?"

"I don't know that, but he came back in immediately and went to the shop window and looked out."

"Did you notice anything about him?"

"He looked frightened and awfully pale."

Mr. Lynch. "Did Dennis come back from the door suddenly?"

"Yes."

"Are you sure he was facing towards the shop window?"

"I am quite sure."

"Did you swear before the magistrates that you thought his face was towards the front of the shop?"

"I did."

"Was that accurate?"

"Yes."

"You said in your deposition that he suddenly came back in, is that an accurate description of what took place, did he suddenly come back in?"

"I think so."

"Did he suddenly come back after he opened the door?"

"I cannot say."

"The door would close if he let it?"

"I think it would sir."

"What hour was it last Saturday when you passed the clock?"

"I can't say."

"Did you never take notice of it before?"

"I did."

Robert Warner, the nephew of the owner of Warner's was next to give evidence. He stated he was in the shop below Mr Bird's office on the day in question. He confirmed he had heard the noises that Fanny Dukelow had referred to.

"I heard two or three shots following each other quickly. I then spoke to Miss Dukelow and as a result of that conversation I went to my uncle's other shop next door to inform him about what we had heard. My uncle sent Mr Brooks and Mr Swords up to Mr Bird's office to see what was happening and I followed the two gentlemen. When we got there we found Mr Bird lying in a stooping position in his office in front of the counter. I then went and got Dr Popham."

Mr Barry. "Did you inform your uncle immediately after you entered the shop?"

"There was a number of customers in the shop when I arrived and there was a bit of a delay before I could speak to him."

"What time elapsed between the time you went to inform your uncle and you going for Dr Popham?"

"Between five and ten minutes."

"Where was the Doctor's?"

"At the top of High Street."

"And how long did that take you?"

"About five minutes."

Dr Lionel Popham was then called to the stand.

"I received a call to attend to Mr Bird's office at about twenty minutes past two on the date in question. I found Mr Bird lying between the door and the counter. I examined him and found him dead. After a superficial examination I found wounds in the breast and skull."

Dr Thomas Popham, the father of the previous witness, corroborated his son's evidence and then went on to give details of the post mortem examination that he carried out.

"I found a circular wound on the outside of the right arm. On the inside of the same arm I found an aberration of the skin. There was a second wound about three inches above the left nipple and half an inch outside the nipple line. This wound was scorched. A third wound was found at the base of the skull. The back of the right hand was scorched extensively. There was recent bruising over the right ear. On examining the skull I found a circular hole about one-eight of an inch in diameter corresponding with the outer wound. On removing the scalp I found a flat bullet lodged at the base of the brain and I found a circular piece of bone corresponding to the size of a hole and a fracture of the base of the skull. I then examined the wound in the chest. Tracing it downwards we found it entered the chest, which when opened, disclosed a circular wound through the lung, and it continued through the principal parts of the body. We found a bullet lodged in the abdominal cavity."

Mr Redmond. "Which of the wounds caused the death of Mr. Bird?"

"Either the wound through the chest or the brain would have caused death."

"Could the wounds have been self-inflicted?"

"There were three distinct wounds and they could not have been self-inflicted."

A third doctor, Dr. Thomas Bennett agreed with the evidence given by his two colleagues.

The next person called was acting Sergeant Driscoll.

"I was stationed in Bantry last February. On the 24th of that month I was standing on the corner of Bridge Street when I got a message from Mr Breen's son, Henry, after which I immediately ran to the rent office of Mr Bird's and found the gentleman lying on the floor dead. Subsequently in company with District Inspector Armstrong, I searched the pockets of the deceased's clothes and found a gold watch and a chain, two £5 Bank of Ireland notes, a pair of spectacles and some address cards in them. I remained twenty minutes in the office and then went down Barrack Street and Main Street and met the witness Michael Hegarty near a baker's shop, he was rushing along. Shortly afterwards and in consequence with a conversation I had with a police constable, I came back again and saw Hegarty on Bridge Street, he appeared to be getting ready to go home. I took him to Mr Bird's office and had a conversation with him. In reply to a question he replied that he had no objection in going to see the District Inspector. At about eight o'clock I went in search of Timothy Cadogan and I found him the following morning at six o'clock in the home of a man named Sullivan in Laharanshermeen. He was asleep and I woke him up and put some questions to him which he said he might answer or not as he thought fit. In reply to a question he said he had been in Bantry the previous day with John Sullivan. They left at about half past ten and got into Bantry about one o'clock. In the town they met another man named Owen Sullivan and had two glasses of lager beer each, he said Owen Sullivan had two halves of whiskey. They remained in Hurst's public house for about an hour and then separated. The prisoner said that he walked about the streets until six o'clock when he went into a shop and bought some biscuits before he started for home. I then told him to get out of bed and dress himself. When we got down to the kitchen I arrested him and charged him with the murder of Mr Bird and cautioned him. Cadogan said he had nothing more to say."

Mr Barry. "As you were arresting the prisoner did he say anything to you?"

"He asked me what the charge was."

"Who told you to look for Cadogan?"

"I got my orders off the District Inspector."

"Were you aware whether Dr Bird had returned to Bantry prior to you receiving your orders?"

"He had."

"After searching the clothes of the deceased; what did you do next?"

"I looked on his desk and saw a book. I inquired into its contents and saw that the last thing written into it was an incomplete entry. It was as a result of this entry that Mr Hegarty was detained. The incomplete entry corresponded with the figure on the receipt given to him."

Acting Sergeant Driscoll then produced the book and the receipt for the court to examine. Dr Bird was recalled and he confirmed that the writing in the book and on the receipt was his late brothers. This concluded the evidence for the day and the court was adjourned until the following morning. The jury were seconded and spent the night in the Imperial Hotel.

The Second Day

The first witness called on the second day of the trial was a part time model maker from Dublin named James Andrew Abbott. He had made partial models of Mr Bird's office and Warner's shop which were produced in court. It is important here to understand the layout of the hall, the stairs, and the door from the shop. The stairs to Mr Bird's office were in two sections consisting of five or six steps each going in opposite directions and separated by a small landing. The hall was accessed from the shop via a storeroom, from this door in the hall it was not possible to see the full extent of the second flight of steps. Throughout the trial the Crown, whether innocently or otherwise, led the jury to believe the door from the hall led directly into the shop and not into a storeroom. However, the effect of this was surely minimal if one assumes that the model produced was correct.

The Solicitor General. "Could a person standing on the first landing be seen by a person standing at the door of the shop in the hallway?"

Mr Abbott. "No he could not."

"At what point in the hallway could a man standing see a person on the first landing between the two flights of stairs?"

"He would want to move out four feet, if he moved out six feet he could see a man anywhere on the landing. To a man standing out six feet in the hallway, no man could conceal himself on the stairs."

"What is the height of the bannisters?"

"The bannisters are the only portion of the place that I did not take measurements of."

"Why not?"

"At the time I thought I only had a few days to prepare the mould and I only took measurements of what I could accurately mould."

"Could you give an opinion on their height?"

"They are about the usual size; around three feet."

"Would a man's face be visible over them?"

"Yes. At the request of a policeman I carried out a test. I observed a man coming down the last three or four steps very well as there was a good light there."

Mr. Barry. "Does the side wall running along the hallway extend up to the top of the house?"

"Yes sir.

"Is it at a right angle to the back wall?"

"No; it joins it at an acute angle."

"Between the ceiling of the hallway and the side wall is there a window?"

"No."

"Where is the window?"

"In the back wall?"

"Whereabouts in the back wall?"

"The window in the back wall is at the head of the landing leading into Mr. Bird's office."

"The light from the one window would be obscured by the ceiling of the stairs and the only way the light could get through was down the stairs?"

"It is reflected everywhere."

"There is no direct light at all?"

"No; except from the street door."

"A man standing at the doorway leading from Warner's shop to the hallway could not see a man on the first landing at all?"

"No; except if he was leaning over the bannisters."

"Leaning over the bannisters, throwing summersaults?"

"He could not see him in the ordinary position."

"And then, if he went out into the hallway, he could not see a person except on the last three or four steps?"

"A man would have to go into the centre of the hall so that a man on the stairs could not conceal himself from him."

"Should not he be practically between the stairs and the hall door to see the man on the landing?"

"Oh no; he could between the door and the stairs about halfway. The height of the first flight is about four feet seven inches and a person's face and upper body would be seen over them."

The Solicitor General. "With His Lordship's permission I would like to recall Walter Dennis and put a few questions to him."

Mr. Barry. "I object; is it right considering the enormous consequences at stake in this case that Mr Dennis should be recalled to amend his evidence?"

Mr Justice Kenny. "I think the evidence of the model should have been given at an earlier stage because there was some difficulty in following the movements considering the model was not before us."

Mr. Barry. "I have called Your Lordship's attention with the fact that we had not been served with notice that a model would be produced."

The Solicitor General. "I think everybody now understands the locality perfectly and if there had been some confusion it has now been removed. What I propose to ask Mr Dennis was if in his answers already he had clearly stated the position in the hall where he was standing when he saw the accused"

Mr Justice Kenny. "It is in my notes, I will not have Mr Dennis recalled."

Mr Justice Kenny then proceeded to have Walter Dennis removed from the courtroom before reading from the notes he had taken regarding Dennis's evidence.

"There is a door opening into the hall, this door has a weight and a cord on it. I went into the hall and could mostly see the steps from the hall. I saw a person half way down between the two flights of stairs. I had a fair view of him. It was Timothy Cadogan, the prisoner. He had a revolver in his hand; his right hand I believe. I just looked at him and then went back into the shop. When I looked at him he was putting the revolver into his pocket. I did not wait to see him start the second flight of stairs. It was only on the landing I saw him. I was at the side of the stairs between him and the hall door. It was near the bannisters I saw him. I saw his face over the bannisters. The bannisters partially concealed him except for his head. In reply to the Solicitor General he said the upper parts of the man's body and head were visible."

The Solicitor General. "I believe that to be sufficient."

"There is just one thing more, in reply to you on re-examination he said the upper portion of the man's body and his face were above the bannister. Now with regard to that do you wish to ask Mr Dennis anything?"

"No; certainly not, I am obliged to Your Lordship. I told you why I didn't produce the model yesterday morning, it was incomplete and though not intentionally misleading it could be regarded as so."

"Oh yes, it was only on the score of convenience I said what I said."

"I quite understand that."

The next witness called was John Sullivan, the man who had accompanied Timothy Cadogan to Bantry on the day of the murder.

"I met Timothy Cadogan on the morning of the 24th of February on the way to Bantry town. The two of us then met Owen Sullivan. The three of us went to Hurst's public house and had two drinks each. When we left Hurst's we met a man named McCarthy outside. I went back into the public house with McCarthy."

The Solicitor General. "Did the prisoner go back in with you?"

"No he didn't."

"At what time was this?"

"Near half past one."

"Did you see Cadogan in Bantry again that day?"

"No."

"When did you hear about Mr. Bird's death?"

"Later that day after I saw a crowd of people running up to his office."

"How long was that after you had parted company with Cadogan?"

"About a half an hour."

"What time did you set off for home?"

"At about seven o'clock."

"Were you alone?"

"No. I was with Tim Sullivan and Pat Mahony before we parted at Dromsullivan West at about eight o'clock."

"Did you meet anyone else on your way?"

"Yes; Timothy Cadogan about a quarter of an hour later."

"Do you remember what you talked about?"

"I said to him wasn't it awful Mr. Bird had done away with himself."

"And what was his reply to that?"

"He said if it wasn't Mr. Bird it was his brother the doctor who had done it."

"Was that all he said about the matter?"

"Yes."

"What was his parting words to you?"

"He asked me had I a newspaper because he had forgot to get one. I said I had got one and invited him into the house so I could read it to him. He then stayed for about three quarters of an hour, leaving at half ten."

Mr Lynch. "Did the prisoner ask you to get him an employer when you were walking to Bantry?"

95

"Yes he did."

"And did you?"

"Yes I did."

"Did you tell the prisoner you had found him work?"

"Yes; I told him on the way home."

"What did he say to you when he heard this news?"

"He said he would go to first mass at Kealkill the following morning and then go and see the man."

Cornelius Sullivan next gave evidence that he saw Timothy Cadogan both on the morning and the night of the murder and on the latter occasion the prisoner had a glass of milk in his house. During the time he was in the house Cadogan made no mention of the tragic event in Bantry. Richard Sullivan was next to take the stand, as well as being Cadogan's employer, he was also a brother of Cornelius Sullivan.

"Previous to the 24th of February Timothy Cadogan was in my employment. He had asked me for an increase in wages and I had told him I couldn't because there was not enough work. He said he was going to Bantry on the day in question to look for new employment. I said that was fine and gave him a pound note that I owed him in wages and asked him to bring me back at newspaper."

The Solicitor General. "When was the next time you saw him?"

"He came back to my house sometime after eleven o'clock that night and we had a drink."

"Did you have a conversation?"

"I asked him if he had any news and he said he hadn't. I then asked him was Mr Bird not shot and he replied that he had heard that."

"Was the prisoner in Bantry the previous Saturday the 17th of February?"

"Yes; he was."

"Did he return home that night?"

"No; he didn't come home until Sunday afternoon between four and five o'clock."

"Do you remember the prisoner ever saying anything about a gun to shoot rabbits?"

"Yes; he said that a number of years ago he was engaged in Kenmare by a man named Herbert. He and the gentleman's sons use to shoot rabbits that were damaging the crops."

"Do you remember him saying anything about a gun and the police?"

"Yes; he said something about the police troubling him for a gun as acting Sergeant Driscoll was calling him a rogue, vagabond and a murderer."

Mr Justice Kenny. "When was this?"

"On the morning after the killing of Mr Bird. The prisoner was in the kitchen and the acting sergeant said this in the outhouse."

The Solicitor General. "I suggest that this has nothing to do with the story about the gun the prisoner told the witness."

Mr Barry. "Was it on the morning of the 24th of February that the prisoner was talking about shooting rabbits?"

Richard Sullivan. "It was not."

The Solicitor General. "I never suggested it was."

Mr Justice Kenny. "He said it was a long time ago and before he was in his employment."

Mr Barry. "Was that the first day that the prisoner went into Bantry?"

Richard Sullivan. "No; he used to go to Mass on a Saturday night."

"Did he ever forget to get your messages before when he went to town?"

"He did."

"Did you ask him did he get you your newspaper when he returned that night?"

"I did and he said he forgot it but he had read it in John Sullivan the masons and that there was a great war in South Africa raging."

The Solicitor General. "How far is Bantry from your house?"

"About five miles."

"And how far is Kealkill chapel?"

"About four miles by road?"

"And how far is it by the short cut?"

"About a mile and three quarters."

"Which chapel do you go to?"

"Kealkill."

"On the night Cadogan came home wasn't the first thing you asked him – is there any news from the town?"

"Yes."

"What was his answer?"

"He said he hadn't any news."

"Did you ask him if he had found employment?"

"I did not."

"Did he say he had been looking for employment that same day?"

"I believe he said something about Mr. Driscoll, a contractor, I don't know exactly what he said."

Mr Justice Kenny. "Was that on that night?"

"I believe it may have been on the Saturday night before."

The Solicitor General. "Is Timothy Cadogan any relation of yours?"

"He is a cousin of mine."

Head Constable McBride was next to take the stand and stated that he had been stationed in Glengarriff between August 1889 and June 1893 and knew where the prisoner lived during this period.

Mr Redmond. "Did you..."

Mr Barry, interrupting. "I know what this question is going to be and I object to it before it is asked. I ask for it to be put in writing and submitted to His Lordship."

Mr Redmond. "I refer His Lordship to the deposition made before the magistrates."

Mr Barry. "What was going on in the Head Constable's mind at the time cannot be given in evidence against the prisoner."

The Solicitor General. "This constable's evidence refers to the period covered by the evidence of the witness Jeremiah McCarthy yesterday."

Mr Justice Kenny. "We can proceed."

Mr Redmond. "Thank you Your Lordship. Head Constable, during your time in Glengarriff had you any dealings with the prisoner?"

"Yes; on four occasions I visited his house in search of firearms."

"Anything else?"

"Yes; in March 1891 I had a conversation with him regarding a murder case..."

Mr Barry, interrupting. "I object to this as evidence. Even if the prisoner had been before convicted it should not be brought as evidence against him in this case. The confession by him of having firearms years and years ago cannot be given as evidence to show the probability of the man being guilty of the present charge. That would be contrary to all the principles of criminal law."

The Solicitor General. "I do not wish to prove a previous crime being committed. What I do press is this; the prisoner knew perfectly well the effect of having firearms or ammunition about him. He knew perfectly well the importance of doing away with them. If His Lordship has any doubt I will not press it."

Mr Justice Kenny. "I think on the whole I best not admit it. The Crown cannot give evidence of character as to show that the prisoner was likely to commit the offence."

District Inspector Armstrong was called next and he gave evidence of going to the deceased's office and finding the body as the previous witnesses had sworn. He stated that while searching the clothes of Mr. Bird he had found a bullet in the lining of his coat.

The Solicitor General. "Were you present at the meeting of the United Irish League in Bantry the week before the murder?"

"I was."

"Was the meeting held on the date it was originally planned?"

"No; it was originally planned for the 11th of February but had to be postponed due to heavy snow on that morning."

"So that when the snow was heavy it was Saturday the 10th or Sunday the 11th."

"Yes."

"Was there any snow on the ground on the 17th or 18th?"

"No."

"Did you in your official capacity attend the meeting on the 18th?"

"I did."

"About what hour did the meeting begin?"

"About one o'clock."

"Where was the meeting held?"

"On the Square in front of the courthouse."

"Do you remember speeches being made?"

"I do."

"Was there a reference made to the White Estate?"

"There were to the evictions on it, I am not entirely sure about the evictions, there were references to the White Estate, the history of the people who had lived on the White Estate and the estate of Lord Kenmare; the suffering they had at the hands of Lord Kenmare and the Whites of Glengarriff Castle."

"And was the White Estate the very estate on which the prisoner was a tenant?"

"Yes."

Mr Lynch. "There was snow on the 11th of February?"

"Yes."

"And you say that there was no snow between that and the 15th?"

"I don't."

"You say there was no snow on the mountains on the 17th?"

"I don't say that; but there was no snow on the Square."

"Do you know a boy by the name of Michael Leary?"

"No I do not and I never heard of him before yesterday."

The next witness was an acting Sergeant Kelleher who testified he travelled to Bantry on the early morning mail train the day before and went to Mr Bird's house to collect papers and then went to his office and took measurements of the staircase leading from the office to the street before returning to Cork that morning.

Mr Barry. "Do you know the boy Michael Leary?"

"No; I never heard of him until yesterday."

"And what did you hear?"

"I made some inquiries regarding him and heard that he had left Bantry on the Monday following the murder because a friend of Cadogan's was seen talking to him."

"Were you aware that a process server named Hurley was looking for Michael Leary that morning to serve him with a subpoena?"

"No; I did not hear that."

Michael Scanlon who had been examined the previous day was then recalled by the Solicitor General.

"Is there a door in the hall which obstructs entry to Mr Bird's office?"

"No there is no door inside the hall which could prevent entry to Mr Bird's office."

Fanny Dukelow was also recalled and was asked about the entrances to the hallway.

"Some distance inside the street door there is a little door which leads to the shop."

The Solicitor General. "Was this door opened or closed during Mr Bird's hours of business?"

"It was always open."

"Could the door close by itself?"

"No."

Mr. Barry. "Is there glass in it?"

"No."

"What entrance do you use when entering the shop?"

"I use the shop door."

"Have you ever used the hall door?"

"No."

Mr Justice Kenny. "Did Mr Bird attend his office daily or only occasionally?"

"He used be there mostly every day."

Head Constable Brennan then deposed that he visited Mr Bird's office on the day of the murder and observed that the hall door into the shop was open, however, under cross-examination he stated that he had to look closely in order to see the doorway at all.

Constable Mulcahy deposed that he had cause to visit Mr Bird's office on a frequent basis due to his job and on each occasion the door in the hall was open.

Mr Barry. "Were there glass panels in this door?"

"Yes."

"What type of glass?"

"Clear glass, but there might be some dust on them."

"Did you hear Miss Dukelow say there was no glass at all in it?"

"I did."

"Did you hear the Head Constable swear that you have to look closely to see the door at all?"

"I did."

"Was he suffering from blindness?"

"I don't know; I saw it at all events."

"Looking at the model of the hallway, is it correct in your opinion?"

"No; in my opinion the door in the hall is hung on the wrong side on the model."

The Solicitor General then asked for Dr. Bird to be recalled and on his reappearance asked him did he agree with Constable Mulcahy in regard to which side the door was hung.

"No; the constable is wrong about that; the door is represented correctly in the model."

"Was this door always open?"

"Yes."

"Was there glass in the door?"

"Yes; the upper portion is glass."

The Solicitor General then declared that the Crown's case was closed.

Mr Barry. "There is a gentleman on the indictment named James Swords and I would ask that he be produced for cross examination."

The Solicitor General. "Mr Barry can call him if he likes and make him a defence witness."

Mr. Barry. "I suggest this witness should be called for cross-examination; however, I have no objection to making him a defence witness."

The Solicitor General. "He made a deposition on utterly immaterial matters and therefore we did not call him."

James Swords then took the stand.

Mr. Barry. "Are you in the employment of Mr Warner of Barrack Street Bantry?"

"Yes; I am."

"Were you in the shop with Mr Dennis and Miss Dukelow when the shots were heard?"

"No; I was in Mr Warner's other shop which is next door. After the shots were fired I passed through the shop and I found Mr Dennis, young Mr Warner, and Mr Brooks at the head of the stairs."

"Did Mr. Dennis say anything to you?"

"No; not a word."

"Did you see him again subsequently?"

"I saw him again that evening."

"Did he say anything to you?"

"No sir; I asked him if he had seen anyone passing up or down and he said no."

"When you asked him this you were alluding to the time that Mr Bird was murdered?"

"Yes sir."

"Was there anyone else present when you asked this question?"

"There was some of the workmen."

The Solicitor General. "Was this on the day of the murder?"

"It was either on the day or the following Monday."

After Swords stood down Mr Barry opened the case for the defence.

"You the jury have a very sad, a very anxious, and a very responsible duty to perform. It seems hard to imagine in this crowded court, full of life and animation that you are practically in a more awful, a more responsible, and a sadder position than if you were standing at the bedside of one who was passing away from this world, and for this reason, that when the hand of death is about to fall on one who is known to you or dear to you, no act you do can arrest it. What you have to say is this; whether you are satisfied about the case that has been made, that the hand of death may fall on the prisoner who is now before them in full strength and vigour; whether you are to pronounce that verdict which can only have one consequence, which once it is issued, a mistake, if a mistake has occurred, it can never, never be retrieved. When you are standing at the bedside of one who is passing from you and when you hear the last sigh and marked the last pulse of life; what would you not give to hear once more the voice that has been stilled forever and see the inanimate form move once more with life. Upon each member of this jury rests the responsibility of the life or death of this man. How would you feel when perhaps soon, when perhaps later – sometime in the fulness of time – the real perpetrator of this murder may be disclosed and you have sent this man to his doom; a doom that is irretrievable for the prisoner at the bar upon evidence which has been submitted for the last day and a half. You have given the case the most painstaking attention. My task is lighter than it otherwise would have been because I know I am addressing gentlemen who will bring their intelligence and their conscientious sense of justice to bear on this case of supreme importance.

In this case the evidence has gone back many years to fix upon the prisoner Cadogan the commission of the crime. They have gone back to Cadogan's eviction in 1895 and to the ejectment obtained in 1894. Having gone back nineteen years to a rabbit shooting expedition that he went on with a gentleman's son in Kerry. They have gone back six or seven years to produce what they call admissions and expressions of revenge against this unfortunate gentleman. The prisoner is not an educated man nor accustomed to polite society. He is an outcast on the world ever since he was removed from his home; and for a man of his class he displayed at his eviction a fairly pardonable ebullition of temper. He made three attempts to get back his home, the last attempt to Mr Bird six months before his death and forsooth he was insulting because he did not go to Mr Bird with cap in hand; with whispering humbleness and bated breath and ask to be reinstated. No, this rough countryman from the mountainside was a miserable outcast and he, after uttering three threats, would be the last man in the world to go in that noonday and commit this crime, for he must have known that the hand of suspicion would fall like a hammer on him. It is said that the prisoner was familiar with the use of firearms but no evidence of this kind was given beyond that years ago he killed a rabbit or a grouse or a woodcock with an old fowling piece. There is no evidence that he ever had or owned a revolver and there is no evidence that he ever fired a shot out of a revolver in his life. There is not in this case one particle of evidence against this man of him having either the skill with firearms or the possession of firearms. Then we are to believe that for the last five years the prisoner was brooding upon his wrongs and harbouring revenge against Mr Bird; when we know for all that time he was wandering about the country looking for work, looking for the wretched pittance to bring body and soul together.

Now, what about Mr Bird? The man whom Cadogan was planning to murder. He was a land agent, and it was necessary for him at times to be walking around the country and possibly through the mountains. If we are to believe that Cadogan was this brooding plotter, the vengeful murderer as represented by the Crown, would he have not availed of the numberless opportunities that would have presented themselves with doing away with Mr Bird while he was in the country? The Crown's answer to this is that Cadogan's feelings were so sluggish, his revenge so softened by the passing of time until; until when? Until Mr William O'Brien and Mr Gilhooly revived all the slumbering passion and simmering rage inside him when they spoke at the United Irish League meeting in Bantry the week before the murder. Do you, as reasonable men and as honest jurors believe that a man would brood on the wrongs done to him for five years, would harbour feelings of revenge and yet wait to do this desperate deed until hearing the eloquence of Mr O'Brien and Mr Gilhooly? And let the jury remember there was no reference to Mr Bird in either of the gentlemen's speeches.

On the day of the murder the prisoner was drinking in Hurst's public house at half past one and was there for a considerable time longer. It is absurd to say he was watching the movements of Mr Bird for the purpose of murdering him. I am sure everybody here in court sympathises with Dr Bird in his affliction with which he seems to struggle with manfully. The murder was either the result of a medley of a quarrel or a row that occurred in the office. It is not up to me to prove which it was. The murder could not have been committed by the prisoner at the time it was committed. Mr Hurst pledged on his oath that the prisoner was in his public house at half past one. Mr Bird left his office at twenty-five minutes past one and it would not have taken him more than five minutes to walk the distance between his office and his club. At that time, the man accused of watching Mr Bird and dogging his footsteps is in the public house. What then of the theory that Cadogan was standing on Hurst's Corner waiting for Mr Bird to return from his club so he could murder him. The perilous moment must have been shortly after a quarter past two, at that time Cadogan was seen going not in the direction of Mr. Bird's office but in the opposite direction. The points in this case depends on seconds; if Timothy Cadogan left his friends on Marino Street, went up the stairs to this office, had the struggle with Mr Bird, shot him, made his way down the stairs and made good his escape all in the span of three minutes, does that sound creditable? Are you satisfied that within this short space of three minutes this crime was committed and the perpetrator made good his escape? How could you know that it is the powerful interests of the locality that is trying to put the result of this crime on the prisoner. There is no disposition on the part of the people to help us. Whether there is a disposition to help the Crown, I don't know. Marino Street on that day was not a desert. If a man after shooting Mr Bird rushed downstairs and out on the street, he would have been sure to be seen.

Had it not been for the suspicion of Dr Bird, even including the identification by Walter Dennis; what plight would Michael Hegarty be in now? I could imagine my friend, the Solicitor General, stating a case against him. I intended to produce a man named Leary who would prove that as he was going up the stairs the conversation ceased and silence reigned. He would further state that Mr Bird seemed angry when he went in and Michael Hegarty was resting his hand on the side of the desk. Hegarty by then had completed his business; had paid his money and gotten his receipt. He was waiting, waiting for what? I am only stating a hypothetical case to show how strong a case could be made against a man regarded as innocent. Now I wish to say a word about this Walter Dennis. Dr Bird's suspicion would not be suspicion enough to convict. Guilt must be brought home beyond reasonable doubt to the minds of reasonable men and if there is the slightest doubt it is their duty to give it in favour of the prisoner. Was there a particle of evidence in the ridiculous conversation about the war in South Africa of which you could find this man guilty of the crime of murder? Was there a scintilla of evidence to connect the prisoner with the crime? Would you on the evidence of Walter Dennis, dismiss a trusted servant, risk a £10 note? Would you hang a dog on such testimony that was asked to bring this man to the gallows? It was said that he knew the prisoner from before. How did he know him? He was not a customer of Warner's and was not in the habit of dropping in and out of the place. It was not stated that he interchanged one syllable with him the whole course of his life. The crucial and vital point of this case is that Walter Dennis never told anybody that he had seen this man on the landing. The strength of this case is that knowing a murder had been committed and seeing the murderer escape, he did not say a word about it at the time. Had he seen Cadogan, surely the first impulse of nature would have been to raise a hue and cry that Cadogan was the man who murdered Mr Bird. But he did not communicate a word of this until acting Sergeant Driscoll came to see him on the following Tuesday. I am sure that you, the jury, will not condemn a man on such a flimsy identification. I ask you are you satisfied that Walter Dennis is a true, sincere, and honest witness. I do not think he is and I ask you to reject as unreliable and as quite insufficient as to warrant you from prescribing a verdict of guilty on this man.

I ask you on the whole of the case to say what I believe you should say that you are not satisfied with the testimony that has been advanced in order to pronounce that dreaded verdict on the accused. Someday in the fullness of time the truth will come out and the real perpetrators of this crime will be brought to justice and then; only then might Mr Bird rest in peace in his grave. I ask you to say that you are not satisfied that vengeance; I do not use that word in any scornful manner, should be visited on this man in the dock. Cadogan is poor, he is an outcast, he is vulgar, he is uncouth, he is a rough ill-tempered, perhaps, a morose fellow if you wish, but he is at least honest. He is one of God's creatures who life is as sacred and precious as the life of the highest gentleman which was taken on the 24th of February. The life of the unfortunate man in the dock is committed to your care and God forbid that by a verdict of yours this man should be sent to his doom that he does not deserve and suffer for a crime he did not commit."

The first witness called by the defence was a man named John Cronin who was in Bantry on the day of the murder.

"I was on Barrack Street at the time of the occurrence on the side opposite Mr Warner's shop when I heard a shot."

Mr Barry. "Had you a view of Mr. Warner's hall door?"

"Yes; I had a good view and I walked slowly towards it. My attention being drawn by the sound of the shot."

"Did you see anyone come out of that hall door?"

"I did not."

"If somebody had come out through that door would you have seen them?"

"Yes; I would have."

"How long did you remain there?"

"For about five minutes after hearing the shot."

"And you had a view of the hall door the entire time you were there?"

"I did."

The Solicitor General. "Were you standing in the street in front of the house?"

"I was."

"How far were you from the shop?"

"I was about thirty yards."

"And you were going towards the door?"

"Yes."

"Where were you when you heard the shots?"

"I only heard one."

"Where were you then?"

"At Biggs's Corner."

"When you heard the shots, how far were you from Mr Bird's office?"

"About thirty yards, I was walking towards it."

"How long was it from the time you heard the shot until you went to the office door?"

"About five minutes."

"Did Constable Hussey take a statement from you in writing?"

"Yes."

"And you signed it in the presence of a man named Denis Sexton."

"Yes."

"Was that true?"

"Yes; I was not on my oath at the time."

"Was the statement true?"

"What I am saying now is true."

"What did you say to Constable Hussey about the shot?"

"I did not tell him about hearing the shot."

"What did you tell him about the shot?"

"I told him I had a view of the place."

"What did you tell him about the shot?"

"I told him I did not see anyone coming out."

"What was the untrue statement you made to Constable Hussey?"

"He may have taken it down wrong."

"You told the jury you were not on your oath by way of excuse. What were you trying to excuse?"

"He may have taken it down wrong."

"Was the statement read back to you in the presence of a man named Denis Sexton?"

"Yes."

"Did you sign it then?"

"I made my mark on it."

"I am going to paraphrase your statement, while standing at a door of a house in Glengarriff Street you saw Timothy Cadogan going down the road between twelve and one o'clock. Further on you make no mention of hearing a shot. Where were you at two o'clock?"

"At Foley's forge."

"Are you helping the defence of Timothy Cadogan in this case?

"No."

"Did you pay any money towards it?"

"No."

"Did any of the people there to your knowledge?

"No."

"Is it not from them that the money is coming?"

"I don't know of any money."

The next witness called was William Foley, a cooper, who stated he was at his forge on Glengarriff Street on the 24th of February.

"After two o'clock I was at the door of my shop from where I had a view of Bigg's Corner and a portion of Warner's shop. I had a full view of the door leading to Mr Bird's office."

Mr Barry. "For how long were you standing at your door?"

"From five minutes past two until twenty-five minutes past thereabouts."

"During that time did you see anyone resembling the prisoner run along the Glengarriff Road?"

"I did not; but I could not be sure if any other man ran along it."

Mr M.J. McMullen, a civil engineer from Cork was next to take the stand and he produced a ground plan of Mr. Warner's shop he had made on the previous Monday.

"When I visited the house it was about half past twelve in the day. There was very bad light on the landing (between the two flights of stairs) with there being no direct light on it either from the street door or the window on the landing above it. The rays of light from the street door would not reach more than eight feet into the hallway."

Mr Barry. "Looking at this plan do you believe a person could get a good look at a man coming down the stairs without standing out in front of the stairs?"

"In my opinion they could not."

"The Solicitor General. "Did you carry out any experiment to ascertain this opinion?"

"I did not, however, to have a good view a man would have to go a couple of feet outside the stairs. The place was dimly lighted and in my opinion a person could not be identified unless the man who purported to identify him was in line with him."

"What is the length of the hallway?"

"About seventeen feet."

"And in that length of hallway you think it is unlikely for a person to identify a person coming down a stairs?"

"If a man got a direct look at a person coming down the stairs he might know them."

Mr Lynch then addressed the jury on behalf of the defence.

"I am conscious as much as it is as possible for a man to be of the terrible responsibility that rests on Mr Barry's and my own shoulders, and I am sure if there is anything that commends itself to your consideration which has escaped our attention and if it is anything reasonable and fair, that you give the prisoner the benefit of it. The Solicitor General, who opened the case in a most able and impressive way, stated many things which I found extraordinary. He said that the prisoner's business in Bantry that day was not for the purpose of looking for employment or to purchase a newspaper for his master, but to perform some dire deed influenced by feelings that were generated and fanned into flames by something he had heard on the previous Sunday. However, witnesses for the prosecution clearly proved contrary. It has been proved that indeed he had come to Bantry to look for employment and that he had obtained some. I ask why the Crown did not produce Tim Sullivan; the man sworn to have been left talking to the prisoner on Hurst's Corner? Where is the servant boy Michael O'Leary who was in the employment of Dr. Bird? Where is he now? No one can trace him; he has disappeared as if the ground had opened up and swallowed him. Where was Cronin and his wife who were also deposed to have been speaking to Cadogan? An extraordinary observation by Dr Bird furnished the keynote of this case, and the reason why the prisoner is on trial for his life and why another man is not in his place, for that man was detained until Dr Bird uttered the words. "If any man did it; it was Tim Cadogan." Then began the hounding down of this wretched man whose life is in your hands. The Crown has laid stress on the fact that the prisoner said he heard it rumoured that Mr Bird had committed suicide. The rumour was common in the town of Bantry that day. A clear and conclusive alibi has been established by the witnesses for the prosecution, as clear as the light shining through that window. Where are the witnesses who proved that Timothy Cadogan went to Mr Bird's office that day? There are none because he did not!

The critical point in this case is the time that Mr Bird was murdered. Why did the Crown not produce the people who were seen standing and talking to Cadogan near the time of the murder? You cannot rely on the evidence of Mr Dennis if you rely on the evidence of Mr Swords. The Crown has proved that Cadogan was on Marino Street up to ten past two, but they have failed to prove that he went to Mr Bird's office because he did not. Walter Dennis in conversation with the witness Mr Swords, who the Crown dropped as a witness, said he saw nobody going up or down; so how can you believe him when he swears he saw Cadogan coming down the stairs with a revolver in his hand? I pray that the prisoner in the dock does not suffer at your hands due to any shortcomings on my behalf and I ask you to consider carefully before passing a verdict which may hurl into eternity a fellow creature, an outcast, a bankrupt, an evicted tenant though he is, on evidence that should not be regarded as satisfactory. Mistakes occur in the administration of law in the most trifling of cases and it is possible for them to occur in the most important ones like this one. Once again I request that you pause for thought before delivering a verdict that may possibly be discovered in future years to be an error which has unjustly deprived a poor creature of his life."

Mr Redmond replied on behalf of the Crown.

"It has been suggested by my learned friends for the defence that this case has been conceived under a mere suspicion, expressed by Dr Bird; that Cadogan had shot his brother, that it has been promoted for the mere purpose of confirming this suspicion so as to bring home a guilty verdict against the prisoner in the dock. I don't think that you, the jury, will entertain such a view of the prosecution, or on having heard the whole case, believe a mistake has been made. We the Crown, have presented the case to you in a way that the clear and concrete evidence against the prisoner demonstrates his guilt as it does to any reasonable person who has heard or read it. This evidence shows that the prisoner, Timothy Cadogan, is guilty in the fullest of senses of wilful murder."

Mr Redmond then reviewed some of this evidence. He went over Cadogan's attendance at the United Irish League meeting in Bantry the week before the murder, the eviction from his farm a few years previous and the threats he had made to Mr Bird after the latter's refusal to reinstate him on his land. He then asked the jury to put out of their mind the hypothetical case made by the defence regarding Michael Hegarty.

"A man who by hypothesis or otherwise could not have had anything to do with this dreadful crime."

He continued.

"Could human evidence, I ask, be more satisfactory or less mistaken than that which has been given in this case on behalf of the Crown? Was there ever in any court of justice a case brought home against an accused person with more certain and inevitable evidence which has been placed before you? With regard to what has been said about the witness Walter Dennis, I ask could our country produce and raise such a breed of monster as young Dennis must be, if out of mere malice of his heart and knowing the terrible consequences of his words, if he without motive, or bribe or inducement of any sort, selected out of all of God's creatures the prisoner at the bar as the man responsible for this crime. Have we met monsters like that in this country; I respectfully say not. The question has been asked had not Walter Dennis lived in Dublin with acting Sergeant Driscoll would his evidence be reliable? Well, enough has transpired in the case to not merely excuse but to justify the conduct of the authorities in removing the boy, Dennis, from his surroundings in Bantry. Some suggestion were made about someone named Michael Leary. Who, in the name of heaven, was Leary. No one knows. He was a servant of Dr Bird's at one time but that is all that is known of him.

The evidence is simply appalling in its weight against the accused. The crime which has been committed is one which has been said is almost without parallel in its determination and audacity. The nature of the wounds prove the resolve of the murdered man's murderer to complete his task that day. It is a crime of the rarest audacity which was committed in the open daylight of the town of Bantry by a desperate and determined man. I am sure that you, the jury, will render a verdict in line with the evidence and show no fear as regards the consequences that the law will attach to it. The protection of the interests of the society that we live in, the safety of the individuals living in this society require that if clear, certain, and understandable evidence has been given against the accused man then you will fearlessly render your verdict according to that evidence. With the consequence of your verdict neither you nor I nor His Lordship has anything to say or do. With an equal sense of responsibility my learned friends have appealed to you to give every consideration and benefit that you can possibly give to the prisoner, however, when you have weighed all the facts, when you have like honourable and courageous , but cautious citizens, considered all the evidence; the terrible evidence given here as part of the prosecution and the absence of evidence on part of the defence, if, when you have done that, you come to the conclusion that all this proves nothing except that the wretched man in the dock committed this most unholy deed, you gentlemen, will have discharged your duty upon you conscience by returning the verdict which the Crown has asked from you in the name of common society."

It was a quarter to six when Mr. Redmond finished his address. Before the court was adjourned Mr Justice Kenny informed the jury that he would charge them the following morning when the court reconvened at ten o'clock. The jury were then taken to the Imperial Hotel to spend a second night.

The Verdict

Shortly after ten o'clock on the morning of the 20th of July 1900, Mr Justice Kenny delivered his charge to the jury.

"For the past two days you have been engaged in the discharge of the most solemn duty that a citizen of this country can be called on to perform, that duty is to determine the issue of life or death for a fellow human being. There can be no question to the nature of this issue. There is no medium course whatsoever in this case. A murder has been committed, a murder of a particularly brutal and atrocious character; and any suggestion of accident, any suggestion of suicide, any suggestion of circumstances that would reduce the crime to the lower and more mitigated crime of manslaughter are absolutely invalid in this case. The perpetrator of this crime whoever he may be; whether it is the prisoner in the dock or whether he is some other person, no member of the community can have any sympathy with. Mr Bird, the gentleman whose life has been taken, was murdered under particularly brutal circumstances because as you remember the medical evidence, he was shot firstly in the arm, secondly in the left breast which resulted in the bullet penetrating the heart, a wound by itself sufficient to kill him. Then, after apparently fallen forward on his knees and with his head lowered, the perpetrator of the crime delivered his parting shot, and that shot was delivered to the back of the man's head as he lay helpless.

The sole question for you to answer is was the perpetrator of this shocking crime the man in the dock. You have taken an oath to make a true deliverance between the Queen and the subject, between the Crown and the prisoner and your duty under that oath is firstly; that no innocent man is sentenced, that is your primary duty. But you also have another duty, that is your duty to society and to yourselves as members of the community. If you are convinced on the evidence beyond any moral doubt that the man in the dock is the man who fired those shots, you are bound, according to the words of the oath that you have taken; to vindicate society and to vindicate the law, and to have no hesitation in reaching a verdict which your solemn oath compels you to do. Within the space of a fortnight I have had to try four cases of homicide, and I have had in every one of them had to state to the juries who were trying them, what the law is in reference to the evidence which was adduced in each particular case and how each jury should act on it. That is my primary duty. I have to call your attention to the facts of the case. I may suggest inference from these facts, but these inferences are only my own and unless you twelve gentlemen, with whom the matter of life and death rests with, agree with the conclusions of fact that I present to you, you are not bound in the least to follow, but instead to draw on your own independent conclusions from those facts and can disregard what I may have suggested. It is my duty to bring before you the salient points of the case and it is then up to you to say whether the facts brought before you by the Crown might lead you to a conclusion which leaves no moral doubt that the prisoner at the bar was the perpetrator of this awful crime.

If you believe the evidence of one of the witnesses of this case, namely Walter Dennis, you might come to the conclusion that his evidence approached direct evidence as closely as any circumstantial evidence could. If you doubt the evidence of this boy Dennis, I can see the greatest difficulty in any of you coming to the conclusion that the prisoner at the bar was guilty. There are circumstances outside Dennis's evidence that might raise a reasonable, nay, a strong suspicion that it was the prisoner's hand who perpetrated this deed, but that if would be sufficient enough evidence without that of Dennis's to send him to his doom; I doubt very much. You have Dennis's evidence and you should take it in connection with every other stem of evidence that has been given, not alone by the Crown but also by the defence, and by knitting together all these circumstances you twelve sensible gentlemen who are accustomed in dealing with the ordinary affairs of life; accustomed to dealing with transactions of your own business will have to come to the conclusion whether you have any moral doubt in your minds of the guilt of the prisoner.

What is the nature of the prisoner's case? I refer your attention to it in the earliest moments of my observations and I beg you in the most solemn manner to bear it in mind from beginning to end. This case is based on three theories. First of all, it has been pointed out the impossibility in regard to the evidence of time, not hours but minutes, moments in which the prisoner could have perpetrated the crime. In other words from finding him with his back up against the wall opposite Breen's workshop at a certain time and within ten minutes the murder had been committed. It is impossible to conceive that he went from that place, where he had been seen by the two Breen's, to Mr. Bird's office and carried out the brutal murder within that short period of ten minutes. That is the first feature of the case and you should bear it in mind very carefully. The second is this, and it relates to the boy Walter Dennis. It was said in regard to the construction of the house, especially the construction of the hall, by the engineer Mr. McMullen who appeared here yesterday, that the place where the boy Dennis recognised the prisoner beyond the possibility of doubt, namely the middle of the landing between the first and second flight of stairs, that it is a place where there is no direct light even in the middle of the day and that it would have been impossible for anyone standing in the hall to recognise someone on the landing the way Dennis said he did. With reference to Dennis's evidence, two suggestions are capable of being made; the first is that Dennis is altogether mistaken to the identity of the man he saw on the landing and secondly, for some purpose of his own, which has not been suggested, has brought both the prisoner's name and fate into this transaction. The third point is this and it may be taken in connection with the previous point. Although Dennis swore before you that he was there and recognised Cadogan, whom he had known for two years and whose name he knew for a year, although there was a great hue and cry concerning the murder, although Michael Hegarty was arrested that night and held, although Timothy Cadogan was arrested the following morning; from twenty past two on the Saturday thereabouts, Walter Dennis gave no information to the police until the following Tuesday the 27th of February. Of course an argument can be naturally made that amidst all the hubbub in the house when Swords came in, when Brooks came in, when Warner came in and then the police and doctors; surely Dennis would have told someone of what he had witnessed regarding seeing a man come down the stairs holding a revolver and not only that, but he could also identify that man. These are the points which the able counsel for the defence has put before you in such an able manner. And I might add there no abler counsel on the circuit in this country than the counsel for the defence, Mr Barry.

Upon the evening of the murder Michael Hegarty was detained by the police in connection with the crime and as I said during the trial, the police would have been guilty of a great dereliction of their duty if they had not arrested a man who had been in such close proximity to the deceased just moments before his death. I concur with a great deal of what Mr Barry has said in relation to the position that Mr Hegarty would be in if he was standing in the dock instead of the prisoner. Why? Because the time he was in the office was between ten and twenty minutes past two, the very office that Mr Bird was found murdered moments later, he was the last man seen in the office, and lastly the ink was not dry in the book which had recorded a payment which he had just made. I tender that a lot of suspicion would fall on the man who was last thought to have been in the deceased's company. But it is up to you to consider if this hypothesis that Mr Barry put forward deserves any credence or whether you believe the evidence given by Mr Hegarty himself. Who is Michael Hegarty? He is a man who had a very close relationship with the deceased. There was absolutely no evidence put before you of a dispute or a quarrel between the two men, no motive at all for believing that Hegarty could have carried out the act. However, there is one slight piece of evidence, I don't know whether you will consider it, and that is the evidence of John Leary who swore that as he went up the stairs he heard the voices of Hegarty and Mr Bird, he did not say in which tone they were speaking, he did not say it was an angry tone, he just said that when he went into the office Mr Bird looked cross. That is the only piece of evidence which could lead you to believe there was the slightest friction between the two men. Nor is there any suggestion that Dr Bird was anywhere near the vicinity of the murder that day. Any suggestion of the sort is absurd. But it was the duty of the Crown to clear up any doubt about his whereabouts.

Every prisoner who is tried is presumed by the law, and you should bear this presumption in mind, to be innocent until the contrary has been proved. This explains the meaning of the phrase "giving the prisoner the benefit of the doubt." A juryman must say to himself, "I must consider this man an innocent man until I am satisfied beyond all reasonable and moral doubt that he is the perpetrator of the deed that is alleged." It is then for a juror to say based on all the facts of the case whether a moral or reasonable doubt as to the guilt of the prisoner is suggested on all the circumstances of the case.

Now, what were the main features of the case presented to you on behalf of the Crown? First of all it was said there was a motive, and the Crown suggest a very strong motive for the perpetration of this deed. They then said that the prisoner was in the vicinity of the place where this deed was carried out. They also said they have the evidence of an eyewitness who saw the prisoner coming down the stairs from where this deed was committed armed with a revolver. Next they suggest the subsequent conduct of the prisoner, his observations or rather his lack of observations to the two Sullivan's on the night of the murder. Finally the statement made by the prisoner to the constable at the time of his arrest that he did not leave Bantry until six o'clock that evening. In all fairness some evidence should be forthcoming regarding his whereabouts between two o'clock and six o'clock. The Crown inquired about this and were met with the answer from the defence counsel that the only period of time that they had to deal with was in or about the time of the murder and about a quarter of an hour beforehand and that it did not fall on them to show the comings and goings of the prisoner over the following hours. The prisoner has been defended by a most able counsel and an indefatigable and zealous solicitor but no evidence is forthcoming of his whereabouts for the three and a half hours after he was last seen, for according to the prisoner's own statement he did not leave Bantry until six o'clock and his movements are accounted for up until at least five minutes past two.

Another piece of the Crown's case was the eviction of the prisoner from his land some years previous. In this eviction Mr Bird had a direct role as he was acting as the receiver for the White Estate. Over the following years the prisoner demanded to be reinstated on this land and on each occasion Mr Bird refused to. On the last occasion that he demanded reinstatement, only six months before the murder, he made a chilling remark which the deceased's brother, Dr Bird, repeated here in this courtroom. "You have done your worst; the devil take you; you may be sorry for it". If you believe the evidence of the witness Levis, it was a strong piece of evidence when taken in connection with the threats made by the prisoner. The defence has stated that matters of ancient history against the prisoner should not be brought up, some of them no doubt are matters of ancient history, but they go to show that the prisoner nourished feelings of revenge against Mr Bird, feelings which he may have put into effect. On the Sunday previous to the murder, Sunday the 18th of February, the prisoner attended a meeting which was held in the public market Square in Bantry. He had come to town the night before and lodged with Mrs Donoghue for the night. He had his breakfast that morning and then went to last Mass before attending the meeting afterwards. It has been proven that he was present. At this meeting, speeches of an inflammatory nature regarding the land were made by several prominent speakers. The Kenmare and White Estates were highlighted for the sufferings endured by their tenants in the past, one of which was the prisoner. However, throughout these fiery speeches there was not a single mention of Mr Bird, the White Estate's agent and receiver, none whatsoever. But here was the prisoner at this meeting, cheering and shouting with his cap in his hand. Did hearing all those speeches relight a fire in his belly which had been dormant for a while? All of this took place just six days before Mr Bird was murdered.

Now to the statement made by Dr Bird on the night of his brother's murder. "If Cadogan was in town; he was the man who did it." This does not prove the prisoner's guilt in the slightest degree. It shows an impression, possibly a wrong impression made by Dr Bird. It is obviously Dr Bird's belief that the prisoner is the guilty man owing to the dealings he and his brother had with him.

The issue of the proximity of the prisoner to the scene of the murder and his ability to get there in time from where he was last seen and all the evidence in regard to that, is an issue for you the jury to decide on. As far as the evidence of the boy Dennis is concerned, undoubtedly he came forward three days after the murder and gave evidence of the strongest character against the prisoner. I agree with one of counsel who said that if Dennis had come forward and foreswore himself, if he has come here and deliberately sworn away the life of one of God's creatures, then yes; he is a monster. But if on the other hand you believe he had the opportunity to see and recognise the prisoner, then he has put beyond all possibility of doubt the guilt of the accused. Whether Cadogan took one minute or three minutes to do the deed, if you believe Dennis's evidence, the deed was done by the prisoner's hand and no other in the town of Bantry that day. His evidence is golden if you believe him, but if he is lying and perjuring himself, if the evidence he has given regarding the identification of the prisoner is a myth, then he must be a monster of iniquity to tell such a story. Was he frightened out of his life or has he concocted the story? Did he see a man on the landing that day putting

122

a revolver in his pocket? Was he afraid to disclose what he saw or was his first thought not to disclose to anyone what he saw? These are all questions for you and in connection to it, you should also bear in mind that when asked by the man Swords if he had seen anyone going up or down the stairs that day, Dennis replied no.

Regarding the observations the prisoner made to the two Sullivan's on the night of the murder, this shows, in my opinion, a disinclination on the prisoner's behalf to talk about the crime.

I am sure the Crown as well as the jury naturally expected more evidence from the defence regarding the movements of the prisoner between ten minutes past two and six o'clock. The defence did not produce Cronin or his wife as it was as much an onus on them to as it was for the Crown. The defence said that the Crown themselves have proven an alibi for the prisoner but that is something for you to decide, they have proved an alibi for him if you believe to your satisfaction that from ten minutes to two until twenty minutes past two he was standing against the wall opposite Breen's workshop on Marino Street. The Crown's evidence has undoubtably proved that he was there for a short time before the actual commission of the crime, but his last movements were contrary to the direction of Mr Bird's office. He had moved down to where the Cronin's were and his back was towards Bridewell Lane. Was it possible in the spell of five, six, seven, eight or nine minutes to have gone to the office and perpetrated the crime? Was he likely to have done so with regard to the evidence? The question of possibility and the evidence of the Breen's is for you to weigh up, but as I have said before, without the evidence of Walter Dennis there is not a case to convict the prisoner in my opinion.

Do you believe the evidence of the boy Dennis? If you believe his evidence, do you believe he had the opportunity to identify the man on the landing? You should bear in mind what he said as well as what the witness Fanny Dukelow said regarding his condition when he came back into the shop and you should also bear in mind what he said to the witness Swords that evening or the next evening when they were in an outhouse that he had seen nobody going up or down the stairs. You should not forget that for three days he did not tell a soul what he has told you. These are circumstances in favour of the prisoner and the law assumes the innocence of a prisoner until the jury is satisfied by cogent reasons that the prisoner is guilty. If you find a reasonable doubt in your minds, then by all means you should give the benefit of that doubt to the prisoner. But if the doubt is substantial and reasonable doubt, such a doubt as a man would act on in the ordinary affairs of life, it is your bounden duty to give the benefit of that doubt to the man who stands here arraigned on the capital charge and if after considering all the circumstances of the case you do not think a reasonable doubt remains, remember the solemnity of your oath, you will only be vindicating the rights of society; of which you are twelve members. You are bound by your oath to find true deliverance between the Queen and the prisoner at the bar. You should consider all the circumstances of the case and weigh them well, and if you do, I have no doubt you will bring in a verdict that will be met with the commendation of all men."

This finished Mr Justice Kenny's charge; he had been speaking for two hours and twenty minutes. After the jury retired to consider their verdict at half past twelve Mr Barry rose and addressed Mr Justice Kenny.

"On behalf of the prisoner I would like to question a point you raised in your direction to the jury. The fact is it is not my defence that the prisoner took ten minutes to do the deed. From the place where Timothy Breen saw the prisoner standing to his house was walked by District Inspector Armstrong in three minutes. So the time the prisoner had to commit the murder was only three minutes."

"That is if Breen's evidence is true."

"He was a Crown witness and I don't suppose they dispute his evidence. District Inspector Armstrong must have took Breen with him when he walked this distance in order to ascertain the pace that he walked on the day of the murder."

"I assume it took him three minutes to walk the distance on the day."

"Your Lordship put it to the jury that I stated that it could not be done within ten minutes. I wish to also remind the jury that when Walter Dennis made his statement on the following Tuesday that he knew at the time that the

124

name of the man arrested and charged with the murder was Timothy Cadogan."

The Solicitor General. "I admit that in his evidence District Inspector Armstrong said that he walked the distance in three to three and a half minutes. In the evidence it was stated that after Timothy Breen saw the prisoner on the street he returned to his workshop for a time. On the day the streets were crowded and the three minutes quick walk bore no comparison to the time taken by Timothy Breen on that day. In my experience, which is very long, I notice that it generally confuses a jury, without any direct result, to bring out a jury and direct their attention to a particular point. I have no objection to Your Lordship reading a portion of the evidence to them."

Mr Justice Kenny. "I will leave no doubt at all about the point with the jury."

The jury was then recalled.

Mr Justice Kenny. "I wish to remove any doubt from your minds as to the time the murder was committed. I may have left the impression on your minds that there was a lapse of ten minutes from the time the prisoner was seen on the footpath opposite Breen's workshop to the time that Mr Bird was murdered. Timothy Breen went home the long way around and it was proven that the murder was committed as he went up the steps of his own house. It only took three minutes to walk around that way and the counsel for the defence has urged then that the prisoner had only three minutes to commit the murder. I am bound to place this fact before you in the case I did not do so in my summation. You will bear in mind that in connection with this that Timothy Breen was sent back into the workshop by his father before he left for his dinner. You should also remember that the prisoner was arrested on Sunday morning, and on that day and on the following Monday and Tuesday, Walter Dennis knew his name was Timothy Cadogan."

The jury were then sent back to deliberate and returned after an hour and fifteen minutes. Their foreman, Mr Hunter, announced that they were unable to agree on a verdict.

Mr Justice Kenny. "Can I give you any assistance? Is there any part of the evidence you would like to have read out?"

Mr Hunter. "No; there is no part of the evidence we would like to have read out. We can get no help from Your Lordship."

"Then I can't help you?"

"Not upon a point of law."

"If you went back again would you be able to come to a conclusion?"

"I believe not."

The Solicitor General. "The jury has heard the case for two and a half days, as they can't agree and say it would be useless to send them back, I can only take their disagreement and ask His Lordship to discharge them."

Justice Kenny, to the jury. "I must discharge you. You have given the case careful consideration and as there is no likelihood of you being able to agree I discharge you."

The Solicitor General asked to have the trial postponed to the next Assizes which would take place the following December. This application was assented to and Timothy Cadogan was remanded in jail until then.

The Second Trial of Timothy Cadogan

'The Crown should not have recourse to 'loose testimony' about character, 'for the purpose of establishing the guilt of the accused. The admission of facts unconnected with the charge on the indictment, or acts alleged to have been done at a different time or place 'would be clearly open to the serious objection of taking the prisoner by surprise.'

'No man should be bound, at the peril of life or liberty, fortune or reputation, to answer at once and unprepared for every action of his life.'

*Taylor and Pitt-Lewis, A Treatise on the Law of Evidence, vol. i, p. 235.

The Munster Winter Assizes opened in the Cork County Courthouse on Saturday the 8th of December 1900. It was presided over by the Lord Chief Justice of Ireland Lord Peter O'Brien. In his earlier years as a Crown Prosecutor, O'Brien had obtained the nickname "Peter the Packer" for his skill in excluding nationalists from juries in agrarian trials. He retorted that this had been necessary because murderers and other criminals were escaping through the intimidation of jurors.

The dangers of this approach were seen in his prosecution of those accused of the 1882 Maamtrasna murders, (a family of five were murdered in Maamtrasna, a part of the Gaeltacht on the border of Galway and Mayo) after which nationalist journalists obtained possession of his brief and revealed that not only had potentially troublesome jurors been excluded, but witness statements had been edited to conceal material from defence lawyers. O'Brien always maintained that all the prisoners convicted had been guilty. However, on the evening before the execution of the three men convicted for the crime, two of them separately admitted their guilt but said the third man, Myles Joyce, was completely innocent of the charge. The Lord Lieutenant, Earl Spencer, refused a stay of execution on Joyce, stating that "The Law must take its course." In 2018 President Michael D. Higgins issued a Presidential Posthumous Pardon to Myles Joyce, it was the first pardon issued for a conviction before the establishment of the State. In Maurice Healy's memoir "The Munster Circuit" he described O'Brien as "a man of considerable legal ability and great natural kindness, who was deservedly very popular. On the other hand, he was rather vain and self-important, and inclined to stand on the dignity of his office. "

Timothy Cadogan's case was not due to be held that day but was scheduled for the following Monday. However, during a case involving a man from Clonmel named James Foley who had been found guilty of sending a threatening letter to a man who had taken possession of an evictee's farm, the Lord Chief Justice made a statement that in retrospect may have had a bearing on Cadogan's case. He stated.

"It would have been better if a Clonmel Jury had found Foley guilty as he plainly was guilty. The substance of Foley's offence was of a boycotting nature. He endeavoured to boycott a very respectable shopkeeper named Phelan because he took a farm for which he paid £525, and he denounced a man named Hunt because of his dealings with Phelan. He was tried in Clonmel but the jury disagreed. In my opinion in none of the counties in the West and South of Ireland is there a real hope of justice being done in certain classes of offences of an agrarian nature. In a trial by a Tipperary jury three men were charged with violent assault. The motive was because the person assaulted had taken an evictee's farm. The moment that fact was brought out the prosecuting counsel knew his case was lost and the three men were acquitted though they were obviously guilty. This is a dreadful example making what is a very solemn proceedings nothing more than an idle one. In my opinion there should be power to change the venue and have special juries when the Attorney General believes it essential for the administration of duty. It is often said to me "Lord Chief Justice is it not a melancholy thing that juries will not convict when the evidence is perfectly plain?" I have invariably replied to this interrogation by saying that if you lived on a lonely mountain and saw a neighbour of yours in the dock, I am not sure that you would not do the same. There is another observation I wish to make; it has been said why has there not being more prosecutions like that at Lixnaw? It has been said to me why was the United Irish League not proclaimed as an unlawful organisation? My answer to that is, and I give it without the smallest hesitation, is that there has been no case made out for the proclamation of the United Irish League as an unlawful organisation. It may be, as some people have said, nothing more than organised intimidation. I am very anxious to speak guardedly, but in my judgement whatever the future might bring, I don't think there has been such overt acts as to justify the proclamation of the United Irish League hitherto. It was a very different case when the Land League was proclaimed. I remember it well; as I was one of the law officers at the time, and all the people of Cork remember it too. Then the overt acts, which the government then thought right to have regard to, were distinctly established. But still it has been said to me why are there not more prosecutions like those of the Lixnaw case? Well that very case illustrates the difficulty in prosecuting, and when people reflect on the administration of criminal law in the country they should bear in mind the difficulty in collecting evidence. Intimidation, though a very far reaching and effective instrument indeed, is a very subtle and impalpable one. The difficulty in getting evidence is very great indeed. Let me illustrate it for you, take Foley's case which we have just dealt with. You will remember the evidence of the man Hunt, who received the letter that denounced him, he said he did not regard it as a threat at all. He regarded it as a mere epistle that appealed generally to his reason or something to that effect. He was quite intimidated as he stood here in the witness box, and this is in Cork, imagine how he felt when he stood in the box in Clonmel? Well again now when people criticise the administration of justice, and as I said, the air is permeated at the present moment with criticism, we must remember the difficulty that exists as to evidence in these cases. I think it my bounded duty to make these suggestions. I suggest the Attorney General have the power to change the venue and have special juries in all cases which he thinks would benefit the country. He should have the power to do so."

The second trial of Timothy Cadogan for the murder of William Symms Bird opened in the County Courthouse in Cork at eleven o'clock on the morning of Monday the 10th of December. The Crown was led once more by the Solicitor General, Mr George Wright, who was assisted on this occasion by Mr J. Bourke Q.C. and Mr J.F. Moriarty B.L.. The defence comprised of the same individuals who represented Cadogan at his first trial, Mr Ralph Brereton Barry Q.C. and Mr P. Lynch B.L.. (As in the previous trial, I shall refer to Mr Brereton Barry as Mr Barry) A jury was selected from a panel of one hundred and forty-six. The twelve selected were Thomas R. Holland, a thirty-seven-year-old corn merchant from Knockrea, who also served as the jury foreman. Edwin Browning aged sixty-three, a seedsman from Great George's Street. Thomas Upward, a forty-five-year-old manure factory manager from Glashgannif. George Abraham Sutton, a forty-eight-year-old coal merchant from Sunday's Well. William Adams aged fifty-seven, a corn merchant from Fishery's Island. Pierce F. Higgins, a forty-nine-year-old tea merchant from Sunday's Well Road. A master baker from Prince's Street named John J. Cranwell who was sixty years old. James Murphy, a sixty-year-old distiller from Mahon. William V. Morris aged forty-five, a shopkeeper and boot manufacturer from Grand Parade. George W. Holland a thirty-eight-year-old butter merchant from Saint Patrick's Hill. Francis Brennan, a commercial traveller aged forty-five from Patrick Street and Richard O'Connor, a sixty-year-old annuitant from Blackrock.

After the jury had been sworn in a number of individuals were told by the Lord Chief Justice to be on standby. One of these men, Mr Patrick H. Meade, stood and addressed the Lord Chief Justice with regard to the make-up of the jury.

"My Lord, I must protest as a Catholic Nationalist Juror against these proceedings. I served on eight Commissions of Assizes and was Mayor of Cork three times. I think it an outrage on the Catholic community of Cork."

The Lord Chief Justice. "This is a mere histrionic performance. I won't permit it. It is a mere theatrical display. Go on now."

Timothy Cadogan, on being arraigned, offered his plea of not guilty in a calm, firm voice, while his appearance showed him none the worse for wear following his long confinement. After the Lord Chief Justice stated that the trial would last at least two days, the Solicitor General rose to make his opening statement.

"In stating the case for the Crown it devolves on me to state as shortly and as clearly as I can the facts of the case as submitted by the Crown that show that the prisoner, Timothy Cadogan, is guilty of the very grave charge which has been made against him, namely, that on the 24th of February of this year in the town of Bantry in this county, he took away the life in circumstances amounting to murder, the life of Mr William Symms Bird. Before I come to the facts of the case that point to the prisoner's guilt or innocence, I would like to tell you what occurred in the town of Bantry on the 24th of February. It was a Saturday and a market day in the town, a tolerably busy day in a town of two or three thousand people. It would be almost a surprise to read of what occurred there in a work of fiction if you did not know that it was a fact that in that town, with business going on the streets, I supposed fairly well full of people, at two o'clock or half past two, at all events, that in the middle of the day, with the light of the day at its brightest and strongest, a well-known gentleman, Mr Bird, was struck down by the hand of an assassin in his office over a shop in one of the business streets. Of this there can be no doubt. When the people rushed in and medical aid sought, there in an office over a busy shop in the business part of a town in which he had lived for over forty years, he lay dead or dying on the floor. Mr Bird received three wounds from revolver bullets, one of which went through his arm, another punctured his left chest causing death and as the wretched man fell forward and was lying on his hands and knees on the floor of the little office, the assassin, for an assassin it was, fired into the defenceless man's skull, inflicting a second wound which could have caused death itself. It is beyond all doubt that on that day and under those circumstances the man who did this deed came into the town determined to do it and influenced by a motive strong enough to induce him to dare the risks to carry out his objective. In this case you will have motive of the strongest character pointing to the prisoner Timothy Cadogan as the author of the deed. This being the state of affairs at two or three o'clock, or whatever the time was, because in cases of this kind, though time is of an importance, it is too easy to attach much importance to matters of minutes or seconds. You should look at the case as a whole and look at the movements of Mr Bird and the movements of Cadogan and see whether these movements were not connected together, and then say if the man who fired the shots was Timothy Cadogan.

Mr Bird was a gentleman well known to many of you as a gentleman. A magistrate, a land agent, and frequently a grand juror. He was about forty-eight years of age and lived his whole life in Bantry. His brother, a retired naval doctor, resided with him. His office was in a block of houses, the second house in what is called Barrack Street. The house to the left of it is called Biggs's shop and as one goes around Biggs's Corner onto Barrack Street, the office of the late Mr Bird, the murdered man was next to Biggs's end on the first floor over Warner's shop. The next house as one goes up Barrack Street is also Warner's shop. So, if one started from the corner at

Biggs's, the next shop is Warner's shop number one and on the first floor directly over this shop was Mr Bird's office.

Now to Mr Bird's connection to the prisoner. There is an estate on the west of the county known as the White Estate. Mr Bird had been for a great many years an agent and latterly a receiver for this estate. On this estate, Timothy Cadogan, was for some years a tenant. He appears to have fallen into arrears on his rent and at the October sessions in 1894, whether it was misfortune or bad management, or whatever it was, it is idle for us to inquire into, the County Court Judge pronounced a decree of ejectment at the suit of the owners of the White Estate against the prisoner to recover possession of the lands at Cooleenlemane, the rent due being four years rent to March 1894. This is, I believe, the origin of this case. It may appear a long way to go back to find a motive, but there have been motives traced back further than this in the history of crime in Ireland. However, you will see the matter will not be left to rest there. I mention it solely as a starting point and I would comment that it was absolutely clear at that time that unless they turned Timothy Cadogan into an owner in fee, it was absolutely vital that any receiver acting under the court and accountable to the court, and bound to take the directions of the court, should take the actions which were taken. You are probably aware that in the Land Code as it exists now, a decree, or an ejectment as this was, is not followed by immediate eviction but instead turns the tenant into a caretaker for a period of six months. If during that time he can redeem himself, well and good, but if not, and especially in the cases of encumbered estates, the landlord is bound in the protection of his own interests to put the law in motion and take possession. Apparently there was no desire to deal harshly with Cadogan, because possession was not taken for ten months after the ejectment order. On the 19th of August, more than five years ago, a whole party consisting of bailiffs, Mr Bird and his brother Dr Bird and members of the constabulary went out to take possession. When they arrived the prisoner was not present but as the eviction commenced he appeared on the scene. Dr Bird and the sergeant of police will tell you what his demeanour was. He was violent and aggressive to such an extent that the sergeant of police thought it incumbent of himself to remain close to Mr Bird in order to protect him from this angered and furious man. I do not wish to exaggerate anything, that is not my duty, in fact it would be a grave dereliction of my duty and an offence on my part to do so, but I will tell you the words which were addressed to Cadogan by Mr Bird, as they were stated at the last trial, namely "Cadogan; you are a bad boy".

After the eviction Cadogan appears to have been a homeless man in the sense that he was without a farm or land of his own. He appears to have been on occasions employed as a farm servant and sometimes he supported himself by shooting game or rabbits in the mountains. That is important because the evidence will point to the fact that he was very well versed in the use of firearms as well as in their concealment, as the police often searched his house for arms that he had no license for and could find none. Following on from this you will find that this man was living a wild life in the mountains.

On more than one occasion, and on one particular occasion especially, he used threats against Mr Bird to induce him to reinstate him. Dr Bird, who assisted his brother in carrying out his business, will tell you that on three separate occasions this man, Cadogan, came into the deceased's office in Bantry with relevance to the land and on the last occasion when the deceased said that he would not reinstate him because the lands were now in the possession of another tenant, Cadogan made a very significant remark. However, before I tell you what the remark was, I will state a conversation Cadogan had with a man named Levis who he met on the mountains one day. Levis said to him that it was a shame he had lost the land, or words to that effect. Cadogan threatened that he would have his revenge on Mr Bird yet and when Levis said that it was not old times anymore when perhaps those things could be done, Cadogan made an elaborate gesture of pointing a gun. My learned friends might find fault with Levis and say he came forward at a late date to give this evidence. Let them say so; there was no desire in that no more than in any other case to help the Crown by volunteering evidence. The tendency was all the other way, Levis kept his knowledge to himself until after the Crown case had been closed and the prisoner was sent forward for trial and it was only then that he ventured to tell anybody what he knew. On the last occasion Cadogan went to Mr Bird's office to ask about being reinstated, sometime about August 1899, the deceased of course refused, and explained that it would be impossible even if he had the money to pay and put it down on the table, which he had not, he could not be reinstated because there was a court letting for seven years pending legal proceedings. In return, Cadogan uttered these remarkable words in the presence of the deceased's brother, Dr Bird. "You have done your worst; you can't do anymore to me; the devil thank you, and you may be sorry for it yet." What the prisoner said to Levis on the mountain some years ago was perhaps said, if you like, irresponsibly and you can attach any weight you like on them, but what will be proved in regard to the instance I am dealing with will be proved by one whom I do not think anybody in court will for a moment doubt, and that is Dr Bird, the only survivor of the family now. (This fact was incorrect, his sister Kate Rebecca Bird resided with him at Beach House.)

After Cadogan's eviction it appears that he entered the service of Richard Sullivan of Laharanshermeen, about six miles outside the town of Bantry. At any rate he had been in the service of Mr Sullivan the season preceding the murder and that was up to January last, when Sullivan practically dismissed him, claiming he had no further work for him. Cadogan asked Sullivan for a favour, to let him stay with him until he found new employment. Mr Sullivan agreed to this. On the 24th of February, Cadogan left Richard Sullivan's house at about eleven o' clock and walked to Bantry. When he was leaving he told Sullivan that he was going to look for new employment for the season. Sullivan asked him to bring back a newspaper from the town. On his way he appears to have met a man named Cornelius Sullivan, and curious to say, he met the same man on his return that evening. After passing Cornelius Sullivan he met another man, John Sullivan a mason from Ards and they travelled to Bantry together. They reached the town by the Glengarriff Road, the only road a person from that district can enter the town. They appear to have first gone to a public house owned by a man named Hurst which is situated on the lower corner of William Street."

The Solicitor General then entered at length into the topography of the town which he explained by means of a large map.

"You will find beyond doubt that Mr Bird visited his club on the Square on three occasions that day, the last time at about half past one. Cadogan, as proved by Sullivan the mason, went into Hurst's public house, and had a drink there immediately on their arrival into town. They both left the public house but then went back in and had more drink. After coming out again Sullivan went away and about the town and did not see Cadogan about the market or the town again that day. He left him standing at Hurst's Corner somewhere about half past one. Thus we have Cadogan taking up his stand to watch Mr Bird. From this station he could see Mr Bird through Bridewell Lane going from his club to his office. I suggest that when he saw the deceased going on his last fateful journey from his club somewhere about two o'clock, Cadogan, who understood the use of firearms, followed him to his office and fired the shots that deprived poor Mr Bird of his life.

Mr Bird was seen in the reading room of the club at about ten minutes to two by Frank Costelloe, the club's steward. When Costelloe went back to the reading room a few minutes later he noticed that Mr Bird had gone and he never saw him again. At about ten minutes to two Cadogan was seen standing at the corner of Hurst's public house. At about the same time Mr Bird was seen through Bridewell Lane heading in the direction of his office. Cadogan was next seen at two o'clock by two Breen's who owned a coach workshop on Marino Street standing on the opposite side of the footpath on Bridewell Lane. He was also seen by other persons who are inclined to help the Crown. After returning to his office Mr Bird conducted some business with persons named Hegarty and Scanlon. Hegarty is a farmer and a blacksmith; a well to do man, who was also a local sub-agent who collected rents at Dunmanus for Mr Bird. On this occasion he paid Mr Bird £10 for which he was issued a receipt. While Mr Bird and Hegarty were transacting their business a fellow named Leary came into the office and Mr Bird said to him in an agitated way "What is the matter with you now?" It appears Leary wanted a few half-crowns for work he had done for Mr Bird. Mr Bird then gave him the money and then drew up a receipt for Hegarty who took it and then went downstairs. In the shop underneath the office there were three employees, a girl named Fanny Dukelow and two boys, Robert Warner, and Walter Dennis. It was a few minutes past two when Dennis, who was standing inside the counter, and the other two heard something like quick hurried movement from the office overhead. They heard some conversation but could not make out what was being said. Suddenly they heard two sounds or reports. Dennis went out into the hallway which led to the stairs up to Mr Bird's office and saw coming down the stairs or standing on the first or second step on the lower floor a man holding a revolver in his right hand. The man walked out and put the revolver in his pocket. That man was Timothy Cadogan. Dennis ran back into the shop, and Fanny Dukelow remarked that he looked awfully pale and frightened. Looking through the shop window he saw the same man running down the Glengarriff Road. Dennis had known Cadogan for the previous two years and had seen him on a previous occasion outside the shop window. Of course Dennis's evidence will be attacked, but what reason does he have for swearing against Cadogan's life? There cannot be a suggestion that either Hegarty or Dr Bird committed the murder. Nobody had a motive except Cadogan who had sworn revenge against Mr Bird.

When Cadogan went home that evening and was asked by his employer was there any news from town; he said there was not but there was a great war in South Africa. When asked did he hear that Mr Bird had been shot; he said it must have been the doctor who did it and if not it was suicide. The Crown has had great difficulty in this case because if it had been anyone else but Cadogan who was seen so much in the vicinity of Mr Bird's office that day, there would have been plenty of people to come forward and give evidence. A great many must have seen Cadogan that day besides Dennis but they have not come forward. If what I have laid out are the facts of the case; surely there can be no room for doubt. You, who are in the position of administering the law and trying to maintain order in this country, are bound to act on the evidence and on your oath. I have had twenty-five years' experience with Cork juries and I need not say that this jury will try the case and will reach the verdict that the Crown has asked them for, that Timothy Cadogan, the prisoner at the bar, murdered Mr Bird, and that his life is therefore forfeited."

Witnesses were then called for the prosecution. The first being Mr Abbott, the part time model maker from Dublin.

"I visited Bantry in February for the purpose of making models. I also visited it again on the 8th of November for the same purpose. The model produced is made to scale and represents Warner's shop and Mr Bird's office. It is made to the scale of a half inch to the foot."

The Solicitor General. "Did you carry out any experiments regarding the light in the hallway?"

"I did."

"Any experiments regarding the view that could be obtained of anybody coming down the stairs?"

"Anybody putting his face through this door (pointing at the door from the shop to the hallway) could not see a person coming down the stairs, but a person advancing six feet into the hallway could see anybody on the stairs."

"What is the height of the bannisters?"

"The height of the handrail on the stairs is two feet six inches but at the bottom it is two feet eight inches."

The Lord Chief Justice. "Could a person hide themselves on the landing?"

"No; not even if they tried."

"Could a person looking in the front door see anybody on the stairs?"

"If the front hall door was open, the face of a man coming down the stairs could be plainly seen, and even if it was closed there is a fanlight on top through which sufficient light also comes for the purpose of observation."

Mr Barry. "Is there a partition under the stairs?

"No."

"How many flights of stairs does the model not show?"

"There are three other flights."

"Is there light on the first landing?"

"The first landing is on a level with the light from the window at the back."

"Does that light come at a straight angle?"

"No; at an acute one."

"Would a person standing behind the counter in the shop see a person going up Barrack Street?"

"Yes; they would."

137

The Lord Chief Justice. "Does the hall door remain open of itself?"

"Yes; it has a weight and a cord on it."

Sheriff's bailiff John Sullivan was next to take the stand and he gave evidence regarding the eviction of Timothy Cadogan on the 19th of August 1895. He swore that he executed the decree produced on the 9th of August 1895 and remembered taking possession of the lands mentioned in it. He handed the possession to Mr Bird who was present with his brother.

The Solicitor General. "The decree was for non-payment of rent for four years at £21 per year. This meant that £84 had been due in March of 1895."

R.I.C. Sergeant Cooper testified next in regard to the same incident.

"When we arrived at the house the prisoner was not there but Mr Bird and his brother were. I recollect observing a man on the mountain about a mile away. This man was Timothy Cadogan. When he arrived the bailiff was in the process of taking his belongings from the house. Cadogan went up to the bailiff and told him very angrily that he should be more careful with his possessions. He then went up to Mr Bird and I heard him ask him to stop the eviction. Mr Bird replied he could not help. The prisoner then went over and deliberately broke several articles of furniture against the wall of the house."

Mr Bourke. "What did you do at this point?"

"I observed the prisoner become very sullen in his demeanour and I considered it necessary to keep very close to Mr Bird."

"What did Cadogan do?"

"While his furniture was being removed he took up some furniture and deliberately smashed them against the wall of the house."

"Did he say anything?"

"He muttered something to Mr Bird which I did not catch. Mr Bird waved him away and said quietly and distinctly. "Cadogan; you are a bad boy.""

"What did Cadogan say?"

"He made no answer but deliberately and coolly began to smash spirit bottles against the side of the house."

Mr. Lynch. "What exactly did the prisoner say to Mr Bird?"

"I only heard the latter part, which was not to go ahead with the eviction."

"Did he say he would pay the rent that was due?"

"I am not sure."

"Will you swear he did not say it?"

"I think he did but I will not swear it."

"It is five years since and you are purporting to swear what he did say?"

"I am."

"But you won't swear that?"

"I won't."

The deceased's brother, Dr Robert Bird was next to take the stand.

"My brother, who was a land agent and a receiver for the Land Judges Court, and I both lived at Beach House Bantry."

Mr Moriarty. "Was your brother the agent for the White Estate?"

"He had been agent first and receiver afterwards for the White Estate."

"Do you know the prisoner?"

"Yes I do."

"How do you know him?"

"He had a farm at a place called Cooleenlemane from which he was evicted."

"Were you present when he was evicted?"

"Yes; I was assisting my brother."

"Have you had any interaction with him since he was evicted."

"Yes; on three separate occasions he called to my brother's office in Bantry when I was present, demanding to be reinstated on the land. Once he said he would get a girl with a fortune to marry him and would pay the rent due, my brother replied that he could not reinstate him on a proposal of that kind. On the last occasion my brother informed him that Miss White was the tenant and paying rent and his reinstatement was impossible."

"What was Cadogan's reply to this news?"

"He said in a sullen type of way; You have done your worst, the devil thank you; you may be sorry for it."

"When did this exchange take place?"

"About six months before my brother was murdered."

"Where were you on the day of the murder?"

"I was out shooting all day, at a place about seven miles from Bantry."

"Do you know if the street door was ever left open when your brother was in the office?"

"I never saw it shut when he was in his office."

"And what about the hall door leading to the shop?"

"It was always open too."

Mr Barry. "Do you know whether the door was open on the day of the murder?"

"I could not say."

"Did the prisoner seem upset at the loss of his farm?"

"Of course he did."

"Was your brother armed on the day of the eviction?"

"Yes; he carried a revolver that day. But I do not believe he carried one since then, even though we would go to the country to collect rents."

An old grey-haired man named William Levis, who had also given evidence at the first trial was called next.

"Sometime after the prisoner's eviction I saw him in the mountains. I waited for him to catch up with me because I wanted to hear what he had to say about the eviction. I said to him that it was a shame for him to allow himself to be evicted, and that Mr Bird, who was a good man, would make a settlement with him. Oh he said, by this and that I will have satisfaction with him yet. I said that the law was too strict now and that he would not be able to waylay or beat him and he said he would have satisfaction another way. At the same time he put up his hand in the gesture of firing a gun."

Mr Lynch. "When did you make this statement to the police?"

"Before the murder occurred."

"Have you made any statement to the police since?"

"No."

"Did you not give evidence before a judge and jury in July of this year?"

"I don't remember."

The Lord Chief Justice. "When did you give this statement to the police?"

"About a year after it occurred."

Mr Lynch. "Do you not remember swearing at the last Assizes that you had only made this statement about a fortnight before that to the police?"

"I don't."

Bantry publican Thomas R. Hurst was the next witness called.

"The prisoner came into my shop on the 24th of February in the company of John Sullivan, a mason from Ards, and another man whom I did not know. They men had two drinks each, one of which the witness paid for."

The Solicitor General. "For how long were they in your shop?"

"For about a quarter of an hour."

Mr Barry. "What time did they come into your pub?"

"At about half past one."

"So you say it was about a quarter to two when they left the pub?"

"Yes."

"Did they return?"

"The prisoner didn't."

"Is the corner where your public house is located a busy spot?"

"Probably the busiest in Bantry."

Kate Harrington from near Mount Corrin, next took the stand.

"I came into Bantry on business on the 24th of February. On my arrival I went to the fish market and I saw the prisoner standing on Hurst's Corner. As I left the market he was still there. I went to Mrs Crowley's for my dinner after which I went to Mr Biggs's store where I heard that Mr Bird had shot himself."

The Solicitor General. "After the second time you saw the prisoner on Hurst's Corner, did you see him again that day?"

"I didn't."

"What made you notice the prisoner on Hurst's Corner?"

"No particular reason. Hurst's Corner is a place where many people congregate because there is a good view from it."

Mr Lynch. "On any day you come into Bantry would there be people on that corner?"

"Yes; always."

Jeremiah McCarthy was next to take the stand.

"Some years ago I was minding a farm for the late Denis McCarthy outside Bantry and I met Timothy Cadogan in the mountains a couple of times carrying a gun."

142

The Solicitor General. "Did you witness him firing a gun?"

"I only ever saw him fire one shot."

"What did he fire at?"

"I couldn't say."

"Did you not swear in your previous deposition that you saw the prisoner fire at birds?"

"What I swore in my deposition was mainly true, but I did not see him fire at birds."

"Do you remember Saturday the 24th of February this year?"

"Yes."

"What were you doing?"

"I was in Bantry that day."

"Did you see the prisoner?"

"When I was passing Bridewell Lane going in the direction of the Square along Marino Street, I saw two or three people and to the best of my belief the prisoner was among them."

"Where exactly was this?"

"It was opposite Breen's workshop on Marino Street."

"At what time was that?"

"It might have been about ten or eleven o'clock."

The Lord Chief Justice. "That is not in your deposition."

"A policeman put many things in my deposition that I was not aware of."

Mr Barry. "How long ago was it when you saw the prisoner on the mountain with a gun?"

"About seven or eight years ago."

The next witness to be called was Henry Breen Snr.

"On Saturday the 24th of February I was standing outside my workshop on Marino Street and I saw the prisoner standing halfway between my workshop and Bridewell Lane."

The Solicitor General. "Was he alone?"

"No; he was talking to two other people."

"Had your employees gone for their dinner at this time?"

"Yes."

Mr Lynch. "What time did they go to dinner at?"

"The men went at two o'clock but one of my sons, Tim, stayed behind to finish the job he was at. I was giving him instructions on how to complete it and he got annoyed and went inside. I followed him in about five minutes later and told him to go for his dinner."

"How long was this after the other men had gone for theirs?"

"About ten minutes."

"In what direction was the prisoner going when you saw him?"

"He was going from Bridewell Lane towards the Square."

"Do you know who he was talking to when you saw him?"

"It was a man and a woman but I don't recall who they were."

"How long had the men gone to dinner before you went out onto the street?"

"I could not say exactly."

"And at what time did your son go for his?"

"I left him in the workshop so I cannot exactly say when he went either."

"When you first saw the prisoner, from what direction was he coming?"

"He was coming from the direction of Bridewell Lane."

A blacksmith named Patrick Cronin was then called to the stand.

Mr Moriarty. "Do you know the prisoner or Michael Hegarty?"

"I know them both."

"Where were you during dinner hour on the day of the murder?"

"I was on Barrack Street in Bantry."

"Did you see Timothy Cadogan?"

"Yes."

"Where did you see him?"

"As I passed Mahony's shop on Barrack Street I saw him standing with his back against the wall of the shop smoking."

"Did you pass anyone else?"

"I passed Michael Hegarty as I approached Mr Bird's office."

"Where did you go then?"

"I remained on Bigg's corner, which is the corner of Barrack Street and Marino Street, until I heard of Mr Bird been killed."

Mr Barry. "Were you examined at the previous trial?"

"No; but I made a deposition before the magistrates."

"What time did you come into town that day?"

"At about twelve o'clock."

"How long were you in the town before you saw Cadogan?"

"I could not tell you."

"How long after you saw Cadogan was it that you heard Mr Bird had been shot?"

"It was something over a half an hour."

Mr Barry then took up a copy of the witnesses sworn deposition.

"In your deposition you swore that you came to town at twelve o'clock and that it was an hour after seeing Timothy Cadogan that you heard of Mr Bird's murder."

"I think it may have been an hour."

"Did you not swear true when you said. "I am sure it was an hour, if not more."?"

"I could not tell you."

"Have you not read your own deposition?"

"I have not seen the deposition since I made it."

"Was it not read over to you so you could correct any errors?"

"No."

The Lord Chief Justice. "How long were you on the corner after passing Michael Hegarty?"

"About a half an hour, then I saw the crowd going towards Warner's."

Constable William Daly next gave evidence of being on street patrol on the day of the murder.

"I was on the corner of Barrack Street when I saw Mr Bird leave his office by the front door at about half past one and proceed in the direction of his club."

The Crown's star witness, Walter Dennis, was next to take the stand.

"The Solicitor General. "Where are you from?"

"I am from Whiddy Island and I am the son of a farmer who is now deceased."

"Where were you employed in February last?"

"I was in the employment of Mr Warner as a messenger boy."

"And for how long were you in Mr Warner's employment?"

"For the last four years."

"In which of Mr Warner's shops were you employed?"

"It is the shop next to Biggs's Corner on Barrack Street."

"Where was Mr Bird's office in relation to the shop you work in?"

"It is directly overhead."

"Did you know Mr Bird?"

"I did."

"Where were you at about two o'clock on the afternoon of the 24th of February last?"

"I was in the shop. I did not go for dinner that day."

"Where abouts in the shop were you?"

"I was behind the counter at the far side of the shop from the door."

"Were you alone?"

"No; Fanny Dukelow and Bob Warner, a nephew of Mr Warner's, were also in the shop. They were behind the counter on the other side"

"As the three of you were there at about two o'clock; did any sound attract your attention?"

"Yes."

"What was the sound like?"

"Footsteps."

"Where did it come from?"

"From overhead."

"Would that have been from Mr Bird's office?"

"Yes."

"Was it a sudden noise?"

"It was the noise of feet."

"Did it last long?"

"Not very long."

"What followed the noise of feet?"

"There was a shot next."

The Lord Chief Justice. "Were the sound of the footsteps slow or hurried?"

"Pretty slow."

The Solicitor General. "And what followed the shot?"

"Another one then."

"From what direction did they come?"

"From overhead."

"Did you hear more than two shots?"

"No."

"While the dragging of feet and the noise was going on did you remain behind the counter?"

"I went back. I passed through the hall door and went into the hall."

"Was this the door that closed by a weight."

"Yes."

"Did you go any distance beyond it?"

"Yes; into the hallway."

"Was this immediately after hearing the report of the second shot?"

"Yes."

"Standing there, did you see anyone coming down the stairs?"

"Yes."

"Is that the stairs coming down from Mr Bird's office?"

"Yes."

"Who was the man you saw?"

"Timothy Cadogan, sir."

"The prisoner at the bar?"

"Yes sir."

"Had he something in his hand?"

"Yes."

"What had he?"

"He had a revolver."

"In which hand had he it?"

"In his right hand."

"Was he moving fast or slow?"

"Pretty slow; not too fast."

"What did he do with the revolver?"

"He was putting it in his pocket when I saw him."

"Did you shift your position then?"

"I went back again sir, into the shop and went to the same place inside the counter."

"When you went back into the shop did you find the same two persons there?"

"Yes."

"And standing there, were you able to see out the window?"

"Yes."

149

"And looking out did you see anyone?"

"Someone like the same fellow going across the street."

"And going in which direction?"

"In the direction of the Glengarriff Road."

"When you saw him was he going fast or slow?"

"He was running."

"Was that the last time you saw him?"

"Yes."

"You say the man was Timothy Cadogan?"

"Yes."

"Was he a stranger to you?"

"No; I had known him before."

"For how long did you know him?"

"I knew his name for a year."

"Did you know him before that?"

"I knew him to see."

"Had you seen him in the town of Bantry before?"

"Yes; once or twice."

"Did you see him near Warner's shop?"

"I saw him once."

"Where?"

"Outside the shop."

"Had you light in the hallway on the 24th of February?"

"I had"

"And were you standing in such a position that you were able to see him?"

"I was."

"Were you able to see his face?"

"Yes."

"You were alone and he was alone?"

"Yes."

"You remember that this was on a Saturday; you did not see him again?"

"I did not."

On the following Tuesday were you up before the resident magistrate?"

"I was."

"Were you sworn?"

"I was."

"Was Cadogan in custody?"

"Yes."

"Did you identify him as the man you saw coming down the stairs?"

"Yes."

"Did Cadogan ask you a question?"

"Yes."

"What was it?"

"Was I sure?"

"Were you then?"

"I was."

"Are you now?"

"I am."

Mr Barry. "What was your position in Warner's?"

"I was a messenger."

"Have you ever seen Michael Hegarty in the shop?"

"A few times."

"Do you know him?"

"Yes."

"How long did you know him?"

"Not very long, I only saw him a few times in the shop."

"Did you ever speak to him?"

"No."

"Have you ever seen Timothy Cadogan in the shop?"

"No; but I saw him outside once."

"Did you not swear the last time that you knew he was a customer of the shop?"

"No; I never saw him in the shop."

"You just saw him once outside the shop and did not know whether he was ever a customer?"

"Yes."

"Might it have been a year before the murder of Mr Bird when you saw him outside the shop?"

"It may."

"Might it have been two years?"

"It might."

"How did you find out his name?"

"I was told what it was."

"When were you told what his name was?"

"I do not know."

"Who told you what his name was?"

"I do not know."

"You had no particular interest in making inquiries about the prisoner's name?"

"No."

"Have you known him a long time?"

"Yes."

"But you never spoke to him?"

"Yes."

"Do you remember the first time you saw him?"

"It was on a fair day or market day."

"Did you go immediately, when you heard the second shot, through this door?"

"Yes."

"And this is the part of the establishment where the barrels of pigs heads are kept?"

"Yes."

"And you would have to go out this way?"

"Yes."

"Did the door close behind you after you went out?"

"Yes."

"Did you walk in and out of this place leisurely?"

"Well, I did."

153

"How long did it take you to go out and back in again?"

"Just a second."

"Did you run out and in?"

"No; I walked."

"And you looked straight out the window on your return?"

"Yes."

"What step was Timothy Cadogan on when you say you saw him coming down the stairs?"

"He was on the second step on the first flight coming down."

"On your oath did you swear at the last trial that he was between the two flights?"

"Yes."

"Was that not the landing?"

"Yes."

"And he had not commenced to come down the last flight?"

"I did not see him come down the last flight."

"This man was taking his time?"

"I did not take much notice of him."

"Was he in a hurry?"

"I just looked at him and walked back again, he was going at a middling pace down the stairs."

"But the man you saw outside was running?"

"Yes."

"When you saw him running; I suppose you had a view of Breen's public house on the other side of the street?"

"Yes."

"Were you looking out in that direction when you heard the shots?"

"I was behind the counter."

"Did you see Harry Breen on the other side of the street?"

"No."

"Was there many people out on the street?"

"Yes; but not too many. I saw people outside but I did not know who they were."

"Did you think that this man who you saw running had done something wrong?"

"Yes; I knew he was after doing something when I heard the shots go off."

"What did you think he had done?"

"I didn't know what he did."

"Whose room was over your head?"

"Mr Bird's room."

"Did you know whether Mr Bird was in?"

"No I did not."

"Don't you know that he is always there on market and fair days?"

"I knew he must have been going in and out."

"What did you think the man did that went out?"

"I didn't know what he had done at the time."

"Did you think he had shot anyone?"

"I did not."

"Did you think he was shooting pigeons up there?"

"I didn't know what he was shooting."

"When you saw him with the revolver did you think he had done any harm?"

"No."

"What did you think he had done?"

"I thought he did something; but I did not know what it was. I did not think anyone was injured."

"When you went out into the hall had you cause to be afraid of anything?"

"I was not afraid. I was frightened when I returned to the shop."

"But you were not frightened at all when you went into the hall?"

"No."

"Is it true that you did not know that anything had happened?"

"I did not."

"And you were frightened?"

"Well I was frightened but not very much."

"In the shop that day was there a girl named Donoghue when the shots were fired?"

"There were some people there but I did not know any of them."

"Do you know a person named Agnes Sullivan?"

"No; I did not know who was there at the time."

"Were there many people in the shop?"

"There was a good deal of people."

"And they, of course, could see as well as you a man running away?"

"They could."

"Did you say Mr Bird was shot dead?"

"No; I did not."

"And did you, when the shots were fired; instead of running into the hall run out into the street?"

"No."

"If anyone said that you did, would it be untrue?"

"I did not go out into the street."

"Did you think this man was running away so that he could not be caught?"

"I did."

"Did you call anyone's attention to the fact that this man was running away with a revolver?"

"No."

"Did some of the clerks from your master's other shop come down?"

"Yes; when they found out what had happened."

"Did you see Mr Bird's body in his office when you went upstairs?"

"I did."

"Did you know Mr Bird?"

"I did; he often spoke to me."

"And when you saw his dead body on the floor, did you tell anyone anything about what you saw?"

"I did not."

"Did Mr Swords ask you had you seen anyone going upstairs?"

"I do not recollect him asking me anything about it."

"How long did you remain in the room where the body was?"

"I just went up and came down again."

"Did you hear anyone asking if anyone knew who shot him?"

"The police were inquiring about it."

"And you didn't tell them?"

"No; I did not."

"Did you hear any rumour that he shot himself or that Dr Bird had done it?"

"I did."

"Did you tell them that there was no truth in it?"

"Why should I tell them?"

"Did you think that Dr. Bird had shot him?"

"I did not know."

"Did you think he didn't?"

"I did."

"Did you not think it right to say he didn't?"

"I didn't want to say anything at all about it. Why should not everyone else tell it as well as me?"

"Now; on your oath, did you tell the clerks when you came back that you knew the man who had murdered Mr. Bird?"

"No; I did not tell them."

"Were you in the office when the remains of Mr. Bird were being removed?"

"Yes; I went down with the remains as far as the chapel."

"Who were you with?"

"I was walking with a son of Thomas Paul's."

"Do you know a man by the name of William Shorten?"

"I do."

"Was he with you on that occasion?"

"I can't recall."

"If William Shorten swore that he asked you if you knew anything about the murder, would you contradict him?"

"No; I would not."

"On that night were you at Beach House?" (The Bird's Residence)

"Yes; I was."

"Do you know a man named Michael Leary?"

"Yes."

"Did you not talk to him at Beach House?"

"I did."

"What did he say to you?"

"He asked me if I knew anything about the murder."

"And what did you say?"

"I told him I didn't."

"Do you know a boy by the name of Timothy Nagle?"

"Yes."

"Did you tell Timothy Nagle the next day after Mass that when you heard the shots you went back into where the pig's heads are kept and stayed there?"

"I did not tell him any such thing."

"Will you swear you did not tell him anything?"

"I did not tell him anything about shots."

"If Nagle swore you made this statement to him, would you on your oath contradict him?"

"I would not."

"Where have you being living since this happened?"

"In Dublin."

"Kept by the police?"

"Yes."

"I am not saying anything about that, you have been very smart. When did you first hear that a man had been arrested for the crime?"

"I heard it that night, that Michael Hegarty had been arrested."

"Did you know a man could be hanged for murdering a man?"

"I didn't know any such thing."

"Do you know it now?"

"No."

The Solicitor General. "He means to say that he didn't know that Hegarty could be hanged for this."

Mr Barry "Did you know Hegarty had been arrested?"

"I did."

"Didn't you know what he had been arrested for; the killing of Mr Bird?"

"Yes; I did."

"And didn't you know that was murder?"

"Yes."

"Didn't you know a man could be hanged for murder?"

"Well, I did."

"And you knew Hegarty didn't do it?"

"Yes; I did."

"Did you go and tell anyone that Hegarty didn't do it?"

"I did not."

The Lord Chief Justice. "As I understand it, he says he did not know that Hegarty would be hung."

Mr Barry. "When did you learn that another man was arrested?"

"On the Sunday."

"Did you hear the name of the man who was arrested?"

"I did."

"And what was his name?"

"Timothy Cadogan."

"You knew the whole of Sunday that Timothy Cadogan had been arrested?"

"I did."

"And the whole of Monday?"

"I did."

"And you never mentioned it to a soul what you had seen?"

"I didn't want to talk about it. Why didn't everyone else talk about it as well as me?"

"When did you tell someone?"

"On the Tuesday."

"Who did you tell?"

"Acting Sergeant Driscoll."

"What time was it when the police came for you on Tuesday?"

"About eleven or twelve o'clock."

"And they brought you to the barracks?"

"Yes."

"Did you know what you were being taken for?"

"Yes; to make a statement."

"About what?"

"About what I had told him."

"On the same day?"

"Yes."

"To identify the man they had in custody as the man you had seen on the stairs?"

"Yes."

"You knew that was Timothy Cadogan?"

"I did not know until I was brought to make the statement."

"What statement?"

"What I saw on the stairs."

"Did you swear to me at the last trial that you did not know why you were being brought to the barracks?"

"I did not."

"There was only one man there when you went there?"

"That is all."

"You said "That is the man."

"Yes."

"You did not go back to Bantry anymore after that?"

"No."

The Solicitor General. "Did you know that Michael Hegarty had been released before you went to the barracks to make your statement?"

"I did not."

"Why did you hesitate to tell the police about what you saw?"

"I knew others had seen the man running away as well."

"Is the evidence you have given here the same as the evidence you gave to the police at the time?"

"It is."

"And do you still stand over it?"

"I do."

The court was then adjourned at a quarter to six until ten o'clock the following morning and the jury were taken by police guard to the Imperial Hotel for the night.

The Final Judgement

When the trial resumed the following morning the first witness to take the stand was Frank Costelloe, who worked as a steward in the Bantry Conservative Club.

"On the 24th of February last I saw Mr Bird in the club's reading room at about ten minute's to two o'clock. When I looked into the room twenty minutes later he was gone.

Mr Bourke. "Would Mr. Bird's route back to his office take him by the Bridewell Lane?"

"Yes; he would pass through it."

Patrick Flynn, a labourer, was next to give evidence.

"On the day of the murder I saw Mr Bird coming from the direction of his club and turning down the Bridewell Lane towards Marino Street before I lost sight of him."

Mr Bourke. "What time was this?"

"At about ten minutes to two."

The next witness called was Michael Scanlon, who worked as a rent collector for Mr Bird.

"On Saturday the 24th of February I went to the office to see Mr Bird at about five minutes to two."

The Solicitor General. "What route did you take?"

"I went by Marino Street."

"Was Mr Bird there when you arrived?"

"No; he was out."

"Did you go up to his office?"

"No; I only went as far as the street door, which was open, where I found Mrs Hourihane waiting for him."

"What did you do next?"

"I talked to Mrs Hourihane for a while before she left and I then waited for Mr Bird to arrive."

"What time did he arrive?"

"At about two o'clock. We both then went upstairs to transact some business."

"Did you stay long?"

"No; only a few minutes."

"As you were leaving did you see anyone?"

"Yes; I met Mrs Hourihane out on the street on her way to see Mr Bird."

"Where did you go then?"

"I went up Barrack Street onto Main Street and then onto New Street."

"When did you hear about Mr Bird's murder?"

"About a half an hour after it happened."

Mrs. Hourihane was next to testify. She corroborated Michael Scanlon's evidence and then stated.

"When I returned I found Mr Bird in his office and I paid him some rent. After a minute or two I left the office. On my way out I saw Mr Hegarty on his way to the office."

Michael Hegarty was then called to take the stand.

The Solicitor General. "Where do you live?"

"In a place called Dunmanus which is about fourteen miles from Bantry."

"What is your occupation?"

"I am a farmer."

"Do you farm much land?"

"I have three farms, one of which I paid rent to Mr Bird for."

"Do you carry out any other business?"

"Yes; I acted as an agent for Mr Bird. I collected rent on his behalf."

"Tell me about your activities on February the 24th last?"

"My wife and myself came into Bantry that day. Between one and half past one I went to Mr Bird's office but I found it locked. I then went away before returning a half an hour later or less. When I came back the office door was open and Mr Bird was in the office speaking to Mrs Hourihane who was standing outside the counter. I waited until she completed her business and then I paid Mr Bird £10 for which I got a receipt. While I was in the office a man named Leary came in and stayed for a minute. I left the office shortly after him"

"What did you do next?"

"On leaving the office I went down Barrack Street, passing O'Mahony's pub to Cullinane's shop on the Main Street where my wife was. From there we went down to Sullivan's in the Square where we were delayed for a few moments. We then went to Vickery's yard before going to Miss O'Shea's on the Square for dinner. It was on the way there that we heard of the murder."

The Lord Chief Justice. "How long were you in Cullinane's?"

"Only a couple of minutes."

Mr Moriarty. "While in Cullinane's did you notice anything?"

"Yes; I saw policemen running up the street."

Mr Lynch. "Had Mr Bird his books open on the counter when you entered the office?"

"Yes; he had."

"Besides your own business, did the pair of you discuss anything else?"

"Yes; we spoke about a Mr Fuller's annuity. Mr Bird told me that a payment of £6 and 17 shillings would bring him up to a certain date."

"How long were you assisting Mr Bird with the collection of rents?"

"About ten or eleven years."

"Were you on friendly terms with him?"

"Yes; I was."

"How long were you in the office for?"

"It could not have been more than five minutes."

"You were at one time an employee of the Property Defence Association?"

"Yes."

"And you have now changed your opinion and become a member of another league?"

"Yes."

"Were you ever a member of the National League?"

"No."

"Did you ever attend any of its meetings?"

"Yes."

"You had a revolver?"

"Yes; and I have it still."

"And you had one in the month of February?"

"I had."

"What time did you come to town that day?"

"Between one and half past one."

"And after you conducted your business with Mr Bird you went to Mr Cullinane's and after that to Mrs Sullivan's?"

"Yes."

"How long did you remain in Cullinane's shop?"

"About a couple of minutes, my wife had her business completed there."

"How long were you at Sullivan's?"

"About the same length."

"While at Cullinane's you saw the police running?"

"Yes."

"And did you see people running?"

"I saw a few people."

"In what direction were they running?"

"Towards the corner of Barrack Street."

"And you did not ask where they were going?"

"No."

"You went along down to Mrs. Sullivan's."

"Yes."

"And you never asked on the way where the police and people were running to?"

"No."

"How long were you in Mr Cullinane's after you saw the police running by?"

"I was only a couple of minutes there altogether."

"And you then went to Mrs. Sullivan's, where you remained a couple of minutes and never asked where or why the police were running?"

"No."

"You then went to Vickery's yard?"

"Yes."

"And you never asked up to that what the police were running up to Biggs's Corner or the Main Street for?"

"No."

"Where did you say you heard Mr Bird had been shot?"

"Between Vickery's Yard and where we were going for dinner near Hurst's Corner."

"And then you heard that Mr Bird had been shot?"

"What I heard there was that Master Willie had shot himself."

"And you did not go back to the office to find out if it was true?"

"No; I went to my dinner."

"On your oath, how long were you there waiting for your dinner?"

"Perhaps ten minutes or a quarter of an hour."

"And did you ask anyone there if the report was true?"

"It is there I heard that he had shot himself."

"Who told you?"

"Miss O'Shea."

"How long were you there before she told you?"

"She told me the moment I came in."

"Miss O'Shea had told you that the man had been shot and you believed her?"

"Yes."

"You had no doubt that he had been shot?"

"I believed he was."

"And that he was dead?"

"Yes."

"On your oath, did you swear before the Coroner that it was when you went back to Vickery's yard you made inquiries as to the truth of the statement?"

"I don't think that is so."

"Was Pat Crowley in Vickery's Yard, the first person whom you inquired as to whether the report was true or not?"

"We came back to get a trap and it is there I made inquiries as to whether it was a fact."

"How long were you at your dinner?"

"The only time that I can give is that while at my dinner the three o'clock train went out."

"And you never went to find out whether Mr Bird had been shot or not?"

"I thought it would be very unusual and an intrusion to go amongst the police and his friends."

"Was it your evidence before the Corner that it was no business of yours as he was not a relative or a friend of yours?"

"And that is my opinion still. As regard the rents I was sending rents to the others as well as him and have since collected it for his successor."

"How long had you been in the office with Mr Bird before Leary came in?"

"Leary must have come in about a minute or two after Mrs Hourihane had gone out?"

"Had you got your receipt then?"

"I had."

"Did you hear Leary coming up the stairs?"

"No; I heard him coming into the office."

"Would it be true that when Leary was coming up the stairs there was loud talking between you and Mr Bird?"

"It would not be true to say there were angry words. The talk was ordinary talk."

"Is that the overcoat you had on in Bantry that day?"

"No."

"You had one on?"

"Yes."

"You had it on when you were driving into town?"

"Yes."

"Where did you take it off?"

"I don't know now."

"You took it off somewhere?"

"I am not sure whether I had it on me in the office or not."

"You had one on when you came into town?"

"I had."

"You had one on as you were walking around the town?"

"I won't swear to that."

"Where did you leave your overcoat when you came into Bantry?"

"I don't know what class of overcoat I had."

"Do you remember having the overcoat?"

"I am sure I must have had one as I would not have travelled that distance without one."

"You won't swear you had it on when you were walking around after you got off the car?"

"I won't."

"You had it on after your dinner when you met the police?"

172

"I had it then because I was in my car going home. Acting Sergeant Driscoll asked me had I been in Mr Bird's office and I said I had."

"Would it be an accurate description of your movements to say you were walking quickly towards Mrs Sullivan's?"

"It may be."

Mr Moriarty. "Where was your revolver on the day of the shooting?"

"It was at home and it still is."

"Have you a licence for it?"

"Yes; for the last fifteen years."

"On the day of the murder did the police search you?"

"Yes and my car and the parcels on it."

The Lord Chief Justice. "Had you any hand, act, or part in the shooting of Mr Bird?"

"Oh dear no; My Lord."

"I thought it my duty to ask the question."

Mr Moriarty. "I did not like to ask, My Lord."

The Lord Chief Justice. "When such evidence is public, I think it is my duty to put the question in order to protect the witness."

The next witness was John Leary.

The Solicitor General. "Were you employed by the deceased?"

"Yes; for the last six or seven years."

"And what did you do for Mr Bird?"

"I cut spurs for thatching."

"On the day of the murder did you visit with Mr Bird in his office?"

"Yes".

173

"At what time?"

"At about two o'clock."

"Was Mr Bird alone?"

"No; Mr Hegarty was also there."

"What did Mr Bird say to you?"

"He asked what was the matter with me and I replied that I wanted money for spurring. He asked me how much I required and I told him two shilling and sixpence which he then gave to me."

Mr Barry. "As you were going upstairs to the office did you hear talking?"

"They were talking."

"As you got near the office did the talking stop?"

"It did."

"Did you notice Mr Bird's demeanour?"

"He was angry looking."

Fanny Dukelow, a shop assistant in Warner's was next on the stand.

"On the day in question I had dined out for my dinner and I returned to the shop at ten minutes past two."

Mr Moriarty. "Was there any other employees there present when you arrived back from your dinner."

"Yes; Mr Warner's nephew Robert and the messenger Walter Dennis."

"After you entered the shop what did you do?"

"I took off my coat and hat and hung them up. Then I took my usual place behind the counter near the window."

"Did you hear anything unusual?"

"Yes; after some time I heard a noise like that of the stamping of feet."

174

"From where did you believe this noise originated from?"

"Overhead in Mr Bird's office."

"What happened next?"

"A piece of mortar fell from the ceiling then there was a noise like someone had struck a door with a rod and the sound like someone had fallen down a stairs. I then heard two noises like that of the shots of a revolver."

"Did you notice what Walter Dennis did?"

"Yes; he went back into the hall leading to Mr Bird's office and when he came back he looked awfully pale and frightened. He returned to where he had been standing behind the counter facing the window."

Mr Lynch. "Now the door that Walter Dennis went out through leads into a storeroom and from the storeroom there is a door that leads to the hallway, is that right?"

"Yes."

And does the door into the storeroom close?"

"Yes."

"Did it close after Walter Dennis that day?"

"Yes."

"So once it closed you could not see where Walter Dennis went?"

"That is correct."

"Was there anyone else in the shop at the time?"

"There was a Mrs Sullivan."

Robert Warner, the seventeen-year-old nephew of the owner of Warner's shop was next to take the stand.

"After I heard the shuffling of feet and then the shots, I walked from the shop through the spring door (into the storeroom) and looked into the hall where I saw Walter Dennis standing in the hall looking up the stairs. I then went back into the shop and said something to Miss Dukelow, as a consequence of this conversation I went to the shop next door where my uncle was to inform him of the noises and then I went up to Mr Bird's office with two clerks from that shop, Brooks and Swords, and I saw him lying dead on the floor. I then went for Dr. Popham."

Mr Barry. "At the first trial you did not say a single word about seeing Walter Dennis in the hall?"

"That is true."

"How did you come to tell it now when you never told it before?"

"I told it to Mr Wright."

"When?"

"When I came up the last time?"

"Before the first trial?"

"No; this one."

"What brought you up here?"

"I was summoned."

"Was it here you told this new story to Mr Wright? Were you brought into his office?"

"I was."

"By whom?"

"District Inspector Armstrong."

"Did you tell it to him?"

"No."

"What day was this?"

"I think it was this day last week."

"And you never told the magistrates and you never told the court at the last trial?"

"No."

"And on last Tuesday when you were brought into Mr Wright's office you told this story for the first time. Tell me who else was there?"

"D.I. Armstrong and two other men."

"Who were they?"

"I think there was a policeman and another man."

"Would you know the other man again?"

"I think I would."

"Was this man in uniform?"

"No."

The Lord Chief Justice. "Was he a civilian?"

Mr Moriarty. "He was Mr Wright's clerk."

The Lord Chief Justice. "How dare you! Are you giving evidence?"

Mr Moriarty. "I beg your pardon."

Mr Barry. "Were you asked any questions as to how you went into the hall?"

Robert Warner. "Yes; they asked me what I did."

"Listen sir, did you tell that before the magistrates?"

"No."

"You were sworn?"

"Yes."

"And you signed your name to it?"

"I did."

"I am going to read out the deposition that you made before the magistrates.

I am in the employment of Mr. J.P. Warner. He is my uncle. I recollect Saturday the 24th of February last. I was in Mr. Warner's shop that day. The shop is under Mr Bird's office. I remember between two and three o'clock that day hearing a noise. It was a loud noise. It sounded to me like the shuffling of feet. After that I heard shots. Miss Dukelow, a shop assistant was in the shop, I spoke to her. In consequence of what she said to me, I went down to the shop where Mr Warner was. There was a good few customers around him. It took me some little time before I could get near him. After I made the communication to Mr Warner he went into the office where Mr Brooks and Mr Swords were. He gave them certain directions and they went to Mr Bird's office. I accompanied them. Brooks was the first to go in and I followed him. I saw the body of Mr Bird lying on the floor. Swords came up after me. I saw Swords lift Mr Bird's head up. I noticed blood under Mr Bird's head. I came downstairs and was sent for Dr Popham. I did not go up to Mr Bird's office again.

You made no mention of following Walter Dennis to the hall in this deposition. Did you tell the truth then?"

"Yes."

The Solicitor General. "These things you have said for the first time about going to the hall after Dennis opened the spring door and seeing Dennis in the hall. Were you ever asked this question until I put it to you last Tuesday?"

"No."

Mr Barry. "Were you asked before the magistrates to tell what occurred?"

"Yes."

The Lord Chief Justice. "You told this to Mr Wright?"

"Yes."

"He was asking you, as is his manifest duty, some questions about the case?"

"Yes."

"And then for the first time you told this to any officer and what you said you said. Is what you said true?"

"It is true."

Fanny Dukelow was then recalled at the request of a juror and stated that she had noticed Robert Warner follow Dennis out into the hall.

Mr Barry. "Were you in court on the day that Robert Warner was examined by the magistrates?"

"I was."

"And did you make this statement that you saw him follow Dennis in to the hall before?"

"No."

Sarah Bevan, a servant of Mr Warner's was next called. She stated that after two o'clock on the day of the murder she was working in the kitchen behind the shop when she heard noises from Mr Bird's office above. She said she remained in the kitchen for a further ten minutes after hearing these noises and during that time nobody entered the kitchen. The kitchen had a back door leading to a yard.

Dr Lionel Popham then gave evidence to having arrived at Mr Bird's office between twenty past two and half past two and finding him deceased. He then repeated the medical evidence given previously.

Acting Sergeant Driscoll was next to give his evidence.

"I was on duty in the town of Bantry on the 24th of February last. I went to Mr Bird's office at about twenty-five past two. On the same day at about eight o'clock in the evening I went in search of Timothy Cadogan and found him in the house of Richard Sullivan, Laharanshermeen, on Sunday morning. When I went in Sullivan told me where Cadogan was and I went to him and spoke to him. I told him any evidence he might give would be taken down. I then questioned him regarding his movements on the previous day, and Cadogan made a statement to me that coincided with the evidence of the previous witnesses up until about half past one in the day. He said he left Bantry at about six o'clock in the evening."

Mr Barry. "Was it you who brought Walter Dennis to the barracks on the following Tuesday to identify the prisoner?"

"It was."

"And Timothy Cadogan was the only man he was asked to identify?"

"He was."

"Why was Cadogan not placed, as is usual, amongst other men for the purpose of identification?"

"Because Dennis told me that it was Cadogan that he had seen on the stairs."

"Didn't you know that the whole town of Bantry knew that the man who was in the police cells was charged with the murder of Mr Bird?"

"I presumed the people knew it, but I didn't know if Dennis knew it."

"It never occurred to you to put Timothy Cadogan amongst other men to see if Dennis really knew him?"

"I hadn't the slightest doubt that he knew him."

"You did not take down in your book at the time you arrested the prisoner that he asked you on what charge he was being arrested on?"

"I did not think it mattered."

John Sullivan from Ards, who had accompanied Timothy Cadogan to Bantry on the day of the murder was next to take the stand.

"It was around one o'clock when we arrived into town."

Mr Moriarty. "What road did you come in?"

"The Glengarriff Road."

"What did you do on your arrival?"

"We went into Hurst's pub and had some drink. We then went outside before going back in for another drink."

"Where was the last place you saw Cadogan in Bantry that day?"

"When I left him he was leaning against the wall outside Hurst's on the corner of William Street."

"Did you see him again that day?"

"Yes; I caught up with him on the way home that evening."

"Did he mention the murder of Mr Bird to you?"

"He said the rumour in town when he had left was that Dr Bird had done it."

Mr Lynch. "Did the prisoner ask you if you had a newspaper?"

"He did and the two of us went into my house to read it."

"On the way to Bantry that morning did the prisoner tell you his reason for going to town?"

"Yes; he told me he was going looking for employment and he asked me to keep my ears open."

"And did you?"

"Yes; on the way home I told him that a Con Sullivan had work for him if he wanted it."

"And what was his reply?"

"He said he would go see him after first Mass in Kealkill the following morning."

Cornelius Sullivan next gave evidence that the prisoner called to his home for a drink on the night of the murder and mentioned nothing about Mr Bird's death. His brother Richard, with whom Cadogan lived with, stated that he had given the prisoner money for a paper on the morning of the murder but he returned without one. He then asked him had he any news to which Cadogan replied that he hadn't. Sullivan then told him that he had heard that Mr Bird had been shot and the prisoner said he had heard that too.

District Inspector Armstrong was next to be questioned. He stated that he visited the scene of the murder on the afternoon and examined the place.

181

The Solicitor General. "Was there any other means of escape for the killer apart from the front door or through the shop?"

"There is a window on the landing of the staircase which I examined immediately after the murder and I came to the conclusion that no one had gone through it as there were no marks on the sash and the lower portion of it was nailed shut. Even if a person had gone through the window he would still be on the property as he would have to go through the kitchen to escape and throughout the period of the murder a servant girl named Sarah Bevin was in the kitchen the whole time and she swore that no one could have passed through without her seeing them."

Mr Barry. "You were in charge of the case?"

"Yes."

"Did you hear the evidence of Timothy Breen at the previous trial?"

"I did."

"Did you hear him make a statement in reference to the prisoner, Cadogan, speaking to a man and woman opposite his father's workshop?"

"I did. I heard the police were talking to a Mr and Mrs Cronin from Sheskin and endeavoured to get information from them but were unsuccessful."

"And did you hear his evidence regarding him leaving the workshop and going to his father's house opposite Mr Bird's office?"

"Yes; before the last trial I walked with Breen from his father's workshop in Marino Street, by the Bridewell Lane, New Street, Main Street and Barrack Street to his father's public house on Barrack Street. We were both examined at the last trial in regard to that experiment which took us three minutes to complete at an unusually smart pace and covering a distance of 304 yards."

"Did you hear Timothy Breen swear at the last trial..."

The Solicitor General. "I object."

The Lord Chief Justice. "I will uphold that objection. There is a grave responsibility imposed on me in a murder trial. If illegal evidence is admitted of any description against the prisoner, it would not be a great reflection on me. If illegal evidence was admitted, no matter how immaterial, and was later ruled inadmissible, the prisoner would get off. The public may not understand it but there is a grave responsibility cast upon me to protect the administration of justice as there is to protect the accused."

Mr Barry. "I am sure His Lordship will acquit me of any intention to introduce illegal evidence."

"Most certainly."

"Might I be allowed to say that my responsibility is a fearful one also."

"It is my duty to see that the rule of law is carried out, and those who know me, I hope give me credit that I have never shrunk from this duty."

The prosecution case then closed.

Mr Barry. "May I see the indictment and in reference to the names of witnesses appearing on the back of it, call them for cross examination?"

The Lord Chief Justice. "That is perfectly right."

Timothy Breen was then called.

Mr Barry. "Were you examined at the last trial as a witness for the Crown?"

"I was."

"Did you make a deposition before the magistrates which you swore to at the last trial?"

"I did."

"Where were you when you saw Timothy Cadogan on the 24th of February last?"

"I was working outside my father's workshop on Marino Street."

"And where was Cadogan when you saw him?"

"He was just to my right on the opposite side of the street."

"In which direction was that?"

"Towards the Square."

"And was he alone?"

"No; he was talking to a man and woman."

"Have you any idea of what time this was?"

"Well; the men had just gone for their dinner."

"What time is their dinner hour?"

"Two o'clock."

"What did you do at this time?"

"I went into the workshop for a few minutes."

"When you came back out did you see Cadogan?"

"Yes; he was still in the same place talking to the couple."

"What did you do then?"

"I went home for my dinner."

"Where is your home?"

"On Barrack Street?"

"And what route did you take?"

"I went by the Bridewell Lane, New Street, Main street and then onto Barrack Street."

"At what pace did you walk?"

"I went at a fairly fast pace."

"Was it at the same pace you walked with District Inspector Armstrong afterwards?"

"Yes."

"When you got to your hall door did you hear anything?"

"I heard shots fired."

"Did you know where they came from?"

"No; but when I got upstairs and looked out the dining room window I saw people outside Mr Bird's office and I saw Mr Warner looking excited outside his shop."

The Solicitor General. "Did you delay on your way home for your dinner?"

"No; I was in a hurry home for my dinner."

"If you were in such a hurry why did you take the longer route home?"

"It is only a minute longer."

James Swords was then called and swore.

"On the Saturday night of the murder I asked Walter Dennis if he had seen anyone passing up or down the stairs at the time the shots were fired and he said he hadn't."

Dr Bird was then recalled at Mr Barry's request and the following question was put to him.

"Was it you who sent the police after Timothy Cadogan?"

"A policeman mentioned Cadogan's name to me, and I said that if Cadogan was in town then it was him who did it and no one else and the policeman said well he was in town."

"When was this?"

"On the night of the murder."

The Lord Chief Justice. "What policeman said this to you?"

"Mulcahy."

Constable Mulcahy was then called to take the stand and was asked by the Lord Chief Justice whether he had mentioned Cadogan to Walter Dennis and he answered that he had not.

Mr. Barry then proceeded with the case for the defence.

"The most heavy and responsible task which can fall on the lot of a man in the profession of which I am a humble member has now fallen on me. And that is to address you, a jury of this city, in a case of life and death. But if this jury which is before me is a responsible an onerous one, the duty cast upon you is still heavier, because I need not remind you that you are here to discharge the most awful duty of citizenship, to pronounce what is in effect a sentence of life or death against the prisoner. You will be told in that stereotypical phrase that comes so readily to the lips of those who have prosecuted such cases that the consequences of your verdict have nothing to do with you. Juries in capital cases are told this over and over with the view of easing their minds and consciences of the apprehensions that rest within them over the enormity of the decision ahead of them. The statement is true in some respects but it is false in the main. You have nothing to do with the result of your verdict in the way it will be the law that carries out the sentence that must necessarily follow on from your verdict, but you have a great deal to do with the consequences of your verdict in respect that upon your verdict comes the dreaded sentence of death being carried out should the verdict you return be a guilty one. On your verdict alone, the dreaded sentence can be carried out, and if you return a verdict of guilty in this case; the prisoner will go to his doom as sure as someday the grave will welcome us who are endeavouring to do our duty here, and then we must answer to a higher tribunal for our actions on this day and in this case.

Before I touch on the evidence, I will say this. The conduct of my learned friends who have conducted this prosecution, on this the second time the prisoner has stood impleaded by them on the issue of his life, has surpassed anything, I venture to say, that has ever been heard in a court of justice. In the Solicitor General's statement, he made his foremost points of this case, points which had not been included in the first trial! And then he closed his case without examining the man who at the last trial who was examined as the principal witness for the Crown and who I was forced to put on the stand; the man who made a deposition before the magistrates and never varied from it, and whose evidence convinced the jury to such an extent that they could not agree on a verdict. The Crown case had closed and that man, Timothy Breen, had not been produced. Why you might ask; because the Crown knew, because the Crown had to know that his evidence would be damaging to their case, they knew that if they asked for a verdict of guilt based on the evidence of Timothy Breen, that would introduce the element of doubt and uncertainty and with that reasonable doubt in your minds they knew the prisoner would be found innocent. I will not venture at the present any particular observations pointing to the nature of the evidence of Timothy Breen, but only make this general statement; I think the prisoner has been placed in a position that he should not have been. I think that the conduct of the Crown, and it is not up to me to dictate to them, but it was their duty to bring forward every witness that they had examined at the first trial, be he for them or against them. To keep back a witness of the truth shows a lack of confidence in their own case.

Why do the Crown say the prisoner, Timothy Cadogan, murdered William Symms Bird on the 24th of February this year? Why and how? All they have said is for some absolutely unexplained reason he did kill Mr Bird. It has been proved that on the morning of the 24th of February Timothy Cadogan went to his master and told him he was going into Bantry to look for employment. The man who had a revolver in his possession on that date has not been traced. It has never being suggested that Timothy Cadogan ever had possession of a revolver or that he had ever fired a revolver in his life. This man went to Bantry on legitimate business; to find employment. He went to the place that any man seeking employment would go; he went to the market where the farmers brought their produce and then he went to the public meeting place on the corner where all the men and women carried out their business. He spent his time there, but because Dr Bird had a bad opinion regarding his character and had come to the conclusion that Timothy Cadogan had killed his brother that day, the police were sent in pursuit of the prisoner that night. Now this jury has been asked, on a great deal of absolutely unreliable evidence, to confirm the suspicion of Dr Bird; to hang the prisoner not on the facts but on Dr Bird's opinion of his character. It is an old saying "Give a dog a bad name and then you can hang him by it". This was part of the modus operandi of my friends representing the Crown, to vilify in the eyes of the jury and degrade this wretched man in the dock, with a view to prejudicing his case; that your minds might be embittered and prejudiced against him. True he was evicted from his farm. True he is a poor outcast in this world, but I as his counsel ask you give him justice, which I am sure you will.

Now it has been said that Timothy Cadogan came into Bantry that day to avenge an eviction that occurred in August 1895. Was there ever such slumbering vengeance? Was there ever such a callous assassin? For five years he slept on the wrong done to him except on three occasions when he asked could he be reinstated on his farm. The last time being six months before the murder of Mr Bird; not a day or a week before. He said something about "somebody being sorry for it". "He was sullen" said Dr Bird, "and morose in his demeanour". And because the prisoner was sullen and morose in his demeanour he is to be hanged on his bad name. Now in 1895 what occurred? What he did at his eviction has been made out to be something dreadful. Mr Bird said. "He was a bad boy." and because he was a bad boy these proceedings have been brought against him. To use the words of the Solicitor General. "He knocked about the furniture and was abusive in his language." What he did do; as a matter of fact, was to break a few whiskey bottles and a cup and saucer. The police had to protect the Bird's from the scattering of the fragments from the broken whiskey bottles. You might think that I am labouring this too much, but I really feel in a case of such enormous magnitude and tremendous importance I have to show that these flimsy details have been introduced to the case for the sole purpose of trying to give the evidence of Walter Dennis some credibility. If Mr Dennis is a credible witness, and you have all seen his demeanour here in court, why was it necessary for the Crown to labour all those antecedent performances, all those ridiculous performances.

The Solicitor General described Timothy Cadogan as a man skilled in the use of firearms and to prove this point he introduced you to the witness William Levis; the old play acting pantaloon, (laughter) who shouldered his stick to show how Cadogan could shoot. (more laughter) Old Levis referred to things which occurred years ago in great detail; however, he could not remember being examined at the last trial. This man was not a reliable witness. Then a man named McCarthy said he saw Cadogan on the same mountain with some old man trying to shoot grouse or other fowl; but as far as he saw Cadogan didn't shoot anything. It was an insult to you the jury to have such evidence presented. Let it go! It proves nothing but the unsubstantiality of the Crown's case. During the years following his eviction, Cadogan showed no inclination of committing this crime for which he is on trial for his life. Why wait five years? It appears that Mr Bird went for his lunch sometime after half past one on the day he was murdered and was back in his office shortly after two o'clock. During this time Cadogan was seen at Hurst's Corner looking for employment. At the time it was said the murder was committed he was seen opposite Breen's workshop on Marino Street. Within three minutes of Cadogan being seen on Marino Street, Mr Bird was murdered in his office. Timothy Breen, the witness the Crown has not dared to produce, saw the prisoner on the footpath in Marino Street opposite his father's workshop. Mr Breen and Detective Inspector Armstrong, according to Breen's evidence, walked around the streets at the same pace as he did when going for his dinner on the day the murder was committed. It is nonsense to say that Breen would have been impeded on a market day by the cars on these streets. It only took three minutes to walk around the way he did and when he arrived at his own house the shots were fired in Mr. Bird's office. How long would it take to get to Breen's house from the workshop by the direct route of Marino Street to Barrack Street? It would take a minute and a half or a minute and a quarter. So, what must have occurred if the prisoner is guilty? He must have made a start when Timothy Breen turned around the corner of Bridewell Lane. He had time in a minute and a half to do the deed. Do you think a man would then escape without peering about to see if there were any witnesses?

I have already commented on the failure of the prosecution to produce Timothy Breen as a witness. They knew that no fair-minded jury could come to any other conclusion except that their star witness, the boy Dennis was wrong in his identification of Timothy Cadogan, as an alibi has been proved for the prisoner. Sometimes you have to look on an alibi with suspicion, but here there can be no suspicion. It was the evidence of a man who made his deposition before the magistrates and has never varied from it, he has stuck by it and it was for this reason he was not called to give his evidence by the Crown now as he had in the first trial. There was no doubt the prisoner was there as old Mr Breen saw him there as well and he has not been discredited, if there had been only the evidence of young Breen the Crown might have said that he was not telling the truth. Walter Dennis was wrong and out of their own mouth they had provided an alibi for the prisoner.

Another man saw Cadogan there, a man named McCarthy, talking to Cronin and his wife. But why, the Crown might ask, why did we not produce Cronin and his wife. What good would that do? The Crown know as well as we do that inquiries were made by both parties to get an opinion out of them. They could not tell for how long they were there talking to Cadogan and have no idea regarding the time. So, any observations they make on the subject would be as unfounded as another statement made by my learned friend that we intended to call half the town of Bantry to prove where Cadogan was after the murder.

Turning to the evidence of the boy Walter Dennis. I submit to you that this evidence in its entirety is wholly unreliable. Assuming he went out into the hall and saw a man coming down the stairs, assuming there was light enough on these stairs, which he did not admit at all, in the glance of a second, assuming all this; I still believe his evidence to be unreliable. A witness, Robert Warner, gave new evidence so that Dennis's story could be corroborated. He swore here that he followed Dennis and saw him standing in the hall. Now this witness had given evidence before a magisterial inquiry, had given evidence at the prisoner's first trial and it was only last week that he thought of giving this crucial new evidence to the Solicitor General. Not only that, but also his colleague, Miss Dukelow, likewise gave evidence twice previously and even at this trial, made no reference to the fact that Robert Warner followed Dennis to the hall. However, after Warner had given his evidence here she was recalled and then remembered that he had followed Dennis. Not only that, Walter Dennis, in any of his evidence makes no mention of Robert Warner following him to the hall. It was also sworn by Miss Dukelow that when Walter Dennis returned to the shop he looked frightened, however, Dennis swore that he was not frightened in the hall, that it was later when he became frightened. Now the jury knows that if such evidence was presented on behalf of the prisoner it would not be believed. Therefore, what is sauce for the goose is sauce for the gander.

We have seen the model of the building and I should say that if we look at the construction of the landing we will see that it is not an ordinary landing. It is a most curiously constructed house, there are no windows in the hall and that tells us of the darkness of the place. There are no means of lighting in the hall, but ironically, it was said by Mr. Abbott, that there was light enough to identify the features of a man on a February afternoon. I know that Mr. Abbott is a man who has a successful business manufacturing

190

beehives in Dublin, but I never heard that he was an expert in the matter of light. He said that the reflection of the light from the houses on the other side of the street was sufficient, notwithstanding that a partition acted as an obstruction to the light.

Dr. Bird was suspicious of Timothy Cadogan and his suspicions were communicated to the police on the night of the murder. Immediately the hue and cry is set up against Cadogan, who his brother had called "a bad boy". Immediately a search is made for him, but that's not necessary, as he is not in hiding or has run away. Instead he has gone home to his employer with whom he has been living with for a couple of months. He is arrested by acting Sergeant Driscoll, who gave us the statement he made when arrested. However, the sergeant failed to tell us the vital words Cadogan said to him at the time; "What charge have you against me?" He was arrested and Michael Hegarty was also practically under arrest that night. It is not a part of my case to say that Hegarty was ever charged with the murder. He was under detention and had been searched. The result of which was obviously unsatisfactory to the police as they prevented him from going home. The boy Dennis knew that Cadogan was under arrest and did not know that anybody was in custody on the same charge. The possibility is if he had been taken down while Hegarty was in the barracks he would have identified him as the man. Had Dennis identified Hegarty, it would be him in the dock instead of Timothy Cadogan. Who was the last man seen and the last man who admitted to have been in Mr Bird's office before the murder? Who was the last man seen conversing with Mr Bird by the witness John Leary? That man is Michael Hegarty. Who is the man skilled in the use of firearms and owns a revolver? Michael Hegarty. And who was the man seen going down the street at a quick pace after the murder? Michael Hegarty. God forbid I should say that Michael Hegarty was the murderer of Mr Bird, I merely state these facts for the purpose of showing the jury that there is a much stronger case against him if Walter Dennis had identified him as the man he saw coming down the stairs.

I suggest that the evidence regarding the newspaper and about Cadogan being asked if he had any news from town should not be an influence on the jury. Was it likely that Cadogan, who was known to have ill feelings towards Mr Bird would go speak to everybody about his death? The only evidence that we will give in this case is the evidence of people who spoke to Walter Dennis and who asked him if he knew anything about Mr Bird's murder. He had followed the body of poor Mr Bird from his office to his residence at Beach House that night and denied, I might almost add in the solemn presence of the dead, that he knew who the perpetrator of this outrage was. He denied it at the door of the chapel the following morning where he had been at his prayers; he denied he knew who the man was or that he knew anything about it. He denied to James Swords that he saw anyone going up or down the stairs. It is absurd to believe a man who has lied persistently on his oath and could give no other excuse for his lies then the shuffling excuse "Why not everybody else tell it as well as I?" He was the only man who saw a man coming down the stairs from Mr Bird's office with a revolver in his hand! Without the evidence of Timothy Breen some credence could be given to that of Dennis's. It is not my business to flatter or cajole you, I can only say this, I know you to be honest men and I cannot say anything higher than that. But I ask you to return a true verdict, the true courageous verdict in this case and perhaps someday the true perpetrator of this heinous crime will be discovered. The mills of God grind slowly but the grind exceedingly small. The hand of the man who killed William Symms Bird may be discovered and then what remorse would be yours knowing that you sent this man to the doom knowing he can never be recalled."

The first witness called for the defence was Henry Breen Jnr, who testified that on the day in question he was standing outside his house on Barrack Street opposite Mr Bird's office when he heard some shots. He said he remained there for a couple of minutes and did not see anyone come out of Mr Bird's office.

The Solicitor General. "Was there many people on the street?"

"There was a good lot of people there."

"Did you know any of them?"

"No."

The Lord Chief Justice. "Where did the shots appear to originate from?"

"From the top window of Mr Bird's office."

A man named John McCarthy, a shoemaker from Bantry was next to take the stand.

Mr Barry. "On Sunday, the day after the murder did you see the boy Walter Dennis?"

"Yes; he was speaking with a number of other boys."

"Did you hear what he was saying?"

"One of the boys asked him if he had seen anyone come out of Mr Bird's office at the time of the murder."

"And what was his answer?"

"He said he hadn't as he could not see from where he had been standing, that all he heard was the stamping of feet overhead. He then demonstrated this by stamping his feet on the footpath."

The next person to take the stand was a woman named Agnes Sullivan.

"On the 24th of February I was in Warner's shop on Barrack Street shortly after two o'clock. I heard the shuffle of feet upstairs and then the sound like as if a stool had fallen over."

Mr Barry. "Did you see Mr Warner's messenger Walter Dennis in the shop at this time?"

"Yes; he was behind the counter at the back end of the shop."

"Did you see him do anything after you heard those noises?"

"Yes; after the noises occurred I saw him run out into the street."

"Did he return?"

"Yes; a short time after."

"Did he say anything upon his return?"

"Yes; he told Miss Dukelow "He is shot!" and I then asked Miss Dukelow who has been shot and she said Mr Bird."

Mr Moriarty. "Was it after the shuffling of feet that he ran out?"

"No; it was after the sound like that of a stool falling that he ran out."

Mr Barry. "Did anyone else run out into the street?"

"Robert Warner also ran out the front door into the street."

"Could you tell how far into the street Walter Dennis ran?"

"No."

"Were you questioned by the police afterwards?"

"Sergeant Bourke asked me to tell him all I knew about the murder on the 27th of February, three days later, and I did."

"Did you say in your deposition that Walter Dennis ran out into the street?"

"I did."

"Did you say in your deposition that Robert Warner ran out into the street?"

"I did, but I don't know why it wasn't taken down."

Michael Leary was next examined.

Mr Barry. "You worked for Mr Bird at Beach House?"

"Yes; I did."

"On the night of the murder were you present at Beach House?"

"I was."

"Did you see Walter Dennis there that night?"

"Yes; I saw him in the kitchen, he had come with a parcel of bread from Warner's."

"Did you speak to him?"

"Yes; I asked him if he knew anything about what happened that day."

"And what was his reply?"

"He said "No Mike, I know nothing about it."

William Shorten took the stand next.

"On the evening of the murder when Mr Bird's remains were being brought to Beach House, I walked with Walter Dennis in the procession behind the coffin."

Mr Barry. "Did you speak to him?"

"Yes; I asked him if he knew anything about the murder?"

"What was his answer?"

"He said he did not as he could see nothing upstairs because the door was shut."

This closed the evidence for the defence. Mr Lynch then addressed the jury on behalf of Timothy Cadogan.

"I fully feel and appreciate this task which has fallen upon me in discharging my duty towards the prisoner and I feel quite conscious of my inability to discuss the matter in a way commensurate with the importance of it. My friend, Mr Barry, to whom I have had the honour to be associated with in this case, has addressed you at considerable length and I shall endeavour in my observations not to trouble you by not repeating any of the matters that he discussed and only to deal as briefly as I can with the great issue that is now before you.

The case was introduced by my friend the Solicitor General in the moderate and fair way that you would expect. But I will confess and suggest to you that both in the address and in the evidence there were a number of incidents introduced which are irrelevant to this case. What is it to us whether six or seven years ago the prisoner walked across the mountains near Bantry and shot some grouse or woodcock? Or whether at about the same time he went through the pantomime performance as described by the old man William Levis? We have reviewed the evidence of the boy Walter Dennis and have come to the conclusion that it should be set aside due to the evidence of Timothy Breen. In conclusion, I have never seen before in a case which I have been connected with, the facts so clearly established as they have been established in this case by the witnesses for the prosecution to prove the absolute impossibility, that this man in the dock, Timothy Cadogan, ever committed this crime." (Applause in the court)

Mr Bourke then replied for the Crown.

"This was a savage and ferocious murder, perpetrated under circumstances of unparalleled audacity, not in the dead of night, nor in a remote and lonely locality, but in the centre of a populous town in broad daylight on a market day when the streets and houses were alive with people. The second shot brought the poor victim to his knees, with his head bowed down. The murderer, mindful that dead men don't tell tales, was determined to make sure of his work and fired a third shot into the head of his victim and lodged a bullet in his brain. He then fled. I tremble to think of the disaster and of the disgrace that would befall society and of the shock and disturbance to public order and the tranquillity amongst us and the blow given to the security of life in our midst, if that criminal's daring confidence in the terrorism he produced by his deed had proven well founded. I think all good citizens must rejoice that his fancied security proved to be an illusion and that there was a young man who confronted him and detected him as he was fresh from his crime with the weapon of his guilt in his hand. The poor peasant boy, Dennis, emerged from adverse circumstances, a conspiracy of silence, a paralysis of terror, he came forward and had the courage and the honesty to brave local odium, local unpopularity, and to tell what he saw.

The character and circumstances of the crime gave the clue to its author. You can form a judgement as to the deliberateness of the deed, plainly it was the act of a man who had long thought it out and premeditated it. Was it not the deed of a man well versed in the habits of Mr Bird? If the Crown have the wrong man in the dock would not Bantry with its quick-witted population supply battalions of testimony to break down the Crown's case? But everyone is hanging back. It is not my duty to inquire into the motive, let it be terrorism, a desire not to be unpopular, or to be mixed up with a prosecution. But the one fact stands out prominently; there was a universal conspiracy of silence. Dennis was hanging back like the rest; he would have rather that other people would have been first with the story that so many knew. The power of truth is omnipotent and the fact that this boy Dennis was in possession of valuable information reached the authorities. On the Tuesday the boy made a clean breast of the affair to his great credit and honour. From that day to this he has not varied one hair's breadth in the statements he has made. Cadogan's movements that day were those of a man watching and dogging his victim."

The Lord Chief Justice then delivered his charge to the jury.

"This case has been so exhaustively spoken to on both sides that I do not feel it incumbent of me to go into the details of the evidence, which Mr Barry with very great ability, and I should say Mr Lynch who was a very able deputy to Mr Barry, have highlighted. Everything that can be done for the accused has been done. Of course this is a very grave case, a man's life is in peril and I will not distract that from your attention.

Now a good deal was said by Mr Barry in his vigorous speech, and I always like to hear a vigorous speech, particularly on the part of the defence. It is the duty of the Crown counsel to put forward their case with firmness and moderation at the same time, but it is the bounden duty of the prisoner's counsel to resort to everything that is consistent with their own honour to defend the man in the dock. It is the bounden duty of the counsel at the bar, and the only thing that should restrain him, that should curtail his eloquence and his enthusiasm, is his own sense of honour. I do not believe that Mr Barry or Mr Lynch have said a word in this case which was not consistent with the highest sense of honour. Of course there were little things here and there that they did not entirely agree with, but anything said deliberately was not inconsistent with a sense of honour. For instance, there was something said about keeping Timothy Breen back, He is the son of the witness Breen who was produced on behalf of the prosecution. One man was supposed to give evidence on behalf of the prosecution and he gave it. Breen gave his evidence on behalf of the prosecution and his son it seems was not at all displeased to contradict any fact his father imparted. Something was said about the non-production of Timothy Breen; however, it is the bounden duty of the Crown not to produce any witness who they cannot rely on; and if at one trial that witness is unreliable, they are therefore bound to view it as a monstrous thing if they were to produce that same witness at the second trial. These expressions that fall from eloquent counsel in the heat of their eloquent speeches should not be taken for granted by the jury. Let us take the example of Timothy Breen. We saw the way he walked for his dinner. He was going to is dinner and why he went that way I do not know. The shortest route would have been by Marino Street. He was obviously not afflicted by the pangs of hunger because he went the way he and the District Inspector later walked and which the latter said was a distance of 304 yards, which they covered in three minutes.

Mr Barry in his most admirable speech said he relied on time as regards the prisoner, Cadogan, and delay regards the witness Walter Dennis. That was his main position. If anyone was dogging the steps of poor Mr Bird that day, in the middle of the day; in the middle of the town of Bantry, they knew very well that time was the essence. Every second was vital for the perpetration of the deed. It is quite plain and common-sense that any man who wished to murder him must have waited for his opportunity with great vigilance and then despatched his victim with great efficiency. Well Timothy Breen went up that way which the District Inspector said took three minutes, and as he went around the long way he was in no hurry. If a man is in a hurry he does not select the longest route. He went that way and I would venture to say on that occasion it took more than three minutes, and that is to say whether he was there at all. You will remember that time is the very essence of the whole thing, not a question of minutes but a question of seconds.

Now there are two or three witnesses which I ask you to allow me to refer to. I intend to address myself to the case by asking you to consider what occurred at the crucial moment; what occurred before it and what occurred after it. If you keep this method in mind you will find that you will follow the case easier than that of following every detail and ramification of it. Let us look at the crucial moment, there are three or four witnesses I call your attention to. The man Scanlon who was on business there, he said when he went to the office at about a quarter to or five minutes to two Mr Bird was not there and he went away and came back to transact his business a very short time later. We have him therefore sometime after two o'clock. Who else have we there? We have Mrs Hourihane there and Mrs Hourihane said that she saw Hegarty. Well Hegarty was there, and he was the last man you might think was with Mr Bird before the assassin came on the scene. I am sure you do not think it necessary for anyone to have to vindicate Hegarty of the charge. The charge was not made against him and it is only right that Mr Barry and Mr Lynch say it was not. It is only a hypothesis that Hegarty was the last man with Mr Bird before the assassin came in. Hegarty had come into town with his wife and had dinner with his wife. It is true that he did not return to the office upon hearing of Mr Bird's shooting, for it is plain to see that he was anxious to get home for he lives fourteen miles away. When Hegarty leaves the office, who comes on the scene at the vital moment, Patrick Cronin. I ask you to mark the brevity, Cronin passes Mahoney's pub on Barrack Street and sees the prisoner standing with his back against the wall of the pub smoking and a little further on he passes Hegarty, the last man to see Mr Bird alive. How far was the prisoner from the front door of Mr Bird's office? Twenty-five yards.

Now let me ask you, who was this man Cadogan who was standing only twenty-five yards from Mr Bird's door? Was he a friend or was he an enemy? He was an unhappy man, a man who had been evicted from his farm and on that occasion had become so violent that a policeman was forced to stand beside Mr Bird. Only six months before the murder he had used violent language against Mr Bird in his office. You will remember that tremendously significant expression of the gentleman who was produced in court, the brother of the deceased. "That if Cadogan was in town, he was the man who did it". This shows the impression the prisoner made on Dr Bird when he witnessed this altercation between his brother and the prisoner after his brother had refused Cadogan's reinstatement on his lands. Who was the witness Dennis? What was his character? It was quite right for my esteemed colleagues at the bar to cross examine him as to his character. Did you hear anything against his character? Was there anything against his character at all? It is up to you to say, and if there was not an attack made on his character then he must be a boy of good character. Had he a motive for swearing against the prisoner? If he is a man of good character he would have no motive to falsely swear against the prisoner.

Now, you should bear in mind the time. You know the whole of Scanlon's evidence. I do not wish to confine yourselves to say five minutes or ten minutes but to look at the evidence. You have the prisoner, who had a motive against the deceased, in the immediate neighbourhood of the house.

You have the boy Dennis, of good character, and as regards him and the prisoner, without motive to convict him. Was Dennis in any way uncertain regarding his identification of the prisoner? I ask you to remember a piece of evidence given. When the prisoner was brought before the witness he asked him. "Are you sure?" and Dennis replied that he was sure, then the learned Solicitor General, in the course of this trial, asked him was he still sure and Dennis said I am sure. Could he have been mistaken? We will take it in steps. He had known the man by appearance for two years and by appearance and name for at least twelve months. We heard Mr Abbot, the model maker, swear about the light and Dennis swear that he saw the prisoner come down the stairs with a pistol in his hand. Dennis went out through the swing door; this was borne out by the girl Dukelow and by young Warner. You must ask yourselves was Dennis there and had he the abundant opportunity to identify the man on the stairs. I would like to refer to one piece of his evidence, when Dennis said he looked out the window and saw the man running up the Glengarriff Road, he said it was like the prisoner, this shows the caution of the boy.

Now the time has been spoken of by Mr Barry, now for the delay. There was one observation made by the Solicitor General during the course of the trial that really struck me with considerable force and that was the wonder that Dennis had given his evidence at all. You know Ireland as well as I do. Perhaps you know the South better than me, but I also know the South. Ask yourselves do people here come forward and try to involve themselves in a case of murder? No; they would rather mind their own business. You have heard the witnesses, you heard Swords say that he asked Dennis whether he had seen anyone come down the stairs and Dennis said he hadn't. Now with reference to Swords, you have heard Dennis give evidence, I consider the boy to have an unemotional and stolidly calm disposition. In his evidence he was asked. "Did Mr Swords ask you if you had seen anybody coming down the stairs?" and the answer was "No; I don't remember him asking me anything". Then there was the evidence of another man named Leary who asked Dennis. "Did you see anyone doing the deed that day?" and the reply was "No". It is for you, however, whether you attach any importance to these matters; it is for you as men with common sense, to say what you think of it. You know that in this county, and indeed, in every other county, people are in a case like this; more anxious to defend a person than condemn him. People are more likely to say something in favour of an accused who was on trial for his life for the charge murder. That is the case before you and you have the evidence of the different witnesses to consider. As to the time of the murder, you should take what Scanlon said, he was there at five minutes to two, that he remained there for some time and that while he was there he saw people running up the street. It is unnecessary to know what time that was.

As to the after events. John Sullivan, the mason, said that Cadogan had said he was going to Bantry to look for employment, if so, why was there no evidence called to show what he was doing that day? If he were looking for employment he would surely have asked for it. He might have been standing on a corner but did he ask anyone for employment? The last time he was seen was standing at Mahony's. After this he said he went home forgetting to get a paper for his master. Then when informed by the first person he met on his way home that Mr Bird had been shot he replied he must have shot himself or have been shot by his brother. The jury should consider the evidence of both sides. You have often being addressed about your responsibility. Well, we all have responsibilities and you should exercise your faculties as God gave them and if you honestly deal with the evidence to the best of your ability you will incur no responsibility before God or man. You should do your honest best. If you have a reasonable doubt, not a fantastic doubt, but such a doubt that as honest men you would entertain in a business transaction of life, you should give the prisoner the benefit of it, and if you do not have any reasonable doubt as towards guilt; then you should convict and as I said, you will incur no responsibility between God and man."

The jury then retired at five minutes to five to consider their verdict. After they left the court Mr Barry asked could he say something to His Lordship.

"I wish to draw your attention to one matter in Your Lordship's charge. With reference to the evidence of the Crown, His Lordship was pleased to say to the jury that by Cronin's evidence the prisoner was placed outside Mahony's at the crucial time."

The Lord Chief Justice. "That is for them to say, with regard to the evidence."

"Cronin's evidence did not show whether it was on the occasion of Hegarty's first or second visit to the office that he met him on Barrack Street. Cronin said it was an hour or a half an hour before seeing Hegarty that he saw the prisoner at Mahony's. His Lordship told the jury that it was the second time, but I submit that there is nothing in the evidence to show the time that Cronin saw him."

"I will tell the jury if you wish."

The Solicitor General. "I ask His Lordship not to recall the jury as, to my mind, bringing out the jury and recharging them on a certain point may upset their ideas altogether. The time the prisoner was seen at Mahony's was on the second occasion that Hegarty visited the office."

Mr Barry. "On the evidence of Henry Breen alone the prisoner was on Marino Street. It is a crucial point and I think it my duty to bring it before His Lordship."

The Lord Chief Justice. "If Mr Barry thinks there is something in this point I will do it for him."

The jury were then recalled.

The Lord Chief Justice. "Mr Barry wishes me to call your attention to one matter and that is Hegarty himself said that he went down Barrack Street twice and Cronin might have seen him on the first occasion which was near the time of the murder. But, gentlemen, you will bear in mind the whole of the evidence with reference to this man Cadogan, and even remember the evidence of the Breen's who had him about their place about the time the men were going to dinner. The two Breen's had him standing there in the middle of the place speaking to some people, but you will remember that if he was watching for Mr Bird, that is one of the places he might have stood."

The jury then retired again at twelve minutes past five and the deliberated for one hour and twenty minutes before returning at twenty-five minutes to seven. On their return it was clear by their demeanour what verdict they had reached. Mr Fraser, the acting Clerk of the Crown, addressed them by name and asked had they agreed on the verdict. The foreman, Mr T. Holland, was then asked for the verdict.

"Guilty." He said in a faltering voice.

Mr Fraser. "You say that Timothy Cadogan is guilty of the murder whereof he stands indicted. That is your verdict; so say you all?"

Mr Holland. "Yes."

Then, in appreciation of the awful consequences of the verdict, he placed his head in his hands. Other members of the jury seemed to be equally effected.

Meanwhile the Solicitor General was heard to say. "Well, well."

Mr Fraser. "Timothy Cadogan, you heretofore stood indicted that on the 24th day of February 1900, did feloniously, wilfully and with malice of forethought murder William Symms Bird at Bantry. To that indictment you pleaded not guilty and put yourself in God and your country, which country has now found you guilty. What have you now to say why sentence of death and execution should not be awarded against you according to law?"

Cadogan remained in his seat and did not reply. He was told to stand up and rose in a dazed manner.

The Lord Chief Justice. "Timothy Cadogan, you have been found guilty by a jury of your countrymen of the crime of murder, and in the propriety of the verdict which has been returned it is only due to the jury who tried you to say that I entirely concur with that verdict. I can hold you out no hope of mercy in this world. You must look to that Great Being who knows all and sees all and to whom I, as your temporal judge, am responsible as well as you. I am but a creature of the law, a humble minister of the law, and as such it is my duty to pass upon you the sentence of it. No one knows how harrowing that duty is but he who discharges it."

Then after donning the black cap he continued.

"Timothy Cadogan, the sentence of the court is and I do hereby order and adjudge that you Timothy Cadogan, be taken from the bar of the court where you now stand to the prison whence you last came and that on Friday the 11th of January in the year of Our Lord 1901, you be taken to the common place of execution in that prison where you shall be bound and you shall be then and there hanged by the neck until you are dead, and that your body

203

be buried within the walls of the prison in which the aforesaid judgement of death shall be executed upon you, and may the Lord have mercy on your soul."

When the Lord Chief Justice finished speaking there was consternation in the court and loud hissing could be heard coming from the public gallery. The policemen present moved swiftly to suppress the unrest. As the Lord Chief Justice ended the death pronouncement, Cadogan gripped with his left hand the front bar of the dock. Looking around the court his face showed utter astonishment at the verdict and it was only as he was being dragged away by two warders that his voice was heard for the first time. While the warders hands were on his shoulders he turned around in the direction of the Grand Jury box and on observing Dr Bird, with more animation than he had exhibited throughout the two trials, pointed his right hand at him and exclaimed.

"I hope I won't be dead twelve months till I have avenged the doctor, the scoundrel, the cut throat. I hope I will be avenged before I am twelve months in my grave."

The Lord Chief Justice had stood to leave as this was occurring and with a look of severity and condemnation shouted.

"Take the man away!"

Cadogan was then taken down but by the time he was being removed to prison a large crowd had gathered outside the court and cheered for him enthusiastically, there were cries of revenge and support echoing in his ears as he departed the scene.

The Execution of Timothy Cadogan

Following Timothy Cadogan's conviction a petition appealing for his release was widely circulated in Cork City. It was signed by a variety of the most important and influential men in the city including a number of magisterial members of the bench in the borough. When the petition was presented to the Lord Mayor, Sir Daniel Hegarty, he did not sign but instead said that he would write a letter to the Lord Lieutenant requesting him to look sympathetically on the case. It was not only in Cork that strong feeling regarding the outcome of the case was held, at a meeting of the Kilmallock District Council in County Limerick on the 4th of January 1901, for example, the following resolution was adopted.

"That this board, while deeply deploring the murder of Mr Bird and all such acts of savage violence, do hereby represent to his Excellency the Lord Lieutenant that the evidence on which Timothy Cadogan was convicted was insufficient and that he belongs to a greatly violated and persecuted class of Her Majesty's subjects, viz the evicted tenants. We are of the opinion that the commutation of Cadogan's sentence to penal servitude would be greatly appreciated and would be an act of clemency benefitting the new century which great, bad, good, and small are entering into."

On the night of the 7th of January, the Lord Lieutenant's decision was published.

"In the case of Timothy Cadogan, a prisoner in the Cork male prison under the sentence of death, the Lord Lieutenant, after most careful consideration of all circumstances, has, in the discharge of a painful duty, has decided that the law must take its course."

The Lord Lieutenant was Lord Cadogan. It was believed that this was the first occasion on which a Lord Lieutenant signed a death warrant for an individual bearing his name.

Two nights before Timothy Cadogan's execution, his executioner James Billington, who had been a hangman for the British Government since 1884, arrived in Cork with his son Thomas who acted as his assistant. On the night

205

before the execution Billington received the fee for his services, £25 was his payment plus £5 in travelling expenses. It was made out in the form of a cheque from Cork County Council. Billington would die in December of 1901 at the age of 54, while his son Thomas would die aged 29 on the 10th of January 1902, exactly one day shy of the anniversary of Timothy Cadogan's execution.

Early on the morning of the execution Cadogan attempted to deny his executioner by taking his own life, he slashed at his neck with the heel of one of his boots before being discovered by one of the prison guards. While he was restrained he stated that "he should have done it a long time ago". At a quarter to seven the prison chaplain, Father O'Leary and a second priest, Father Thomas, visited with Cadogan. Both had been regular visitors with him since his conviction. Mass was celebrated at seven o'clock by Father O'Leary and Cadogan received Holy Communion. He then returned to his cell and had breakfast which consisted of two eggs. After this he returned to the prison chapel for a few more minutes for last prayers. A small procession then made their way to the execution chamber consisting of the Prison Governor Mr Andrews, the Sub-Sheriff Mr Gale, the Prison Surgeon Dr Moriarty, the condemned man, the two priests and some prison guards. The walk from the chapel to the execution chamber took about one minute. Cadogan walked steadily and responded to the final prayers being said by the priests in a firm tone.

On his arrival at the scaffold, Billington and his son proceeded to tie his hands. He was then motioned to the trapdoor and once upon it his legs were strapped. While this was going on Cadogan continued to respond to the prayers. The death bell began to ring and at one minute to eight the preparations were completed. Cadogan was asked for any last words but did not speak. Quickly, Billington drew the black hood over Cadogan's head and stepped back, he then looked at the governor who gave him the nod to pull the leaver which opened the trap door. A drop of seven feet had been allowed for the prisoner who had put on over a stone and a half in weight since his incarceration. Cadogan dropped and was left swaying in the pit. Dr Moriarty descended into the pit and after a superficial examination declared that death had been almost instantaneous. The announcement that the death sentence had been carried out was signified in the usual manner by the hoisting of a black flag above the prison tower. Representatives of the press were then allowed into the execution chamber to view the hanging body while in the meantime all the principals who had participated in the execution left the prison. Outside the prison a sizeable crowd had gathered and the only sound heard from them was their prayers. At a quarter past ten an inquest was opened in the prison guard room by the Coroner John J Horgan. (A man who served as coroner in the city of Cork for fifty years and was simply known as Coroner Horgan. Famously in 1915 while presiding at the inquest into the victims of the Lusitania, which had been sunk by a German submarine, he pronounced a verdict of wilful murder against the Kaiser.) A small group of people were in attendance including members of the press and prison officials. District Inspector Morrison represented the constabulary. After the jury of fourteen men had been sworn in, Coroner Horgan instructed them to go and see Cadogan's remains and also asked the Governor, Mr Andrews, to show them the cells in which he had been confined for the last month of his life. The jury returned after ten minutes and then the first person to be examined was Mr Andrews.

Coroner Horgan. "Give me any information you have with regard to this execution, have you the warrant?"

"Here is the rule of court. This was the document given to me by the court, but the sheriff has left the death warrant here with me should you require it."

"That is what I want. (Looking at the document) The prisoner was sentenced on this date to be hanged, was the execution carried out?"

"Yes; in accordance with the sentence."

"Have you seen the body since the execution?"

"Yes; it is the body of Timothy Cadogan."

"What is the mode of treatment of prisoners under the sentence of death?"

"They get any dietary they desire for. He was allowed two bottles of stout in the day but he only took one. He preferred to take a cup of leaf tea in its place."

"I suppose he got everything necessary?"

"Yes. With regard to his accommodation he was allowed to exercise anytime he wished in the yard which was close to his cell where he had all his meals."

"Where did he sleep?"

"He slept during the night in a large triple cell, with two warders with him there."

"Also there?"

"Yes."

"How long was he in the triple cell?"

"From eight at night."

"How long before his death?"

"The first week of his confinement he asked for a larger cell than he had."

"Than the first cell?"

"It was the cell in which all other prisoners previously under sentence of death were confined."

"What is the size of it?"

"I don't know the exact measurement of it."

"Have you any idea?"

"It is fully seven feet long?"

"How many feet wide?"

"About ten feet but that is only a rough guess."

"That was the last cell he was in?"

"No; he was in the triple cell last."

"Did he complain about the treatment of being confined in the first cell?"

"He complained the air would be too close for three of them in a cell and as soon as he complained he was moved."

"That would be two warders and himself?"

"Yes."

"I may tell you that someone sent me a letter signed "A Prisoner" and requests me to ask you why were Cadogan and the two warders locked up day and night for the first fourteen days in a cell only intended for one prisoner, although Cadogan and the two warders complained about being nearly smothered and made sick from the want of pure air to the governor and the doctor."

"The first time he complained about it…"

"It is not because an unfortunate man was sentenced to death that he should be sentenced beforehand."

"Our object was to be as kind as possible to him and give him every indulgence."

"That is what I would expect. Does it occur to you that a little seven by ten cell is not the place for three men to spend the night in shut up?"

"It is the largest cell."

"Is it or is it not? The jury saw the cell. I sent them to see it. I am asking you a simple question and please try to answer it, yes or no?"

"I think the doctor would be able to answer that question."

"What do you think? Try and give me a candid answer, it will do you know harm, you are only doing your duty. It won't affect you in the least with your authorities. Do you consider a cell measuring seven feet by ten sufficient accommodation for three men to spend the night? Answer yes or no."

"That cell in my opinion was sufficient in all other similar cases."

"I am not asking you about similar cases. That is a matter for public opinion. Do you consider it sufficient accommodation? Answer the question."

"I consider it sufficient."

"You do?"

"I do."

Mr Brookes, a member of the jury. "Were there three men sleeping in the last cell we went into?"

Mr Andrews. "Yes."

The jury foreman, Mr Malone, who was the Chair of Philosophy at Cork University. "Why wasn't he placed in the first cell we visited originally?"

Mr Andrews. "He was kept there for the purpose of observation and it is the cell usually used by prisoners under the sentence of death. It has been used as such for years and years."

Coroner Horgan. "My complaint is this; you don't seem to understand it yet, that any medical man or any man under common understanding ought to know and I am sure your prison inspectors if it had been brought to their attention, would see that a cell seven feet by ten was not a place to confine three men for a whole night locked up."

"That is an entirely medical question."

"I consider it grossly insufficient, and to think that a government can spend a hundred million pounds on a most infamous war can surely build a cell necessary for the accommodation for a man or person under the sentence of death."

"The moment I heard the complaint made about I had the change made forthwith."

"You should not have waited to have your attention drawn to it. It was no place for him and he should not have been placed there. That is all I have to ask you on the matter, but the communication I got said that the prisoner and warders were sent to sleep in a disused part of the prison where they had to keep blankets rolled around them to keep them from being frozen. Cadogan had to go to bed without proper light to see his prayer book, the gas being at the furthest part of the cell near the ceiling."

"That is untrue."

"Is it?"

"It is."

"I am glad to hear it. Was there any fireplace in the cell?"

"No."

"Or any heating apparatus?"

"Yes; hot water pipes running through the cell."

"How far is the heating apparatus from this large cell?"

"It is at the end of the wings."

"From the cell?"

"Yes; it is a good distance from it but it heats it well, it is a new apparatus too; for heating purposes."

"This communication tells me it is a long distance away. Does it heat all the intervening cells?"

"It does but it heats that one well."

"I read from the communication again, "these are but a small sample of the treatment of Cadogan and the warders. Complaints don't suit in prison." Any thoughts on that?"

"I know nothing about it; it is an anonymous communication."

"Yes; it is anonymous but it contains some truth for you to admit some of the statements in it."

"No. I don't admit it."

"Don't you admit he was in a small cell?"

"Certainly; but it was a cell which people who have been under the sentence of death for years and years have been confined."

"It should not continue any longer and the Prison Board ought to provide proper accommodation."

Mr Malone. "Did the prisoner attempt to commit suicide this morning?"

"Yes he made an attempt to cut himself across the throat with the heel of his boot."

Mr Malone. "How did he manage to get his boot off with two warders about him?"

"I have no idea. The two warders were present when it occurred and one was standing by his bed."

Coroner Horgan. "Now we shall call the next witness, James Billington; the executioner."

A call was then put out for Billington but there was no answer. Coroner Horgan than asked R.I.C. Sergeant Kinahan where the witness was.

Sergeant Kinahan. "This morning I personally served the executioner and his son a copy of the Coroner's summons which directed them to attend the inquest and give evidence."

Coroner Horgan. "Where is this man Mr Andrews?"

"I do not know sir."

"Do you swear that?"

"I swear that he left here. I saw him go away from my own house, get into a car and go away, and I may tell you I understand that he has gone off home."

"Well gentlemen, I will adjourn this inquest for ten days; until the 22nd of this month, and if the executioner is not here I will dismiss you. Now District Inspector Morrison you will please have him here then."

District Inspector Morrison. "I can't bring him if he does not want to come. Personally I will do all I can in the matter."

"I will issue my warrant for his appearance. Will you please call to my office for it?"

"I will."

Following the news of Timothy Cadogan's execution the constabulary in West Cork were placed on high alert for disturbances. Over one hundred extra constables were brought to Bantry in order to maintain order. Intelligence had been received that there was to be a demonstration in the town and that Cadogan's body was to be brought from his homeplace in Coomhola for burial in the Abbey Burial Ground in Bantry a distance of six miles. However none of this came to pass.

On the morning of the 22nd of January the inquest into Timothy Cadogan's death was resumed in the prison guard room. The participants being the same as the first day. Coroner Horgan opened proceedings by addressing the jury.

"As you are aware the inquest was adjourned for what I consider the appearance of a necessary witness whom I have been officially told this morning is not present. Consequently I deem it my duty to say a few words to you in regard to the duties you have to perform. These duties are essentially inquisitorial. The word inquest conveys that. You are here under a special Act of Parliament passed about twenty-five years ago after the abolition of public executions in this country. You were sworn in the words of your oath to diligently enquire when, where and by what means death had taken place. The Act of Parliament requires you to be satisfied as to the identification of the deceased, the person on whom the sentence of death has been carried out, namely Timothy Cadogan. That identification has been proved, I hope, to your satisfaction by Mr Andrews, the Governor of the Gaol. You are to be satisfied that the sentence of death has been properly performed. The means by which the sentence was carried out was by the executioner engaged for the purpose, Billington. His testimony, in my opinion, was of primary importance. When I got word of this execution on the 10th of January I wrote to District Inspector Morrison and I enclosed the writ and summons for the executioner, in the letter I stated that I would require his evidence as I would not accept second hand evidence in such a serious matter of this kind. District Inspector Morrison courteously acknowledged the documents and said they would have his prompt attention. Evidence was given here the last day that the summons had been served on Billington that day in this establishment. He was here up to half an hour before you all assembled, but he deliberately ignored the summons and left here, according to all accounts, under police protection. I am quite satisfied that Billington would not have adopted that course unless he had not been assured by someone in authority that he could do so with impunity. Therefore it had been my duty to adjourn the inquest on the previous day and issue a warrant to have him brought back. After a week or so this warrant was returned to me by District Inspector Morrison with the intimation that the Inspector of Constabulary declined to have it executed. To my own knowledge Billington has been examined at inquests in England and I have read his evidence from several inquests there. I have even examined him here myself on a previous occasion. He was, as I have said before, the means of which the execution was carried out and is therefore an essential witness. Suppose for arguments sake, that this execution was unduly carried out, what is more natural for this man to disappear so to avoid being examined as to how he had performed his duties. In England the law is observed. In Ireland the Inspector General is the law and he has decided what the jury on their oath are supposed to accept. The law as laid down in Jervis, which is the recognised authority on inquests, states, "It is the duty of all persons who are acquainted with the circumstances attending the subject of the Coroner's inquiry to appear before the inquest as witness. Should they neglect or refuse to do so the Coroner, as an incident of his office has authority to issue a summons to compel their appearance and commit them for contempt should they fail to appear, or having appeared to give evidence upon the subject of the inquiry, because the proceedings are not so much an accusation on an indictment as an inquisition of office to truly inquire how the party came to his death which cannot be ascertained unless all the witnesses who know anything about the death are examined". Well as I have said, the authority and jurisdiction of this court has been flouted and the matter is now for you. You are the people to find a verdict and with those observations I will proceed to take evidence and finish the matter as best I can. I will first examine the prison surgeon."

District Inspector Morrison. "May I make a remark?"

Coroner Horgan. "Go ahead."

"As regards the service of the summons on the executioner, the Coroner told the jury quite truly that this had been duly carried out."

"I said so."

"The summons was duly executed on Billington, but not inside the precincts of the prison."

"That is a detail."

"I believe he was served outside the prison just as he was going home. The Coroner also stated that he had left under escort, that is quite true, but that escort was for the purpose of his protection. They were for his safety and they did not have any authority over him. Their instructions were to go with him and if he had obeyed the summons they would have remained with him. If they had detained him it would have been an unlawful arrest."

"I did not impute anything to them or say it."

"It would have been an unlawful arrest if they had detained the executioner against his will, and if I had done an illegal act, I would have been responsible for it and Billington could have had an action for damages for being detained. The executioner could disobey the summons if he wished as there was no warrant at the time for his detention. His escort were bound to accompany him wherever he went and I am sure the Coroner did not mean to impute anything about me when he said that Billington received a hint not to appear."

"Not in the least; you have done your job perfectly."

"Nothing of the kind occurred as far as I am concerned. I don't care if all the executioners in England are here. It is a matter of complete indifference to me whether the executioner went away or remained here. As regard the return of the warrant, I wish to read a paragraph from my letter with reference to the matter..."

Coroner Horgan. "I shall read it for you – I beg to return the inquest warrant by the direction of the Inspector General and must decline to execute it. At the same time I am asked to call your attention to the provisions of 31 and 32, Vic. cap 24, under which inquests are held and to inform you that several of the prison officials are ready and willing to come forward and give evidence on the only two subjects of inquiry, namely, the identification of the body and whether the judgement of death was duly executed. I must, therefore, ask you to proceed with the inquiry."

District Inspector Morrison. "The statute with special bearing on this subject, 31 and 32, Vic. cap 24, section 5 which says in effect that the Coroner shall within twenty-four hours of an execution hold an inquest on the body of the offender and the jury shall inquire into and ascertain as to the identity of the body and to whether the judgement of death was duly executed. As to the identity of the body, the Coroner has said that evidence of identification was given the last day by the Governor of the prison. All that remains now is for the jury to decide whether the sentence of death had been duly carried out. I think I can confidently say that the officials of the prison, especially the prison surgeon will be a much more competent witness to whether the sentence was duly executed than the executioner could possibly be."

Coroner Horgan. "I have called the prison surgeon for examination. District Inspector Morrison should keep his observations until afterwards."

District Inspector Morrison. "I don't suppose the executioner was allowed to examine the body after death as the doctor was?"

"The executioner did handle the body afterwards. It was he who coffined it and all that. I saw it done."

"Yes; but he could not give scientific evidence to whether death was instantaneous or not. A similar inquest was held in Belfast the other day and as far as I know the executioner was not examined."

"That is a matter for themselves."

"I thank the Coroner for allowing me to refer to these matters."

"I think I referred to them fully myself and fairly. Now I call Dr Moriarty."

Dr Moriarty the prison surgeon was then called and sworn in.

Coroner Horgan. "There is only one question which appears necessary to me to ask you and that is what was the cause of death?"

216

Dr Moriarty. "Fracture of the cervical vertebrae. Death appeared to me to be instantaneous."

"I suppose you examined the body immediately afterwards?"

"As soon as I could."

"How soon?"

"I suppose not more than a minute elapsed after the drop."

Mr Malone, jury foreman. "How long after the body had fallen into the pit did you make your examination?"

"Not more than a minute, as I said as soon as the drop fell I got down. The hangman's son was in my way pulling back up the trap and he obstructed me just a little."

Mr Hurley, a juror. "Was there any sign of life doctor, when you made your examination?"

"No; death was almost instantaneous in this case."

Mr Malone. "Was it the ring attached to the noose that caused death and broke the cervical vertebrae?"

"No; it was not. It was the weight of the man's body, that is the drop. A man weighing about eleven or twelve stone would get a drop of about six feet, Cadogan got a longer drop than is usual."

"Had Billington no rules to guide him?"

"There is a standard rule laid down on the subject."

"Are you aware of the statements made by Professor Haughton on the subject of the drop to be given at executions by hanging?"

"I am."

"He states that under certain conditions if a man was given too long a drop his head could be cut off. I suppose Billington was aware of the rules on this point?"

"I fancy there are regulations in the Home Secretary's office on this point. It is altogether a very gruesome theme."

Mr Hurley. "Did Billington do his duty without any blame attached to him?"

"There is no blame whatsoever."

"And no injury was done to the body beyond that necessary in the carrying out of the sentence?"

"There was no injury to be done."

District Inspector Morrison. "As a matter of fact the execution could not have been better carried out?"

Dr Moriarty. "Yes; as far as I know."

Mr Malone. "Could we have the warder who brought the body out of the pit examined?"

A juror, Mr Brooks. "We have had the evidence of the doctor to the cause of death, I don't know what more we want."

Coroner Horgan. "I am satisfied."

Mr Brooks. "I object to calling more witnesses. We have been given the evidence of a highly competent witness."

Coroner Horgan. "Mr Brooks, you are only one of the jurors."

"I understand that; I object on my own part."

Chief Warder Webb. "It was the executioner who brought up the body but Warder Houston was with him at the time."

Coroner Horgan. "We will examine him."

Warder Thomas Houston was then called and examined.

Mr Malone. "You were present and saw Billington remove the noose from Cadogan's neck?"

"Yes."

"Did you notice anything peculiar about that noose?"

"No."

"There was a brass ring attached to it?"

"Yes."

"Was that ring embedded in Cadogan's neck?"

"No."

"It was rumoured it was."

"The executioner told me that it was the same rope he had used on a previous occasion."

This concluded all the evidence. Coroner Horgan then suggested that the jury should adopt the following verdict which he had written for them.

"That the deceased died from fracture of the cervical vertebrae from the effects of hanging in Cork Male Prison on the 11th of January 1901 in obedience to sentence of death passed on him on the 11th of December 1900."

Mr Malone. "I don't believe we can come to any verdict without the evidence of Billington."

The Corner said that the jury should deliberate on that and while they did he would retire. The jury deliberated for ten minutes and then Coroner Horgan was recalled.

Mr Malone. "I am sorry to announce but we could not agree to a verdict. Some are in favour in agreeing with the evidence given while some are not. We have had a long discussion regarding the non-appearance of Billington. It was rather a heated discussion and I think I can say that the majority of the jury believe he should appear. He had a most important role on the morning of the 11th of January and his non-appearance is a slight on this court and the action of the authorities to allow him to take the course he did is also a slight. The Coroner issued a warrant to have him here. That was disregarded. Warrants have been issued for our Irish Members of Parliament. They were not disregarded. On the strength of these warrants they have been brought back to Ireland and imprisoned, but we have it now

219

that Billington can defy the law and that the law supports a creature of this class. His evidence is most material, especially because of the rumour circulating in the Cork Press that death was not instantaneous."

Mr. Brooks. "I object to all this."

Coroner Horgan. "You can speak Mr Brooks, when this gentleman is done."

Mr Malone. "Undoubtably there are very strong reasons why Billington should be here to give us full disclosure as to the manner in which he carried out the sentence of death. This matter should not be allowed to drop and I believe some Irish Members should ask questions in the House of Commons."

Mr Brooks. "We have had the evidence of a very eminent physician who said that death was instantaneous and that it was carried out as merciful as possible. I think the matters introduced now are perfectly extraneous."

Coroner Horgan. "Twelve of the jury will be sufficient to sign the verdict paper. Would you be satisfied do you think if you had the evidence you speak of?"

Mr Malone. "I believe so."

"Twelve of you cannot agree?"

"No."

"I will fix no date but I shall adjourn the inquest sine die* and if the authorities believe it worthwhile to have Billington appear we can possibly come here again."

(*Sine die - A court may adjourn a matter *sine die*, which means that the matter is stayed until further notice. In a *sine die* adjournment of this type, the hearing stands open indefinitely, and could theoretically be resumed if the situation changed.)

Mr Hurley. "Some of us did not want that evidence at all. We believe the sentence of the law was carried out and we do not want to come back here again."

Coroner Horgan once again read out the verdict he had drawn up and District Inspector Morrison then asked the coroner to give the jury a direction in law.

Coroner Horgan. "I have already done that."

District Inspector Morrison. "Unless the jury wish to question the evidence of the doctor I fail to see why they cannot agree. If they do wish to question it, it would be a most extraordinary position."

Mr Foley, another member of the jury. "I think we will be stultifying ourselves if we are to reconsider the doctor's evidence. He is a professional gentleman with a lot of experience and we believe his evidence, that is my opinion anyway."

Dr Moriarty. "I hope everybody else thinks the same."

Coroner Horgan took a show of hands and there were nine members of the jury in favour of signing the verdict paper.

Mr Brooks. "I think the Corner has put the matter very fairly before us."

District Inspector Morrison. "Some of the jury have made their protest but now I think they should find a verdict."

Mr Hurley. "I think we should find a verdict or we will be the laughing stock of the press and the country."

Mr Brooks. "We should find a verdict and be done with it."

After some further conversation Coroner Horgan asked for another show of hands and eleven jurors were prepared to agree the verdict suggested on this occasion. After this result he said.

"Well gentlemen, I will waste no more time about it. I will adjourn this inquest sine die."

A month later the outcome of the inquest was brought up in the House of Commons. Questions were put to the Attorney General for Ireland Mr John Atkinson by members of the Irish Parliamentary Party.

Mr William O'Doherty, M.P. for North Donegal. "Why was a summons, issued by the Coroner of Cork for the attendance of Billington as a witness, not executed?"

The Attorney General. "It was obvious from the proceedings which took place before the coroner issued his warrant that the presence of the executioner, Billington, was not required at the inquest for the purpose of the only inquiry on which the coroner had jurisdiction to enter, but for an indirect and improper purpose. The practice in England and Ireland, I believe, is identical. The presence of the executioner at inquests, I believe, was never required. Whether a coroner's warrant for the arrest of a witness for contempt of court is as efficacious as a warrant issued by a magistrate? The answer is that they are both equally efficacious."

Mr O'Doherty. "Can the right honourable gentleman say if the police authorities are a court of appeal to whom a coroner's court is subject?"

"No sir."

Mr James Flynn, M.P. for North Cork. "With regard to the warrant issued by the Coroner for the city of Cork, what is the right honourable gentleman's grounds for stating that the attendance of the executioner was required for an improper purpose?"

"It is quite impossible to discuss this matter in the form of a question and answer, but if the right honourable gentleman brings it forward on the Estimates I should be happy to explain and defend the action which has been taken."

Mr Pat O'Brien, M.P. for Kilkenny City. "May I ask whether it is a fact that the law in Ireland requires that in all cases of death in prison an inquest should be held and a record kept of the verdict."

The Speaker of the House. "Order. Order. That is a general question which does not arise out of the question on the paper. General questions of law cannot be raised in this manner."

Mr O'Brien. "I want to know is there any record of the death and of the verdict of the jury in this case, and if not, what is the reason?"

The Attorney General. "The reason is the coroner most improperly and illegally refused to complete the inquest."

Mr O'Doherty. "If the corner acted improperly why was he not dismissed by the Lord Chancellor?" (cheers from the Nationalist benches)

The Speaker of the House. "Order. Order."

No further action was ever taken regarding the inquest into the death of Timothy Cadogan and no official verdict was ever issued. Timothy Cadogan was the last man to be hanged in Cork Jail.

A Question of Timing

"This being the state of affairs at two or three o'clock, or whatever the time was, because in cases of this kind, though time is of an importance, it is too easy to attach much importance to matters of minutes or seconds."
From the opening address of the Solicitor General, Mr George Wright, at Timothy Cadogan's second trial.

So, justice was served. But was it really? In the following chapters we will examine the case closely and see if Timothy Cadogan was guilty beyond a reasonable doubt.

"A reasonable doubt exists when a factfinder cannot say with moral certainty that a person is guilty or a particular fact exists. It must be more than an imaginary doubt, and it is often defined judicially as such doubt as would cause a reasonable person to hesitate before acting in a matter of importance."
Merriam-Webster

"Beyond a reasonable doubt is the legal burden of proof required to affirm a conviction in a criminal case. In a criminal case, the prosecution bears the burden of proving that the defendant is guilty beyond all reasonable doubt. This means that the prosecution must convince the jury that there is no other reasonable explanation that can come from the evidence presented at trial. In other words, the jury must be virtually certain of the defendant's guilt in order to render a guilty verdict."
Cornell Law School

According to the evidence Timothy Cadogan arrived in Bantry at one o'clock on the day of the murder. He was in the company of a man named John Sullivan who he had met on his way to town. Once the two men arrived they went to a public house on the corner of William Street owned by Thomas Hurst. They met a man named Owen Sullivan and had two drinks each before leaving the pub and standing outside on the corner. They talked here for several minutes before another man, Tom Sullivan, arrived and they then joined him for a drink inside. After this drink they returned to the corner. John Sullivan stated that he met a man named John McCarthy on the corner and after a few minutes went up the town with him leaving Timothy

Cadogan on the corner leaning against the wall. The publican, Thomas Hurst, swore that he only remembered Cadogan on his premises once that day and this was at about half past one and that he stayed for about fifteen or twenty minutes. Under cross examination he stated that he could not remember if Cadogan had been in earlier that day.

Looking at this evidence I think we can come to the conclusion that Cadogan was either inside Hurst's pub or standing on the corner outside between one o'clock and at least a quarter to two. Thomas Hurst's evidence puts Cadogan on his premises at half past one, where he remained for fifteen to twenty minutes. In the evidence we do not know if Hurst himself was in the pub at one o'clock when Cadogan and Sullivan first arrived. He only stated he saw him at half past one and when pressed could not give a definitive answer as to whether he had been in earlier. In his opening statement for the prosecution at the second trial, the Solicitor General, George Wright stated that Timothy Cadogan had gone into Hurst's on two occasions during this timeline. Three men who could have shed some light on these occurrences, Owen Sullivan, Tom Sullivan and John McCarthy were never called to either prove or disprove Timothy Cadogan's whereabouts during this time.

William Bird left his office for his club on the Square between twenty-five past and half past one. It was a walk of about five minutes. Frank Costelloe, the club steward testified that he saw Mr Bird on three different occasions on the day in question, the last being at ten minutes to two in the club's reading room. Costelloe then said he had left the club on some business before returning twenty minutes later and when he did Mr Bird was gone. A local labourer named Patrick Flynn stated that he met Mr. Bird heading in the direction of his office at about two o'clock walking at a smart pace. We may gather from this evidence that Mr Bird arrived back at his office at two o'clock or a minute or two after. Where was Timothy Cadogan at two o'clock? According to the Crown he was watching Mr Bird from his viewpoint on Hurst's Corner as he made his way down Bridewell Lane and onto Marino Street. The Crown suggested Cadogan then followed him and watched his office from outside Mahony's public house on Barrack Street from where he saw Michael Hegarty leave, he then entered the office and carried out the dastardly deed. This version of events relied heavily on the evidence of Patrick Cronin who testified that he saw Timothy Cadogan

226

leaning against the wall of Mahony's pub smoking, as he walked up Barrack Street. He also swore that he passed Michael Hegarty after he had come out of Mr Bird's office. Cronin then said he remained on Biggs's Corner until he heard about the murder. Under cross examination by the defence he stated that he was unsure of how much time had elapsed between him seeing Cadogan and hearing of the murder. Initially he said it was a half an hour and then he said it was a full hour. No one else saw Cadogan, no one saw him follow Mr Bird down Bridewell Lane, no one saw him walk up Marino Street and turn onto Barrack Street and no one saw him enter Mr Bird's office. So where was he?

According to Henry Breen Snr, he saw Timothy Cadogan shortly after two o'clock walking along Marino Street in the direction of the Square before he stopped to speak to a couple on the opposite side of the street to the workshop. He was positive it was after two o'clock because his employees had already gone for their dinner, the dinner hour being two o'clock. This is a crucial statement, for it indicates that Cadogan was walking in the opposite direction to Mr Bird's office shortly after two o'clock. This automatically renders the theory put forward by the Crown, that Timothy Cadogan had spent his time watching and following Mr Bird, incorrect. The couple that Cadogan stopped to talk to were later identified as Dan Cronin and his wife from Sheskin. They were later questioned in regard to their interaction with Cadogan, however, bar from admitting that they spoke to him that day, they could not furnish any details to the length of their conversation or the actual time that it took place. One question they should have been asked was on how many occasions that day did they speak to Cadogan, if only the once then that time would correspond with Henry and Timothy Breen's evidence. Henry Breen swore that during the time that he saw Cadogan his son, Timothy, was working on a cart outside the workshop. He stated that after he gave his son instructions on how to complete the task he was working on, Timothy got annoyed and went into the workshop. After five minutes Henry Breen went into the workshop and told his son to go home for his dinner. At that stage he said his other employees had been gone for ten minutes. Before he entered the workshop he said that Cadogan was still talking to the couple. Under examination Timothy Breen corroborated his father's evidence of seeing Cadogan on the opposite side of the street from the workshop. He also swore that after he

227

was told to go for his dinner by his father, Cadogan was still standing in the same spot conversing with the Cronin's and this was at least ten minutes past two. Another witness named Jeremiah Sullivan, believed he saw Cadogan in the same location talking to the couple.

As Mr Brereton Barry asked at the first trial. "Where are the witnesses who saw Cadogan go to Mr Bird's office?"

The answer? There are none, or if there were any on that busy day in the town, none came forward or none were found. Surely it would be reasonable to think that the prosecution would have found such a witness, even if it was only one. Instead the best they could offer was Patrick Cronin, who they produced at the second trial, he claimed to have seen Cadogan leaning against the wall of Mahony's pub on Barrack Street smoking. However, if Cronin's evidence was to be true then the two Breen's were mistaken. No other witness claimed to have seen Cadogan in the vicinity of Mr Bird's office. The only locations he was seen at between his arrival in Bantry at one o'clock and ten minutes past two was on Marino Street near the Square, in Hurst's pub and standing on Hurst's Corner, where he was seen by another witness named Kate Harrington.

Mary Hourihane testified that she went to Mr Bird's office to pay rent at about a quarter to two. As she climbed the stairs she noticed that the office door was closed so she turned around and as she was leaving the building she met Michael Scanlon, Mr Bird's rent collector. She informed him that Mr Bird was not there. According to her evidence they spoke for about ten minutes before she went back down Barrack Street and turned on to Main Street, leaving Scanlon at the door. She returned a short time after and met Scanlon on his way out of the building, he informed her that Mr Bird was now in his office. She then went upstairs to the office where she found Mr Bird alone writing a letter. She paid her rent and was only there a minute or two before Michael Hegarty entered the office. She then left leaving the two men talking. Mrs Hourihane went home, her house was only three doors from Breen's workshop on Marino Street. She stated this was shortly after two o'clock. There is no evidence to suggest whether she was asked if she saw Timothy Cadogan on her way home. This would have been important as it might have shown whether Cadogan was on his way to Mr Bird's office.

228

For if indeed he was the murderer he would have had to be on his way to the office in order to fit the timeline. Michael Scanlon's version of events was that he met Mrs Hourihane shortly before two o'clock and the two of them spoke for a while before she went down Barrack Street. He remained there until Mr Bird came around Biggs's Corner and then he followed him up to the office. He stated that he stayed in the office for about five minutes before leaving. He met nobody on his way out except for the returning Mrs Hourihane at the street door.

Evaluating the evidence of Hourihane and Scanlon I believe that when Mr Bird arrived back at his office he had a brief conversation with Scanlon at the door and then the two of them went upstairs. Bird would have had to unlock the office door and most likely remove his hat and coat. Then the two men transacted their business. If we believe that Scanlon stayed for five minutes in the office then it would have been close to seven minutes past before Mrs Hourihane entered the office. She swore she was only there for a minute or two before Michael Hegarty arrived. She then left the office meeting nobody on her way out. This suggests that Hegarty arrived in the office between eight and nine minutes past two.

Michael Hegarty who was believed to be the last man to see William Bird alive before he was murdered, stated at the Coroner's Inquest that he went to Mr Bird's office sometime after half past one and found the office locked. He said that he then went to Sullivan's shop on Bridge Street before returning a quarter of an hour later. However, at the first trial he swore that from Sullivan's shop he went to Cullinane's shop on Main Street before returning to the office, while at the second trial he swore that he had went to Mr Bird's office between one and half past one before returning a half an hour later. When he did return he went upstairs and found Mary Hourihane paying her rent. He stated that she left shortly after his arrival and then he proceeded to pay his rent for which Mr Bird issued him with a receipt. When the police investigated the scene after the murder the discovered an incomplete entry regarding this transaction in Mr Bird's ledger on his counter. Hegarty also stated at the Coroner's Inquest that while he was making this payment a man came into the office looking for money for thatching work off Mr Bird. He stated he did not look at this man for the length of time he was there. After the man, John Leary, left, Hegarty stated

229

that he remained speaking to Mr Bird for a few minutes before he left himself. During his opening statement at the second trial the Solicitor General stated that it was after Leary left the office that Mr Bird wrote out the receipt for Hegarty. However, in his own evidence Hegarty swore that he had been given the receipt before Leary's arrival.

On the occasions Michael Hegarty gave evidence, he was vague about the length of time he spent in Mr Bird's office. At the inquest he swore that he was in the office between six and ten minutes and that three or four of those minutes were spent after John Leary had left. During the second trial he swore he was not more than five minutes in total in the office. That is a significant difference. The inquest took place two days after the murder when events should have been fresh in his mind, but by the time of the second trial ten months later, minutes have vanished. If Mary Hourihane left Mr Bird's office at eight or nine minutes past two then Michael Hegarty would have entered the office at around the same time. If we then take his evidence at the inquest when he swore he was in the office between six and ten minutes, that would place him at the scene of the crime between eight and eighteen minutes past two.

John Leary testified at the Magisterial Inquiry that he had called to Mr Bird's office at about two o'clock. From looking at the evidence of Scanlon, Hourihane and Hegarty, we know it must have been about ten minutes past two when he got there, for neither Scanlon or Hourihane mentioned seeing him on their way out and Hegarty was already in the office. On his way up the stairs Leary stated that he heard raised voices which ceased once he had entered the office. He said that Mr Bird was sitting behind his desk looking angry and agitated, while Michael Hegarty, who he did not know at the time, was leaning against the counter resting his head in one hand. After a brief discussion with Mr Bird over money that he was owed for thatching he left the office. He stated that he was in the office for only a minute which would mean he left at twelve minutes past two if taken together with the previous evidence. John Leary swore that he heard about the murder a mere five or six minutes after leaving Mr Bird's office.

Timothy Breen swore that as he set off for his dinner at ten minutes past two, Timothy Cadogan was still in conversation with the Cronin's'. Breen went home via Bridewell Lane, New Street and Main Street before turning up Barrack Street. At the first trial District Inspector Armstrong confirmed he had carried out an experiment with Timothy Breen on the 9th of March regarding his route home. He testified that they had walked up Bridewell Lane along New Street and Main Street to Breen's public house on Barrack Street. He entered the house as far as the foot of the stairs before turning around and walking fifteen yards into the middle of the street. As he did this two policemen who had walked from the workshop to Mr Bird's office via Marino Street came out the street door of the office. They then compared times and distances. The District Inspector and Timothy Breen covered a distance of 304 yards in three minutes while the two policemen covered a distance of 137 yards in just over a minute and a half. (On the 18th of October 2022, I visited Bantry and walked both routes from Breen's workshop to Mr Bird's office. The longer route via Main Street took me three minutes and twelve seconds, while the shorter route along Marino Street I did in a minute and twenty seconds) At the second trial while being cross examined about this experiment the District Inspector was asked about the sworn evidence given by Timothy Breen at the first trial. Before he could answer the Solicitor General objected and his objection was upheld by the Lord Chief Justice who regarded the evidence given at a previous trial as being illegal. What this experiment hoped to prove was that by the time that Timothy Breen arrived home Cadogan had made his way up Marino Street and murdered Mr Bird in the three minutes that it had taken Breen to walk home. Instead what they managed to do was narrow the window of time that Cadogan had to carry out the murder. As Mr Brereton Barry observed, Cadogan would have had to set off immediately after Breen had turned into Bridewell Lane, reached the office unobserved, struggled with Mr Bird before shooting him three times and then making his escape. The time difference between the two routes was a minute and a half, so logically one presumes that Cadogan had a minute and a half between entering through the street door, going upstairs to the office, struggling with, and then shooting Mr Bird three times before making his way downstairs and escaping. This is one of the main reasons the evidence of Walter Dennis was vital to the Crown, and remember, he stated that when he saw Cadogan he was moving slowly! Timothy Breen, who had been a witness for the Crown at the first trial, was regarded by them as now being a hindrance to their case by the time of the second trial

231

and therefore had to be called by the defence. Breen's house and pub was directly across the road from Warner's shop and Mr Bird's office. As Timothy Breen started up the stairs he heard the report of gunshots. Once upstairs he went into the dining room and looked out the window. He observed Mr Warner and his son outside their shop in an excitable state. Breen's brother, Henry Jr, swore that he had been standing in the doorway of his father's pub when he heard two shots which according to his evidence he believed had originated from Mr Bird's office. He remained standing in the doorway for a short period and later swore that he did not see anyone exit the street door from Mr Bird's office. Like his brother, he then went upstairs and observed the people on the footpath outside Mr Bird's door.

If we take it that Timothy Breen left the workshop at ten minutes past two and it took him three minutes to walk to his house, then the murder occurred between thirteen and fourteen minutes past two. Henry Breen Jr's evidence is not as reliable as his brother Timothy's regarding the timing of the murder. Although he swore that he had wound his clock to twenty-five past two, just prior to hearing the shots and that he knew his watch was five minutes fast, the rest of his recollections match those of other witnesses. Like Henry Breen Jr, Fanny Dukelow's account of the time is not correct. She swore that as she returned from her lunch she looked at the town clock which showed it was ten past two as she passed by. On her return to Warner's shop she hung up her hat and coat before taking her place behind the counter near the window. She stated she was there for about ten minutes before hearing the noises from the upstairs office. If her timing was correct it would mean the murder occurred after twenty past two and as we shall see as we go on, that was an impossibility. I believe Fanny Dukelow was mistaken when she said the time by the clock was ten past two. It was most likely ten minutes to two and if that was the case her evidence of hearing the shots upstairs corresponds with the other witnesses.

Along with Fanny Dukelow in the shop were Robert Warner and Walter Dennis. There were also some customers including a Mrs Agnes Sullivan and a Mrs Matilda Donovan. Fanny Dukelow stated that she was standing behind the counter nearest the window to the street alongside Robert Warner. Dukelow stated that she heard a noise like that of a scuffle coming from Mr Bird's office overhead and also a sharp sound as that of a rod hitting a door. She also said that a piece of mortar fell from the ceiling. Her colleague Robert Warner in his deposition before the magistrates was very vague in regard to the time he heard the noises from Mr Bird's office, he only stated it was between two and three o'clock. Upon hearing the noises he had a brief conversation with Fanny Dukelow and then he ran to his uncle's other shop next door. He stated that his uncle was dealing with a customer and he had to wait a short time before informing him of what had occurred. Once he told him, his uncle went into his office and instructed two of his clerks, Edward Brooks and James Swords, to go and see what had happened. It was about this time that the Breen brothers looked out their windows. Henry stated that he had just looked out the window and saw Edward Brooks rushing out of the shop, while Timothy stated that when he looked out he saw Mr Warner and his son acting excitedly on the street outside their shop.

According to Robert Warner he followed Brooks and Swords to Mr Bird's office. He stated that Brooks was the first to go up the stairs and he followed immediately behind him. When he reached the office he saw Mr Bird lying on the ground. Swords was right behind him, and Brooks went back downstairs. Robert Warner then stated that he saw Swords lift Mr Bird's head up and that he saw blood underneath him. He then went back downstairs and was instructed to get Dr Popham. By the time James Swords arrived in the office the two Breen brothers were right behind him. Timothy swore that Mr Bird was lying partly on his knees with his face downwards leaning in the direction of the door, while Henry added that Bird was on his hands and knees and that there was blood underneath him. Timothy assisted in trying to raise Mr Bird up and also opened his shirt and felt his chest. He thought he heard a sigh come from Mr Bird but at the same time his face turned black. Henry Breen was instructed to go for the police and he found acting Sergeant Driscoll on the corner of Bridge Street and Main Street.

Driscoll later testified that he arrived on the scene of the murder at twenty-five minutes past two. However, under questioning he admitted he later discovered that his watch was three and a half minutes fast. This made the time of his arrival on the scene between twenty-one and twenty-two minutes past two. Twenty past two was the time that Dr Lionel Popham

233

stated that he received word from Robert Warner about the incident and he arrived in Mr Bird's office at twenty-five past two where he was met by the waiting acting Sergeant Driscoll. In his evidence Robert Warner swore that he called for Dr Popham on High Street, the Popham's residence was on Blackrock Terrace which was off High Street. When asked how long it was between hearing the shots and calling for the doctor Warner said between five and ten minutes. If we take the gap as being seven minutes this would indicate the murder occurred at approximately thirteen minutes past two. Dr Popham's father, Dr Thomas Popham arrived at the scene at twenty minutes to three o'clock, he was asked by District Inspector Armstrong at the Coroner's Inquest how long he believed Mr Bird was dead before he saw him and he answered about twenty-five minutes.

At Timothy Cadogan's second trial, one of the women present in the shop, Agnes Sullivan, gave evidence. She swore that she had heard the scuffle of feet and then the sound like that of a stool falling over. She was asked if she had seen Walter Dennis during this time. She stated that he was standing behind the counter at the rear of the shop and after the noises occurred she saw him run out into the street along with Robert Warner. On face value this contradicts Dennis's evidence of going out into the hallway but it was also possible Mrs Sullivan saw him after coming back in from the hall and then running out into the street. However, what he said when he returned to the shop is very interesting if Agnes Sullivan was correct. She stated that on his return he told Fanny Dukelow that Mr Bird had been shot. If this is true then why did Dennis not tell anyone including the police that he had witnessed Timothy Cadogan coming down the stairs from Mr Bird's office with a gun in his hand?

The Eye Witness

"I am employed at Mr Warner's at Barrack Street. I was in Warner's shop on Saturday last the 24th of February 1900. I was in No.2 shop. I was attending my business there. Mr. Bird's room is over the shop in which I was. I heard some noises in Mr Bird's room, like as if hurried footsteps around the room. I heard some shots next. I heard two shots. The sound appeared to come from Mr Bird's room. It was between twenty past two and twenty to three. After I heard the shots I went to the door that leads from the shop to the hallway leading to Mr Bird's office. I opened the door and went through about half ways into the hall. I had a clear view of the bottom part of the stairs and as I looked at that portion I saw a man coming down the stairs. The man I saw was Timothy Cadogan. I now see him present and I identify him. He was walking down the stairs, not in a great hurry. I saw he had a revolver in his hand next to me. I am perfectly sure it was a revolver. I saw him put it into his coat pocket, the side of his pocket next to me. I then walked back into the shop as I was afraid. When I went into the shop I stood where I was before and looked out the window. I saw Cadogan running up the road, the Glengarriff Road. I did not see him after that until now. I am perfectly sure it was Cadogan I saw coming down the stairs and afterwards running towards the Glengarriff Road. I know Cadogan for about two years by eyesight, but not his name until twelve months ago. I often saw him in Bantry. I am sure of this".

This was the full deposition of the chief prosecution witness, Walter Dennis, which was read out on the 25th of April 1900 at the final sitting of the magisterial inquiry into the murder of William Symms Bird two months previously on the 24th of February. This deposition was taken three days after the murder on the 27th of February. In all the evidence heard at the inquiry and the following two trials, Dennis was the only person who claimed to have seen Timothy Cadogan on the actual premises where the murder occurred. He was the only witness to see Cadogan with a gun in his hand and he was the only witness to see a man running from the premises on a busy Saturday afternoon. But despite seeing these things he never said a word to anyone for a full three days until acting Sergeant Driscoll brought him to the police barrack on the following Tuesday to make the above statement.

Walter Dennis was nineteen years old and originally from Whiddy Island. He had been in the employment of J.S. Warner for four years at the time of the murder. At Timothy Cadogan's first trial, Dennis swore that while he was working in Mr Warner's shop on the day of the murder he heard footsteps upstairs in Mr Bird's office "shortly" after two o'clock. This was followed by the sound of two shots. This already contradicts his deposition, as he claimed it was between twenty past two and twenty to three that he first heard the noises. At that stage Dr Popham and acting Sergeant Driscoll were already upstairs in Mr Bird's office. After hearing the shots he made his way into a back storeroom which had a door leading to the hallway. Dennis swore he went out into the hallway to a position from where he could see "most" of the two flights of stairs which led to Mr Bird's office. From there he stated he saw Timothy Cadogan "halfway" down the stairs with a gun in his hand. He was asked by the Crown if he remained in the hallway as Cadogan came down the lower flight and he replied that he had not, that he just looked at him and then went back into the shop. The Crown pressed him further by asking him if Cadogan did anything with the gun and Dennis said he put it in his pocket while he was looking at him. Under cross examination Dennis swore that he only saw Cadogan for the moment he was on the small landing between the first and second flight of stairs and that he did not wait for him to start down the first flight before he went back into the shop. If that is the case he could have only being looking at the man for a couple of seconds at the most since that would be the maximum time it would take for someone to cover that distance. When asked how much of Cadogan he could see over the bannisters of the stairs he replied that he could see his face and "that was all I looked at too". So how did he see the man put a revolver in his pocket? Dennis agreed with the defence that the bannisters partially covered the man except for his head and that the man was wearing a cap. At the second trial when asked where abouts he saw Cadogan on the stairs, he said, "He was on the second step of the first flight coming down". When reminded that he had sworn at the first trial that he was on the landing between the first and second flights, Dennis agreed with that evidence and then swore, "I did not see him come down the last flight". When he was then asked was the man he saw in a hurry coming down the stairs he made the extraordinary reply. "I did not take much notice of him, I just looked at him and walked back again". Asked by the defence how long it took him to go out into the hall and back he replied, "Just a second". He also swore that there was enough light in the hallway for him to identify Timothy Cadogan.

At the two trials a part time model maker from Dublin named Abbott gave evidence in regard to the hallway and the stairs. It is important here to understand the layout of the hall, the stairs, and the door from the shop. The stairs to Mr. Bird's office were in two sections consisting of five or six steps each going in opposite directions and separated by a small landing. From the shop door in the hall which was about eight feet from the foot of the stairs and about twenty-five feet from the street door, it was not possible to see the full extent of the second flight of steps. At the first trial Abbott stated that a person standing on the landing between the two flights could not be seen by anyone standing in the doorway to the shop. He stated that you would have to stand out four feet into the hall in order to see someone on the landing and a further two feet to see the person fully. He also testified that the only direct light in the hall came from the open street door. A civil engineer from Cork name McMullen appeared for the defence at the first trial and stated he had examined the stairs and hall the week prior to the trial at half past twelve in the day. The conditions in July being brighter than those in February, he stated that the landing between the two flights was very badly lit as there was no direct light on it from either the street door or the window on the landing above it. He said that the rays of light from the open street door would not reach more than eight feet into the hallway while the foot of the stairs was seventeen feet from the doorway. In his opinion a man would have to be just a couple of feet from the stairs to be able to identify a person on it. This evidence adds weight to the testimony of Head Constable Brennan at the first trial who swore that he found it difficult to see the shop door in the hall on the day of the murder.

During Cadogan's second trial Dennis elaborated on where he was exactly when he heard the shots. He stated he was behind the counter at the furthest point from the street door. When he returned to the shop he swore that he took his place back behind the counter and looked out the street window. He stated that he saw a man run across the street and along the Glengarriff Road. Dennis "thought" that this was the same man he had seen coming down the stairs, but, in his deposition he had sworn it was Cadogan. In the

Solicitor General's opening statement at the first trial he said that on Dennis's return to the shop he went straight to the street window to look out, while at the second trial this changed to Dennis just looking out the window with no mention of where he was actually standing. The Solicitor General was not the only one to say something different in regard to Dennis's return to the shop. In Fanny Dukelow's evidence at the first trial she swore that on his return he immediately went to the shop window and looked out, however, her evidence at the second trial corroborates Dennis's, she stated that on his return to the shop he went back to where he was originally standing behind the rear counter. Asked whether he looked out the window she stated that he was looking "towards" it. In any case one would assume if Dennis was so adamant that it was Timothy Cadogan coming down the stairs he would have been more certain that it was Cadogan he saw run across the street in the daylight. Also in her evidence Dukelow never said that she saw Dennis go into the hallway, this was implied by the Crown. What Dukelow actually saw was Dennis go into the storeroom which led to the hallway. Under cross examination she stated that the door of the storeroom closed behind him, so in fact she had no way of knowing whether he went into the hall or not. The Crown put great emphasis on Dukelow's statement that Dennis appeared frightened and looked pale on his return, but she also stated that he "immediately" returned to the shop after leaving it. In the evidence of the witness Agnes Sullivan she states that both Warner and Dennis ran out onto the street immediately after the shots were fired. In Warner's case this was more than likely after he had his brief discussion with Fanny Dukelow and was on his way to the shop next door. In Dennis's case the evidence is a bit more problematic for the Crown because she also stated that Dennis returned and informed Fanny Dukelow that Mr Bird had been shot. Now if we are to believe that Dennis saw Timothy Cadogan coming down the stairs and then running across the street, why if he told Fanny Dukelow that Mr Bird had been shot, did he not tell her also he had seen the man who had possibly done the deed? Surely in all this excitement he would have mentioned it to her.

But as we will see not only did he not mention it to Fanny Dukelow, but he did not mention it to anyone until he was brought to the barracks by acting Sergeant Driscoll the following Tuesday morning. James Swords swore in his evidence that when he went to Mr Bird's office he found Walter Dennis, Robert Warner and Edward Brooks ahead of him at the top of the stairs and when he asked Dennis that night in the presence of other men, had he seen anyone going up or down the stairs at the time of the murder, Dennis replied that he had seen no one. Michael Leary was an employee of the Birds' who worked at their residence at Beach House. He testified at the second trial that on the night of the murder he was at Beach House when Walter Dennis called with a parcel of bread from Warner's, Leary said he asked him did he know anything about the murder and Dennis's reply was "No Mike, I know nothing about it." Interestingly, at the first trial Dennis denied knowing who Michael Leary was, but by the second trial he admitted that he had known who he was. Also at the second trial a man named William Shorten testified that on the night of the murder he walked alongside Walter Dennis in the procession that brought the remains of Mr Bird back to Beach House. Shorten swore that he asked Dennis if he knew anything about the murder and that Dennis replied that he did not as he could see nothing upstairs because the door was shut. Another witness named John McCarthy swore that on the day after the murder he was in company with Dennis and some others. He stated that one of the others asked Dennis if he had seen anybody come out of Mr Bird's office at the time of the murder and Dennis answered that he had not because he could not see from where he had been standing, that all he heard was the stamping of feet overhead. McCarthy said that Dennis then demonstrated this by stamping his feet on the footpath. At the second trial Dennis was asked whether he knew a boy named Timothy Nagle, he replied that he did. He was then asked if he had told Nagle on the day following the murder after Mass that when he heard the shots he went into the back storeroom and stayed there. Dennis replied that he said no such thing. However, when Mr Brereton Barry asked him if Nagle swore that he had made this statement, would he on his oath contradict him. Dennis's answer? He would not.

In order for the prosecution to convince the jury of the validity of his evidence, they had to show that Dennis knew Timothy Cadogan. In his opening statement at the first trial, the Solicitor General stated that Dennis had known Timothy Cadogan for "a considerable time and knew him by name for about twelve months". He then made a crucial statement. "He saw him frequently in the shop". However, by the time the second trial came around the frequency of Dennis seeing Cadogan in the shop had been replaced by having seen him on one occasion "outside the shop window". At Cadogan's first trial Walter Dennis agreed with the Solicitor General regarding the length of time he had known Cadogan and when asked how often he had seen him in Bantry, he replied "A few times". However, under cross examination he told a different story. Asked if Cadogan was a customer of the shop he worked in, he said. "No never; he was never a customer of Mr Warner's". So much for being a frequent visitor to the shop as stated by the Solicitor General. Asked if Cadogan was often in Bantry, he replied that he did not know that. Asked if he ever spoke to Cadogan in his life he said he had not. Asked how many times he had seen him outside the shop, Dennis replied once. Asked who had told him Cadogan's name, Dennis replied belligerently, "I don't know that. I don't know who told me his name. I know a great many people and I can't say who told me their names". At the second trial when asked by the Solicitor General if he knew Cadogan, Dennis stated that he knew him "well enough". He swore under cross examination that he had known Cadogan for a long time after already swearing that he only knew him by appearance for the previous two years, then he swore that he had only seen him once or twice in Bantry. Further, he could not tell when this was, only that it was on a fair day or a market day and it was possible that it was two years since he saw him outside the shop. One has to wonder how Cadogan made such an impression on Dennis that after only seeing him once or twice he was able to identify him as the man he claimed to have seen for a couple of seconds coming down the unlit stairs from Mr Bird's office following the murder. Maybe it was the one-man identity line up in the barracks three days after the murder that helped to jog his memory!

Looking at both Mr Justice Kenny's and Lord Chief Justice O'Brien's views on the evidence of Walter Dennis, there is a distinct divergence in their opinions. In Mr Justice Kenny's summation he states that there are circumstances outside Dennis's evidence that raise a strong suspicion that Cadogan was the guilty party, but he doubted that this evidence would be sufficient to find him guilty without that of Dennis's. Mr Justice Kenny gave credence to the evidence of the civil engineer, McMullen, stating that the place where Dennis, namely the middle of the landing between the first and second flight of stairs, recognised the prisoner beyond the "possibility of a doubt" was a place where there was no direct light in the middle of the day, making it "impossible" for anyone standing in the hall to recognise someone on the landing. After making such an impression on Mr Justice Kenny one has to wonder why McMullen was not called at the second trial to give evidence. In reference to Dennis's evidence Mr Justice Kenny said that two suggestions were capable of being made, one was simply that he was mistaken in his identity of Cadogan or secondly he perjured himself on purpose. The final issue the judge had with Dennis's evidence was the passage of time between the murder and his identification of Timothy Cadogan as the culprit three days later. He suggested that between the witnesses, including the police and the doctors surely he would have said something to someone about what he had witnessed. It would be fair to say that Mr Justice Kenny's summation played an integral part in the failure of the jury to reach a verdict. Recalling the length of time the jury deliberated for, one hour and fifteen minutes, there was no coaxing by Mr Justice Kenny or the Solicitor General for them to take more time. Indeed the Solicitor General was more than happy for Timothy Cadogan to be remanded and sent forward for retrial in December. This is noteworthy because in later years when the Solicitor General, Mr Wright was himself a Justice, he presided over a trial in which he sent the jury back on multiple occasions to try and reach a verdict. (The Crown vs William Scanlan, 1910) Coincidentally the Crown prosecutor in that case was one Mr Redmond Barry, who was also Attorney General at the time. I believe Mr Wright feared that if the jury were given more time they would return with a verdict of not guilty.

At the second trial the Lord Chief Justice brought up the character of Walter Dennis. He asked the jury had there been an attack on his character and he answered the question himself by saying that as there was no attack on his character, then he was a boy of good character and a boy of such character would have no motive to falsely swear against the prisoner. He asked was Dennis in anyway uncertain regarding his identification of Cadogan, his simple answer to this was that Dennis said he was sure when asked by the Solicitor General. If one was to use this logic then what about the witnesses who were sure that Dennis said that he had seen nothing? According to the Chief Justice this was because he was afraid due to the atmosphere in the town which had already been stoked by the meeting held on the previous

Sunday regarding the land issue and Dennis thought if he told what he knew he would be ostracised. This was the reason he waited three days to tell what he saw because he could no longer withhold what he knew. The Chief Justice left the jury in no doubt of what he thought about Dennis's evidence. He described Dennis's demeanour as being unemotional and steadily calm and that he had an "abundant opportunity to identify the man on the stairs". That statement was frankly ridiculous in lieu of the evidence. He referred to Dennis looking out the shop window and seeing the man run across the street and stating that it looked like the prisoner and this showed "the caution of the boy". One must remember the extraordinary statement that the Lord Chief Justice made before Cadogan's case was heard in relation to the case from Clonmel. It seems that his mind was made up about Timothy Cadogan's guilt before the trial even began.

Suspects and Motives

In a murder case one of the first objectives of an investigation is to try and discover what was the motive for the crime. In this case the first motive ruled out was that of robbery. The first policeman on the scene was acting Sergeant Driscoll and in his evidence he said the office had not been ransacked like it would have been in the normal course of a robbery. He also swore that along with District Inspector Armstrong he searched the clothes of Mr Bird and found cash and a gold watch still on his person. The police soon came to the conclusion that the person who had murdered Mr Bird had come to the office with the intention of killing him, or else, something had provoked a visitor in to killing him. But who?

The first rumour that swept the town was that Mr Bird had shot himself, but that was never a suspicion held by anyone who came upon the scene. Take James Swords who swore that when he went into the office he searched for a firearm, as he assumed that Mr Bird had shot himself, but found none. The second rumour was that he had been shot by his brother, Dr Robert Bird, however he had an alibi since he was several miles away with a shooting party. Also the witness John Leary stated that Dr Bird was not in the office when he was there a few minutes prior to the murder. The first person to come under suspicion was Michael Hegarty, the last man believed to be with Mr Bird in his office before he was murdered. Acting Sergeant Driscoll testified that after he left the crime scene he went down Barrack Street and on to Main Street where he swore he met a "rushing" Michael Hegarty near a baker's shop. Shortly after this he met a constable who informed him that Hegarty was believed to be the last man to see Mr Bird alive in his office. Driscoll went looking for Hegarty and found him on Bridge Street as he was getting ready to go home to Dunmanus. He took him back to Mr Bird's office and from there to the barracks to see the District Inspector. Unfortunately we have no record of the discussion which took place in either the barracks or the office, all we have to go on is Hegarty's deposition and his evidence given at the Coroner's Inquest and the two trials to try and piece together his movements after the murder. After leaving Mr Bird's office Hegarty told the Coroner's Inquest that he went to Cullinane's shop on Main Street to meet his wife. He stated he was not five minutes in the shop when he saw three policemen running up the street and then he heard that "Master Willie" had shot himself. When asked by the Coroner how much time had elapsed between him leaving Mr Bird's office and seeing the three policemen run up the street, he stated about a quarter of an hour. This means according to Hegarty it was close to half past two when he saw the policemen. By this stage acting Sergeant Driscoll and Dr Lionel Popham were already at the scene of the murder. If we take a brief look at this evidence it would imply that it took Hegarty ten minutes to cover the distance between Mr Bird's office on Barrack Street and Cullinane's shop on Main Street, a distance of less than two hundred yards. At the first trial Hegarty's five minutes in Cullinane's had now been reduced to "only a couple of minutes". However, his evidence of seeing the policemen running up the street while in the shop remained, the only difference being he did not state how many he saw. This was the same evidence he gave at the second trial. As we have seen the first policeman on the scene of the murder was acting Sergeant Driscoll, who had been called from the corner of Bridge Street by young Henry Breen shortly after a quarter past two, for although Driscoll stated he arrived at the office at twenty-five past two he admitted his watch was some three and a half minutes fast, making his arrival at the scene shortly after twenty minutes past two.

Let's recap. Timothy Breen swore he left his father's workshop on Marino Street around ten minutes past two, it takes him three minutes to arrive home. A few seconds later he hears shots and within a minute he observes people on the street outside the entrance to Mr Bird's office. Henry Breen Jr hears the same shots and also observes people outside shortly after going upstairs. The two Breen's then run across the street and up to the office where along with James Swords, they see the body of the slain William Symms Bird. Henry Breen Jr is sent for the police while Robert Warner is sent for a doctor. Dr Lionel Popham swears that "a messenger from Mr Warner's" calls for him at twenty past two and he reaches the office at twenty-five past where he finds acting Sergeant Driscoll already there.

Michael Hegarty, in his evidence before the Coroner's Inquest stated the length of time he was in Mr Bird's office was between six and ten minutes. However, during the two trials he swore he was no more than five minutes

244

there. Also in his evidence at the Coroner's Inquest Hegarty swore he had "a long conversation" with Mr Bird and remained in the office for up to four minutes after the departure of John Leary. Even if we believe his statement that he was no more than five minutes, this means he was leaving the office at the approximate time Timothy Breen heard the shots just after thirteen minutes past two. This indicates that he left by the street door in the time it took the two Breen brothers to go upstairs and look out their window because neither said they saw him leave. Hegarty swore he met no one on his way out which would mean the killer still had to go upstairs. One unanswered question is where was Michael Hegarty in the time he left Mr Bird's office and meeting up with his wife in Cullinane's some ten minutes later?

One of the most intriguing aspects of Hegarty's visit to Mr Bird's office is the half-completed entry in Mr Bird's ledger, the ink was still wet, regarding Hegarty's payment. Hegarty produced the receipt for this payment and Dr Bird confirmed that it had been made out in his brother's handwriting. One can easily imagine that both the receipt and the entry into the ledger would have been done at the same time especially when you consider Hegarty swore the two men spoke for several minutes. The Crown's view of this was that Mr Bird wrote out the receipt and then waited until Hegarty had left the office before writing the transaction into the ledger. But this does not correspond with the evidence given by Hegarty at the first trial, asked if Mr Bird enter his payment into the ledger, he replied that the book was open on the counter but he did not know whether he recorded the payment. Hegarty was then asked did Mr Bird write in the ledger while he was present and Hegarty stated that he did. In his evidence John Leary swore that when he entered the office Mr Bird was sitting behind his desk while Hegarty was leaning on the counter. At some point Mr Bird rose from his desk to write in the ledger which was found on the counter. A striking piece of Leary's evidence was his observation of Mr Bird's mood, which he stated was one of anger and agitation. This totally contradicts Hegarty's version, he stated at the Coroner's Inquest that when he arrived Mr Bird was writing some letters and on seeing Hegarty he put them aside to ask how his wife was and then they had a general chat until Hegarty was leaving. He testified that he felt Mr Bird wished to speak to him for longer but he had to leave. He also said that Mr Bird was in his "usual good humour" during his visit. This again goes against the testimony of John Leary who swore that he heard loud talking as he went up the stairs to the office. Asked at the second trial whether this was true Hegarty answered vaguely by saying "It would not be true to say there were angry words". Thus answering a question he was not asked.

Now let's look at what Hegarty did upon leaving Cullinane's shop. He testified at the first trial that it was his wife who informed him that Mr Bird had been shot, she told him she had overheard two girls saying it, asked at what time she told him he replied at twenty-five past two. Another important point here is that Mrs Hegarty was never called to corroborate her husband's testimony. One would consider her evidence valuable since her husband had been the last person to see Mr Bird alive. Even if Hegarty was correct in his timing on hearing the news of the shooting, his lack of interest in finding out the truth is wholly shocking. In his own words he stated, "My wife made some enquiries and she was told that Mr Bird had been shot. I did not make any enquiries until after my dinner". It was a full three quarters of an hour after the news of the shooting broke that Hegarty made any enquiry into the event. This was when he returned to collect his horse and trap in Vickery's Yard and he asked the man attaching the trap, Pat Crowley, whether the news was true.

At the Coroner's Inquest Hegarty made an emotional statement after admitting Mr Bird and himself were friends, he said. "There is no man in the County Cork who will miss him more than myself. Not only on one occasion, but every occasion he was a very good and useful friend to me." However a short time later when asked why he did not return to the office after hearing the terrible news, he replied. "If he had been a relative of mine I would have went back, but I only collected some rents for him". So much for being a good friend. Hegarty was slow to make enquiries into the wellbeing of his friend and did not bother to go to the office to offer his assistance knowing well he was possibly the last man to see Mr Bird alive. Instead he went for his dinner. At Timothy Cadogan's first trial Hegarty was asked once more why he did not go back to the office. This time he said. "He was not a relative of mine and I did not think it was any of my business". When asked the same question at Cadogan's second trial his reply was "I thought it would be very unusual and an intrusion to go amongst the police

246

and his friends". So much for missing the man more than any man in the County of Cork! When asked was it his opinion that it was no business of his as he was not a relative or friend of Mr Bird. Hegarty stated that was his opinion and "as regard the rents I was sending rents to the others as well as him and have since collected it for his successor". This is crucial evidence, for between the Coroner's Inquest and the second trial we can categorically say that Michael Hegarty lied about his relationship with William Symms Bird.

In the defence brief that Ralph Brereton Barry wrote prior to the first trial it was obvious that he regarded Michael Hegarty as the prime suspect in the murder of William Bird. He stated that Hegarty was a man who was not regarded as having an "upright" character. In the brief he delved into Hegarty's background and of his role as an "emergency blacksmith" during the time of the Land Wars. An "emergency blacksmith" was a blacksmith, who under police protection, travelled the county to carry out work for land owners who were the subject of a boycott in their local area. Brereton Barry wrote "He acted as a bailiff on the Ponsonby Estate in East Cork and use to take a type of travelling forge with him to shoe boycotted horses". Brereton Barry goes on to say that at the time Hegarty was considered "a man of notorious character who would stop at nothing", and a man who was well versed in the use of firearms. One might wonder where Brereton Barry obtained this information on Hegarty, the answer is that he had personal dealings with him. In 1888 Brereton Barry represented Hegarty as the Crown prosecutor in a case which Hegarty brought against James Gilhooly M.P. for intimidation. Hegarty stated that Gilhooly had named him at public meetings as an emergency blacksmith and a supplier of carts to the police, which led to him being boycotted and unable to sell his cattle or produce. The case was heard in Schull and during the hearing it was revealed that Hegarty had been expelled from the Cork Defence Union for gross misconduct. (The Cork Defence Union was opposed to Home Rule and the National League. The Union consisted of landowners, merchants, farmers, shopkeepers, artisans and labourers united under the presidency of the Earl of Bandon and his assistant Viscount Doneraile to help those who had become victims of the National League boycotting campaign) Hegarty was found to have sold cattle at a higher price to members of the Union by pretending that he had no other buyers due to the boycott. After his expulsion Hegarty attempted to join the National League. During that case, in which he defended himself, Mr Gilhooly requested the presence of a magistrate from Bantry in order to examine him, the name of this magistrate? William Symms Bird. This was perhaps another reason why Mr Gilhooly's presence at the magisterial inquiry in to the murder of Mr Bird was so vigorously opposed. During the two trials Hegarty admitted that he was the owner of a revolver, however, he swore that it was not in his possession that day, but at his home in Dunmanus. Both the police and Hegarty stated that he was searched after being picked up, he also said his trap and parcels were also searched but no firearm was found. However, there was an intriguing exchange between Mr Lynch and Hegarty during his cross examination at the second trial. Hegarty was asked whether the overcoat he was wearing was the same one he was wearing on the day of the murder. Hegarty said it wasn't and admitted he had been wearing a different one. He was then asked whether he had taken off the overcoat while in Mr Bird's office and he replied he was not sure whether he had it on or not in the office. He was then asked whether he had it on as he walked about the town and to this he stated that he couldn't swear he had. Asked where he had left his overcoat when he came to town, Hegarty's answer was he didn't know what class of overcoat he had that day, but he was sure he must have had one that day, since he would not have travelled the distance he did without one. One wonders was Mr Lynch hinting here at the possibility that Hegarty had placed his coat with the revolver in it, in a secure location until he was going home. Taken with the evidence of the ten missing minutes after he left Mr Bird's office and Sergeant Driscoll seeing him "rushing" along Bridge Street after the murder, the mystery of the overcoat could have been a viable line of inquiry.

Throughout the two trials Mr Brereton Barry cast suspicion on Michael Hegarty. He stated that was it not for the evidence of Walter Dennis "what plight would Michael Hegarty be in now?" He mentioned the evidence of John Leary, who by Hegarty's own account arrived in the office after he had completed his business with Mr Bird. "Why was he still there and what was he waiting for?" Brereton Barry's concluding remark about Hegarty was. "In fact if Cadogan committed the murder, Hegarty should have met him on the stairs after leaving Mr. Bird". I have to agree that concurs with the timeline we have established.

In Mr Justice Kenny's summation of the evidence at the first trial he agreed with Mr Brereton Barry's opinion in relation to Hegarty being in the dock instead of Timothy Cadogan had it not been for the evidence of Walter Dennis. He also stated his reasons for this opinion. "Because the time he was in the office was between ten and twenty minutes past two, the very office that Mr. Bird was found murdered moments later, he was the last man seen in the office, and lastly the ink was not dry in the book which had recorded a payment which he had just made. I tender that a lot of suspicion would fall on the man who was last thought to have been in the deceased's company". He told the jury that it was up to them whether that theory deserved any credence or whether they believed the evidence of Hegarty. In discussing Hegarty he asked what motive would he have had for committing the crime since no evidence had been produced of a dispute or a quarrel existing between the two men, but Mr Justice Kenny then went on to mention the evidence of John Leary stating that his was the only piece of evidence which could attribute friction between the two men.

In his summation of the evidence at the second trial of Timothy Cadogan, Lord Chief Justice O'Brien showed considerable bias in favour of Michael Hegarty, in fact at one stage during his summing up he stated to the jury. "I am sure you do not think it necessary for anyone to have to vindicate Hegarty of the charge". He went on to say that Hegarty had come into town on business, then had dinner with his wife and the simple reason for him not returning to Mr Bird's office following the news of the shooting was that he was anxious to get home before it got dark. He completely glossed over testimony, which was prejudicial against Hegarty, preferring to rely on the evidence of Patrick Cronin. He told the jury "Cronin passes Mahony's pub on Barrack Street and sees the prisoner standing with his back against the wall of the pub smoking and a little further on he passes Hegarty, the last man to see Mr. Bird alive. How far was the prisoner from the front door of Mr. Bird's office? Twenty-five yards". In placing this evidence to the fore the Lord Chief Justice may as well as called Timothy Breen and his father liars. For they both stated firmly that Cadogan was opposite their workshop at ten minutes past two and never veered from this evidence, while Cronin got muddled up in his evidence and confirmed he had not read the deposition he had given. The Lord Chief Justice went as far as trying to put a different spin on the Breen's evidence, he stated. "Remember the evidence of the Breen's who had him about their place about the time the men were going to dinner. The two Breen's had him standing there in the middle of the place speaking to some people, but you will remember that if he was watching for Mr. Bird, that is one of the places he might have stood". Yes he might have stood there, but not if Mr Bird was already back in his office ten minutes earlier and Cadogan was walking towards the Square before he stopped to talk to the Cronin's. At this point I think it important to remind ourselves about the Lord Chief Justice's history, he was the lead prosecutor in the case of the infamous Maamtrasna murders for which an innocent man, Myles Joyce, was among those hung for the crime. Lord Chief Justice O'Brien left no doubt in the juries mind about the verdict he was expecting them to reach.

As regards a motive for Michael Hegarty murdering William Symms Bird, there is not an obvious one. One can only speculate like the way the Crown speculated regarding Timothy Cadogan. Was there a business disagreement between the two men? Had Bird discovered something about Hegarty? Did Hegarty go to the office with the intention of murdering Bird or was it a spur of the moment decision in the heat of an argument? We will never know because once Timothy Cadogan was arrested all other lines of enquiries were closed.

Now let us look at the case against Timothy Cadogan without the evidence of Walter Dennis. He was in Bantry on the day of the murder, that is it! During the two trials the Crown tried to place great emphasis on Cadogan's whereabouts from ten minutes past two until six o'clock when he claimed he left the town for home. They also placed emphasis on his demeanour when he met John Sullivan with regard to the news of Mr Bird's shooting. Cadogan stated that he spent the afternoon in Bantry wandering around the town before buying some biscuits and heading home at around six o'clock. According to the Crown and Walter Dennis's evidence he was last seen running along the Glengarriff Road making his escape. John Sullivan stated in his evidence that he caught up with Cadogan not long after half past eight on his way home. If the Crown's evidence was right then Cadogan must have been hiding out in the country for over six hours. When Sullivan mentioned the shooting of Mr Bird to him, Cadogan's short answer tells a lot. He said. "The rumour around town was that Mr. Bird had done it himself or his brother the doctor had done it". These indeed were the rumours sweeping Bantry after the shooting. If Cadogan had scarpered down the Glengarriff Road out into the country like the Crown had said he did, when and where did he hear those rumours? Does it sound more plausible that a man who claimed to have been around the town for the afternoon to hear such things then a man hiding out in the country for over six hours? One other point regarding Cadogan's statement and that is him buying biscuits, surely it would have been simple enough to find out where he said he had bought them and then ask whoever sold them to him did they remember his purchase. It seems that this was not done.

What made the authorities turn their attention to Timothy Cadogan? The deceased's brother, Dr Robert Bird, heard of his brother's murder as he was returning home from shooting that evening. Upon his arrival he was told that Michael Hegarty was been held in the barracks in connection with the murder. He was informed that Hegarty had been the last man seen in the presence of his brother before he was murdered. During both Timothy Cadogan's trials the doctor was asked was it him who mentioned Cadogan to the police that night and he replied that he had not, he said it was a constable named Mulcahy who brought up his name. Asked what he said when he heard the name he stated. "I said that if Cadogan was in town then it was him who did it and no one else, Hegarty had no cause to. Then the policeman said well, he was in town". This was the only evidence the police had on the night of the murder regarding the involvement of Timothy Cadogan, a statement made by the brother of the deceased who had not been in the town that day and had not known Cadogan had been until mentioned to him by a policeman. This was enough for the police to set out that night in search of Cadogan, who had returned to his home and gone to bed. Not exactly the actions of a man who a few hours earlier had carried out a cold-blooded murder. If Cadogan was the murderer, and if all the things said about him during the trial in regard to his supposed hatred of Mr Bird was true, one would imagine he knew he would be the prime suspect for the murder. However, when he was taken from his bed at quarter past five on the Sunday morning by acting Sergeant Driscoll he asked him what the charge was that he was being arrested for. In his evidence, Richard Sullivan, Cadogan's employer swore that the acting sergeant called Cadogan "a rogue, a vagabond and a murderer". Is it any wonder that Cadogan clamed up and refused to answer any more questions?

In order to find a motive for Cadogan murdering Bird, the prosecution had to delve into his past. They cited his eviction from his farm in 1895 as the principal motive for the murder. At his eviction the Bird brothers were present. The bailiff and one of the policemen who carried out the eviction gave evidence regarding the proceedings. At the magisterial inquiry R.I.C. Sergeant, George Cooper, who was based in Glengarriff swore. "The late Mr. W.S. Bird and his brother Dr. Bird were present and possession was handed to Mr. Bird by the bailiff. I saw the prisoner there and heard him addressing Mr. Bird when he came on the scene about the way the bailiff was handling his belongings. The prisoner asked Mr Bird not to go ahead with the eviction that he would pay him the rent as soon as possible but Mr Bird replied that it had to go ahead. The prisoner then muttered something and became rude and dogged in his demeanour, he went towards a heap of bottles and crockery wares which had been removed by the bailiff from the house. He grabbed some of them and threw them violently, smashing them against a wall. Mr Bird said to him. "Cadogan, you are a bad boy". The prisoner made no remark and continued to smash the bottles. I remained with Mr Bird in consequence of these actions". During the first trial while being cross examined, Sergeant Cooper was asked by the defence did Cadogan say he would pay the rent he owed to Mr Bird and he replied that he could not say whether he did or not. When reminded that he had sworn at the magisterial inquiry that he had, Cooper replied that this was only his opinion. At the second trial the sergeant was asked what exactly did Cadogan say to Mr Bird. He answered that he had only heard the latter part of the conversation which was not to go ahead with the eviction. He was then asked had Cadogan offered to pay the rent which was due. The sergeant replied that he was not sure. He was then asked would he swear on his oath that Cadogan had not offered to pay the rent, "I think he did, but I will not swear it". Mr Lynch then retorted. "It is five years since and you are purporting to swear what he did say but you won't swear that?" Sergeant Cooper confirmed he would not.

The next link in the Crown strategy with regard placing Cadogan's eviction front and centre as his motive for murdering Mr Bird relied heavily on the evidence of Dr Bird and specifically on his claim of being present in his brother's office on three separate occasions when Cadogan call demanding reinstatement on his farm. At the first trial he stated he remembered two of those occasions "vividly" especially the last occasion which he said occurred around six months prior to the murder when he said the demeanour of Cadogan was rude and sullen. Asked what Cadogan had said at the time, Dr Bird replied. "On thinking it over I recollect what he said was. You have done your worst – you can't do anymore, or the devil thank you and something in the way of you may be sorry for it". By the time the second trial came around Dr Bird was more definitive in his evidence regarding what Cadogan had said on the final occasion he was in the office. "He said in a sullen type of way. You have done your worst; the devil thank you; you may be sorry for it". This was crucial evidence for the Crown, for it had Timothy Cadogan directly threatening William Symms Bird.

But should the evidence have been admitted? Is it not hearsay? In the narrow and commonly understood sense of hearsay, a witness may not generally relay what another person said on a particular occasion as evidence of the truth of what that person said. The Crown had nobody who could corroborate Dr Bird's evidence. However, this was not the only occasion that the Crown relied on hearsay evidence. Their most grievous use of hearsay evidence was that of seventy-six-year-old William Levis. In his opening address at the first trial the Solicitor General stated. "It was with the greatest difficulty that we secured evidence from a man named Levis, who evidence was given a short time ago and after the prisoner had been returned for trial. In his evidence Levis states that he met the prisoner on the mountain a short time after his eviction and he was cussing and swearing and saying he was going to take Mr. Bird's life and other things of that kind". During his evidence Levis made the gesture of firing a gun and said this was what Cadogan had done when talking about Mr Bird. The defence had only received a couple of days' notice of Levis appearance but were still able to cast doubt on the credibility of his evidence. When they asked him how long was it since this meeting occurred Levis replied "two or three years ago". This contradicted what the Solicitor General said in his opening address. But it was during the second trial that Levis credibility was destroyed. Asked when he had made his statement to the police about meeting Cadogan and the threat he had made, Levis swore he had told them the year before Mr Bird was murdered. However, worse was to follow. Asked if he had made a statement to the police since that occasion he replied no he hadn't. Asked if he remembered giving evidence before a judge and jury at the first trial, Levis said he could not remember if he had. Finally asked if he remembered making his statement to police shortly before the first trial, he stated he did not. Looking at the evidence of William Levis through a modern prism it would not be far-fetched to state that he was possibly suffering from some form of dementia, in fact he died just over a year after the completion of the second trial. Yet along with Dr Bird he was feted as the Crown's most important witness regarding threats by Timothy Cadogan on Mr Bird's life.

Another area the Crown concentrated on was Cadogan's supposed proficiency with firearms. They also put emphasis on the suggestion he was well versed in the concealment of weapons. This was done no doubt due to the fact they could not find the murder weapon on his person or in his home. This strategy began at the magisterial inquiry when the Head Constable from Borrisokane in County Tipperary gave evidence. He swore that while serving as a constable in Glengarriff from 1887 until 1893 he had searched Cadogan's home for unlicensed firearms on four separate occasions. Asked had he found any he said no. Then there was the witness Jeremiah McCarthy, he had sworn that he thought he saw Cadogan talking to the Cronin's on Marino Street on the day of the murder, however, this was not the evidence the Crown was interested in. They wanted to know about an incident seven or eight years beforehand. At the magisterial inquiry he was asked if he had ever seen Cadogan in possession of a gun and McCarthy replied he had seen him more than once with a gun on the mountain. Asked if he saw him fire the gun he said he had seen him once shoot at birds. He was then asked was Cadogan a good shot and he replied that he did not know. At the first trial McCarthy's evidence changed to that he didn't know what Cadogan was firing at on that occasion, claiming that at the magisterial inquiry he stated that he only thought Cadogan was firing at birds. At the second trial McCarthy swore that he had only seen Cadogan fire one shot ever and did not know what he fired at because he was too far away. Even if one was to take that the incident McCarthy was trying to recall had happened the year prior to the murder instead of seven or eight years previous you could discount this evidence as irrelevant to the murder of Mr

Bird. The Crown's attempt to portray Cadogan as an expert in firearms should have proved the opposite. Despite many police searches he was never found in possession of a gun of any type let alone a revolver. They did not say where this near destitute man laid his hands on the murder weapon. The only admission Cadogan made about handling guns was to his employer Richard Sullivan who said that Cadogan had told him "That a number of years ago he was engaged in Kenmare by a man named Herbert. He and the gentleman's sons use to shoot rabbits that were damaging the crops". This and the evidence of Jeremiah Sullivan was the only evidence given in regard to Cadogan actually firing a weapon and in the former case it would have been most likely a licensed weapon he was using.

I am not trying to make out that Timothy Cadogan was an angel. He spent two months hard labour in Cork Jail during the 1880's for allegedly shooting at a man named Hallisey, for which he pleaded his innocence. However, even if Cadogan was guilty of that charge, when it came to the murder of William Symms Bird, he should have been tried only on the factual evidence presented at trial and not on what his character may have been in the past.

Beyond Reasonable Doubt?

There can be no doubt that without the evidence of Walter Dennis, Timothy Cadogan would not have been on trial let alone convicted and hung for the murder of William Symms Bird. He was arrested on the word of Dr Robert Bird and held for two days before Dennis identified him. What occurred during those two days one can only speculate. But one thing is for sure, Timothy Cadogan did not confess to the murder. Even throughout the magisterial inquiry and the two trials, the newspapers commented on his calm demeanour. His only outbreak of emotion came when he was found guilty, then in a state of shock he looked at Dr Bird and roared at him. "I hope I won't be dead twelve months till I have avenged the doctor, the scoundrel, the cut throat. I hope I will be avenged before I am twelve months in my grave". To me this is the statement of an innocent man.

Even from the beginning this case was treated differently. The press were denied access to all the hearings the magisterial inquiry held. The Crown and presiding magistrate tried to prevent the local Nationalist M.P. and magistrate, James Gilhooly, from adjudicating on the case. Cadogan was remanded on six occasions before being sent for trial. But probably the most baffling point is the treatment of Walter Dennis. After giving his evidence he was spirited away by train to Cork and then on to Dublin where he was joined by the very man who had arrested Cadogan, acting Sergeant Driscoll. The reason given for this was for the witness's safety, to protect him from the baying mob who had turned against him for testifying against Cadogan. There may be an element of truth in this as Dennis never returned to live in Bantry after the conclusion of the trial. Collusion with the police would not have gone down well at that time, however, there may have been another reason. It would have been a lot easier for the authorities to apply pressure on a naive twenty-year-old from the wilds of West Cork in metropolitan Dublin than in Bantry. Living with Driscoll one can imagine what their main topic of conversation was.

Why did it take Walter Dennis three days after the murder to inform the police, and no one else, what he claimed to have witnessed in that hallway? During the first trial Dennis was asked did acting Sergeant Driscoll call for him at his workplace on the Tuesday morning to bring him to the barracks, he replied. "No he did not; he came for me in the middle of the day after I had told him". This is an important point because it implies that Dennis had told Driscoll about Cadogan on the Monday. However, and not for the only time, Dennis contradicts himself a few minutes later. He said that when acting Sergeant Driscoll called for him he went to the barracks and told him all about it. Asked by the defence if this was on the Tuesday Dennis replied yes. Then Mr Brereton Barry on behalf of the defence asked the vital question. "And it was only when acting Sergeant Driscoll came to you the next Tuesday that you told anyone about what you saw?" Walter Dennis made no reply, he must have recognised that he had slipped up. The pretence he had given of informing the police on the Monday about Cadogan was shattered. It is not outside the bounds of possibility to suggest that acting Sergeant Driscoll, under the orders of a higher power, was told to pick up Dennis and bring him to the barracks. Once there pressure was placed on him to say that he saw Cadogan, and to make sure that it was Cadogan he identified they came up with the one-man line up. Due process was completely ignored for a man facing a capital crime. Not only with the farce of the line-up, but the denial of counsel for the defendant when he requested it. In modern times everything that happened in the barracks would surely be ruled as inadmissible.

Walter Dennis was not the only person who was pressurised, how else can you explain the evidence of Robert Warner at the second trial? Warner stated that he had followed Dennis out into the hall after hearing the shots, in fact it was the first time he mentioned Walter Dennis. He shared this evidence when he was summoned to Cork, for a meeting with the Solicitor General a week before the trial began, having failed to mention it before in his deposition before the magisterial inquiry and in his evidence at the first trial. At the first trial he had sworn that as a result of hearing two or three rapid shots he spoke to Fanny Dukelow and then went immediately to the shop next door for his uncle. He seemed flustered on the stand at the second trial as he agreed with the defence that his first version of events was true. After Warner finished his evidence Fanny Dukelow was re-called and now she amazingly remembered that Warner had followed Dennis into the hall, this despite her giving her evidence just prior to Warner's with no mention at all about it. I believe some pressure was applied to these witnesses in

258

order for them to recall this a full ten months after the murder. In fact when Dennis was asked during his testimony at the second trial whether Dukelow and Warner were still in the shop when he returned he said they were. It had already being sworn that Dukelow and Warner were behind the counter at the front of the shop. If Warner had followed Dennis and saw him standing in the hallway he would have had to come out from behind the counter, cross the shop floor and go through the storeroom, and as Dennis and Dukelow swore, Dennis was only gone a few seconds before he returned to the shop. Throughout his evidence Dennis only ever said Warner was in the shop behind the front counter. Is it conceivable to think a seventeen-year-old boy who had been summoned from Bantry to come to Cork would not have been influenced by the Solicitor General of Ireland and a District Inspector when questioned about his evidence?

During the second trial Walter Dennis was asked when he first heard a man had been arrested for the crime and he stated that he had heard on the night of the murder that Michael Hegarty had been arrested. He also swore that he did not know that Hegarty had been released before he went to the barracks on the Tuesday. This seems strange since he admitted that he knew Cadogan had been arrested on the Sunday. In his summation the Lord Chief Justice stated that Dennis was a man of obvious good character and the reason he had waited to tell what he knew was because he was torn. He explained it as such. "During the course of the trial what really struck me with considerable force and that was the wonder that Dennis had given his evidence at all. You know Ireland as well as I do. Perhaps you know the South better than me, but I also know the South. Ask yourselves do people here come forward and try to involve themselves in a case of murder? No; they would rather mind their own business". What a sweeping statement! In a couple of lines the Chief Justice basically told the jury not to bother about the length of time involved between the murder and Dennis's identification of Cadogan. In the same breath he was discounting the evidence of men like James Swords, Michael Leary and others who had sworn Dennis had told them nothing of what he had seen. He was also ignoring human nature. Surely when one has experienced a trauma as alleged by Dennis he would have told someone. But no, Walter Dennis did not mention it to a soul, not even the people he was with at the scene of the crime in the minutes following the murder, surely he would have said something. Even after seeing Cadogan race across the street and along the Glengarriff Road, why did he not call attention to him? At the second trial his answer to this was. "I knew others had seen the man running away as well". But others did not see what he said he saw. Nobody else stated that the saw a man run out onto Barrack Street and down the Glengarriff Road. According to the Crown and the Lord Chief Justice the reason for this was a code of silence amongst the townspeople of Bantry. It was them who were lying, it was them who knew Timothy Cadogan had murdered Mr Bird and it was them who chose to remain silent while Walter Dennis was the only brave man to come forward with the truth. One is left to wonder if Walter Dennis was a man of such bravery and good character as implied by the Lord Chief Justice, why did he say nothing when Michael Hegarty had been arrested for murder. Maybe the answer was in his own testimony. "Why should I?"

After all these years no one can say with any certainty who murdered William Symms Bird on the 24th of February 1900. Was it possible that it was Timothy Cadogan? Well, anything is possible. But was it Timothy Cadogan beyond any reasonable doubt then I would say no. I believe that the evidence if heard today would not stand up in a court of law. Without doubt another person would have been standing in the dock in his place without the evidence of Walter Dennis.

Michael Hegarty died on the 5th of March 1941 at the age of 86. Dr Robert Bird died on Christmas Eve 1909, in West Kensington London where he had relocated to, at the age of 61. The beneficiary of his will was his sister Kate Rebecca Bird who died herself on Christmas Day in 1923 at Hove, Sussex at the age of 74. Her will provides some interesting information. She bequeathed £500 each to Walter Dennis and Fanny Dukelow (which in today's money would equate to over £38,000 each). She also left £200 to acting Sergeant Driscoll (which equates to over £15,000), and £100 for Constable Mulcahy (which equates to over £7,000). This was in thanks for their evidence at the trial of the murderer of her brother William Symms Bird according to the Ballymena Observer on the 2nd of May 1924. This is also the only mention of Walter Dennis that I came across after the trial in any newspapers or genealogy sites. He would have been forty-four years old at this time.

The Ballad of Timothy Cadogan

Tim Cadogan was a farmer's son,
his lawful debts he paid,
Of landlords nor of bailiffs
he never was afraid.

No bird nor crow nor magpie
his spirit proud could tame.
That rough and rugged son of toil,
from the Kerry Hills he came

One day he went to Bantry,
twas Saturday afternoon
As he had often done before
in wintertime & June.

A bird was winged that morning,
a minion of the crown
He was no loss to Bantry
or any other town.

The peelers in pursuit of him,
no evidence could find
Through treachery they did conspire
to gain this hero's mind.

Cadogan in his prison cell
no danger did he fear
He knew that he was innocent,
this gallant mountaineer.

The jury thought the same of him
and twice decreed it so
Despite the perjured evidence
of Dennis and Dukelow

Third time they packed a jury,
the spawn of Cromwell's breed
To hang this gallant farmer's son,
at last they did succeed.

The jury found him guilty,
and the judge to him did say,
"The 11th day of January
shall be your dying day"

Long life to Paddy Meade,
his name won't ever die.
For the judge and jury in the court,
he boldy did defy

He knew the trial would be a farce,
presided by O'Brien,
The Judas of the Irish race,
from Cork to Ballyline.

Gilhooly, Flynn, and Barry,
tried by might and main,
To save the life of Cadogan,
their efforts were in vain

The names of Dennis and his gang,
they're loathsome now to hear
They do not visit Bantry Town,
their hearts are filled with fear,

As like the owl that sleeps the day,
until darkness comes around,
They crawl out of their hiding place,
where reptiles doth abound.

The grass they thread shall wither,
and ne'er again will grow
When trampled by Dennis,
Fanny Dukelow and rats

He is buried in old Ireland,
so far across the sea
And a thousand men like Cadogan,
would set old Ireland free.

That Cadogan's soul may rest in peace,
on that bright celestial shore,
Before the count above the clouds,
where sorrow is no more.

This poem about Timothy Cadogan was written in California by Patrick O'Brien, commonly known as "Rocky Mountain O'Brien". He was a native of Bantry.

(SKETCHED IN COURT BY OUR SPECIAL ARTIST.)

A sketch drawing of Timothy Cadogan which appeared in the Cork Weekly News on the 15th of December 1900.

THE NEW LORD CHIEF JUSTICE OF IRELAND,
MR. PETER O'BRIEN.

Photo Robinson, Dublin.

MR. WILLIAM KENNY, Q.C., M.P.,

Resources

Ballymena Observer. 02/05/1924

Ballymena Weekly Telegraph. 22/12/1900.

Belfast Newsletter. 06/05/1886, 20/07/1900, 12/01/1901

Belfast Telegraph. 17/05/1910

Bray and South Dublin Herald. 12/01/1901

Cavan Weekly News. 03/03/1900, 10/03/1900, 17/03/1900

Cork Constitution. 03/03/1884, 12/11/1887, 06/03/1888, 06/10/1888, 09/06/1891, 17/11/1892, 30/11/1893, 28/03/1895.

Cork Daily Herald. 08/06/1891, 15/11/1892, 24/09/1895, 26/02/1900, 27/02/1900, 03/03/1900, 06/03/1900, 20/07/1900, 11/12/1900, 12/12/1900, 12/01/1901,

Cork Examiner. 26/02/1900, 27/02/1900, 28/02/1900, 03/03/1900, 12/03/1900, 14/03/1900, 23/03/1900, 02/04/1900, 17/04/1900, 14/07/1900, 17/07/1900, 19/07/1900, 06/08/1900, 16/11/1900, 11/12/1900, 12/12/1900, 11/01/1901, 12/01/1901, 19/01/1901, 23/01/1901.

Cork Weekly Examiner. 03/03/1900, 17/03/1900, 21/07/1900, 27/07/1900, 11/08/1900, 15/12/1900, 19/01/1901.

Cork Weekly News. 21/07/1900, 28/07/1900, 15/12/1900.

Derry Journal. 23/07/1900, 11/12/1900.

Drogheda Argus and Leinster Journal. 03/03/1900.

Dublin Daily Nation. 26/02/1900, 06/03/1900, 10/03/1900, 27/04/1900, 17/07/1900, 19/07/1900, 20/07/1900.

Dublin Evening Mail. 26/02/1900, 02/03/1900,.

Dublin Evening Telegraph. 11/12/1900, 12/12/1900, 23/01/1901.

Dublin Weekly Nation. 16/10/1886, 03/03/1900.

Dungannon News. 01/03/1900, 17/01/1901.

Enniscorthy Guardian. 03/03/1900

Evening Herald. 20/07/1900, 11/01/1901.

Flag of Ireland. 10/03/1888.

Freeman's Journal. 05/03/1890, 09/061891, 03/03/1900, 26/04/1900

Irish Independent. 12/03/1900, 14/03/1900, 26/04/1900, 19/07/1900, 06/08/1900, 11/12/1900.

Irish News & Belfast Morning News. 06/03/1900, 15/12/1900.

Irish Times. 27/11/1888

Kerry Reporter. 03/03/1900, 21/07/1900, 15/12/1900, 19/01/1901.

London Evening Standard. 26/02/1900.

Londonderry Sentinel. 27/02/1900, 01/03/1900, 19/07/1900, 07/08/1900, 13/12/1900.

Leinster Reporter. 22/12/1900, 19/01/1901.

Mid Ulster Mail. 28/07/1900.

New Ross Standard. 03/03/1900

Newry Reporter. 28/02/1900, 16/03/1900, 27/04/1900, 23/07/1900.

Newry Telegraph. 13/12/1900, 12/01/1901.

North Down Herald & Co. Down Independent. 16/03/1900.

Northern Constitution. 03/03/1900.

Northern Whig. 26/2/1900, 06/03/1900, 06/08/1900, 11/12/1900.

People's Advocate & Monaghan, Fermanagh & Tyrone News. 28/04/1900.

Sligo Independent. 12/01/1901.

Warder & Dublin Weekly. 03/03/1900, 19/01/1901.

Weekly Freeman's Journal. 10/03/1888.

Weekly Irish Times. 15/12/1900, 12/01/1901.

Wicklow Newsletter & County Advertiser. 12/12/1900.

Bull, Philip. "The Formation of the United Irish League, 1898-1900: The Dynamics of Irish Agrarian Agitation." *Irish Historical Studies*, vol. 33, no. 132, 2003, pp. 404–23. *JSTOR*, https://www.jstor.org/stable/30006910

O'Donovan, John. "Class, Conflict, and the United Irish League in Cork, 1900-1903." *Saothar*, vol. 37, 2012, pp. 19–29. *JSTOR*, https://www.jstor.org/stable/24897201

Expert Report on the Trial of John Twiss 1895 by Dr Niamh Howlin, April 2021.   https://www.gov.ie/en/publication/23410-expert-report-by-dr-niamh-howlin-on-the-trial-of-john-twiss/?referrer=http://www.justice.ie/en/JELR/Report-on-the-Trial-of-John-Twiss-by-Dr-Niamh-Howlin.pdf/Files/Report-on-the-Trial-of-John-Twiss-by-Dr-Niamh-Howlin.pdf

A Dictionary of Irish History, D.J. Hickey & J.E. Doherty, Gill and Macmillan, Dublin, 1980. Pp. page 95. ISBN 0-7171-1567-4

Murder Most Local, Historic Murders of West Cork by Peter O'Shea. 2020.

The Ballad of Timothy Cadogan
https://www.duchas.ie/en/cbes/4921577/4881131

National Archives.ie

findmypast.ie

Also by Pat Doran

Enniscorthy The Forgotten Republic.

County Wexford in the Year 1900.

Printed in Great Britain
by Amazon

32064108R00162